THE LIFE OF EVELYN
UNDERHILL

Other Books in the SkyLight Lives series

Simone Weil: A Modern Pilgrimage
by Robert Coles, M.D.

Zen Effects: The Life of Alan Watts
by Monica Furlong

Evelyn Underhill in the garden at Pleshey

THE LIFE OF EVELYN UNDERHILL

AN INTIMATE PORTRAIT OF THE GROUNDBREAKING AUTHOR OF
MYSTICISM

Margaret Cropper

With a new foreword by
Dana Greene

Walking Together, Finding the Way
SKYLIGHT PATHS Publishing
Woodstock, Vermont

The Life of Evelyn Underhill: An Intimate Portrait of the Groundbreaking Author of Mysticism

2003 First SkyLight Paths Publishing Edition
Foreword © 2003 by Dana Greene

Library of Congress Cataloging-in-Publication Data
Cropper, Margaret.
The life of Evelyn Underhill : an intimate portrait of the groundbreaking author of Mysticism / Margaret Cropper ; with a new foreword by Dana Greene.— 1st SkyLight Paths Pub. ed.
    p.   cm. — (SkyLight lives)
Originally published: 1958. With new foreword.
Includes index.
ISBN 1-893361-70-5
1. Underhill, Evelyn, 1875–1941. I. Title. II. Series.
BV5095.U5 C7 2002
248.2'2'092—dc21

2002013528

10 9 8 7 6 5 4 3 2 1
Manufactured in the United States of America

SkyLight Paths Publishing is creating a place where people of different spiritual traditions come together for challenge and inspiration, a place where we can help each other understand the mystery that lies at the heart of our existence.

SkyLight Paths sees both believers and seekers as a community that increasingly transcends traditional boundaries of religion and denomination—people wanting to learn from each other, *walking together, finding the way.*

SkyLight Paths, "Walking Together, Finding the Way" and colophon are trademarks of LongHill Partners, Inc. registered in the U.S. Patent and Trademark Office.

Walking Together, Finding the Way
Published by SkyLight Paths Publishing
A Division of LongHill Partners, Inc.
Sunset Farm Offices, Route 4, P.O. Box 237
Woodstock, VT 05091
Tel: (802) 457-4000   Fax: (802) 457-4004
www.skylightpaths.com

Contents

Foreword to the SkyLight Lives Edition

Acclaimed in her own Edwardian era, Evelyn Underhill was then briefly forgotten only to emerge again today as one of the fore-mothers of contemporary spirituality. The passage of time burned away the inessential, leaving the core of her insight to finally be appreciated. A lucid and prolific writer, in her novels, poetry, biographies, text editions, analytical pieces, and "devotional" writing, she serves as a mediator of God's reality in the world. She is best known for her groundbreaking book *Mysticism: A Study of the Nature and Development of Man's Spiritual Consciousness,* published in 1911 and continuously in print since then. In this "big book" she did what no one writing in the English language had ever done before, that is, examine the elements of mystic experience and track its developmental stages. In this, and in all her work, she was not theological but anthropological, exploring the human quest for the divine.

It was Underhill's experience of the mystics—those she defined as claiming to know for certain the love of God—which first inspired her. But at mid-life in 1921 she moved away from a schol-arly consideration of mysticism and set out on a new course to help "normal" people, those who would not call themselves mys-tics, deepen their experience of the love of God. This "care of souls" was largely unknown amongst Christians. Self-trained and with no ecclesiastical or academic standing, she begin to give retreats and serve as a spiritual guide. Her friend T. S. Eliot claimed that her genius was that she understood the grievous need of her contemporaries for the contemplative element in their lives. Through her writing, which was both elegant and accessible,

Underhill compelled her readers to go to their center where they are "anchored in God."

In all of her efforts she held up not so much institutional religion, but human holiness, those models of sanctity who radiate God because God is within them. For Underhill, to be human was to be born with a capacity for God, but only the holy ones, the saints, became "pure capacities for God." Underhill's vocation was to bring these "great souls" before her contemporaries, reminding them that they were kin, different only from themselves in degree, not kind.

Underhill's torrent of writing poured from what has been described as her "quiet" life, a stable, married existence in London's charming Kensington section. But this barrister's wife lived her life in the company of what she called "the great pioneers of humanity," the mystics. And it was that company which made all the difference in her life and work.

Margaret Cropper, friend and fellow author, captures Underhill's "quiet" life and its inner adventure in her biography published in 1958, seventeen years after Underhill's death. In 1945, Charles Williams had gathered up much of Underhill's correspondence and published *The Letters of Evelyn Underhill,* but Cropper's was the first biography. Her *Evelyn Underhill* is testimony to friendship and the kind of knowing and insight it provides. Based on manuscript sources and an unfinished biography by Lucy Menzies, another of Underhill's intimate colleagues, Cropper illuminates the center of Underhill's personality. She weaves a life that captures both the discipline and constraint of a prolific writer and the abandon of one who knows there is "a splendor burning in the heart of things."

Through Cropper's prism we see a life which points beyond itself. There are first the early days as a lonely child and Underhill's beginning efforts as a writer. There are her travels to the continent, especially Italy, a place she called "the holy land of Europe, the only place left that is really medicinal to the soul." It was there through art and architecture that she came to what she called a "gradual unconscious growing into an understanding of things." We see her pursuit of the mystics, her scholarly efforts to preserve their insights and then her own personal torment during the first world war. She emerges with a new vocation to bring the mystic insights to ordinary people through years of retreat work and sustaining the inner life of others. As World War II began she made a final vocational decision to embrace pacifism. This was her darkest moment, yet it followed from her life "a free and unconditional response to that spirit's pressure and call whatever the cost may be."

Margaret Cropper was the first to capture this life, which now in this new century can continue to inspire, challenge and point the way for those on the ancient quest for the holy.

Dana Greene
August 2002
Oxford, Georgia

Introduction

It is important that I should introduce this book as in part the work of Lucy Menzies, though she did not give it its final form. When she died, I had her draft of Evelyn Underhill's life up to 1922. She did not feel at all sure that this had taken the shape that she would have liked, and I gathered that she meant to alter it considerably. There were besides a file of precious personal letters, a box full of unsorted reviews, and articles, and letters, various diaries and notebooks, and, above all, the letters to and from Baron von Hügel all collected by her diligent and brave researches. I had gone north to see if I could help her with the book; we had one day together looking at these things before she fell ill, afterwards we had only snatches of talk, for she was too ill to say much. In the spring of that year she had asked me if I would write the book, but I had to reply then that I was not free enough to do so; after she died it seemed right to take on the work for which she had prepared with so much courage and devotion, in spite of feeling myself very unequal to the opportunity, and, so that the book might have a unity, I rewrote the early part of it, using her draft freely.

I knew Lucy Menzies and Evelyn Underhill with a good degree of intimacy, and loved them both, and always feel myself deeply indebted to them. To see them together was to have a sight of a very dear friendship, full of heavenly values, and fun, and freedom to say anything, and a love which warmed and comforted their friends. Life was supremely with them an adoring search for the Will of God, sometimes in great darkness and suffering, sometimes in the Light.

Evelyn was Lucy's spiritual director for many years, and always had a sort of motherly care for her. Lucy was Evelyn's devoted disciple, and delighted in spoiling her in all sorts of endearing ways, to Evelyn's sometimes dismayed pleasure. Lucy continued her devoted work after Evelyn's death, bringing out works that had not been published, steering a steady course as Evelyn's literary executor, a not too easy trust, and giving to her friends a sense that they were part of the enduring circle of her love.

I am very grateful for help in discovering many facts and records to Miss Clara Smith, who was for long Evelyn Underhill's secretary, to the Rev. R. Somerset Ward for much help and encouragement, to Miss Audrey Duff, Miss Dorothy Swayne, and many other of Evelyn Underhill's friends for letters and reminiscences. I should also like to thank Lucy Menzies' family and her executor, for entrusting to me the books, papers and letters which I needed for completing the work she had begun.

The draft of the first part of the book which Lucy Menzies herself prepared has been lodged in the Library of the University of St. Andrews.

Margaret Cropper
1958

Note

Many friends of Lucy Menzies, who know how much this life of Evelyn Underhill owed to her courageous research, and her costly work, asked that some memorial of her might be included in it, and that Bishop Barkway, lately Bishop of St. Andrews, who knew her most intimately, should write it.

I was of course more than willing that this should be done, for I could not have written the book without the material that she had collected, and the work that she had already begun on it.

Margaret Cropper

Lucy Menzies: A Memoir

The title of Lucy Menzies' best-known book is an admirable clue to her own character. She was truly a "Mirror of the Holy." She reflected that with which her thoughts were constantly occupied, and like a mirror hid herself behind its reflection. The self-renunciation after which others strive is often distorted and unattractive because it is self-conscious and artificial; her self-abandonment was so complete that it drew no attention to itself. The words on her book-plate represent what she was—a lantern for the divine Light: *"Ego sum lux; tu es lucerna."* Her slight and fragile form at times seemed almost luminous. Her name, Lucy, suited her nature.

"Sacrifice is always fruitful, and there is nothing fruitful else." "Without shedding of blood there is no…" There can be little doubt that Lucy Menzies sacrificed her life in the preparation of her last work, as a final tribute to what she owed to Evelyn Underhill. She shrank from it, as if she already knew in advance what it would cost her. But it was not the cost that deterred her, but her sense of inadequacy. No one else, however, could have done what she has done. In addition to her own intimate knowledge of Evelyn Underhill, greater than anyone else's, there went the indefatigable search (involving toilsome journeys and interviews) for lost letters, such as the von Hügel correspondence, which she recovered, and other relics, without which the materials for the biography would have been very incomplete. Two months before her death she spent a short holiday in Austria (Obergurgl), to reorient herself for the travail of completing the biography which was now filling her thoughts, but in spite of her concentrated work death came before completion.

1

So reticent was she that it is now impossible to trace the stages of her youthful development in St. Andrews. Writing to a friend in later years she said: "We are both very self-contained"; and another, who lived with her for years in Pleshey, says: "We never chatted, as women do." But some memories remain. Dr. Dorothy Douglas reports that she was born and brought up at Inchture, a village in the Carse of Gowrie, between Perth and Dundee, where her father, Allan Menzies, was minister. He was appointed to the Chair of Biblical Criticism in St. Andrews University; and they moved there about 1890 or 1892. Lucy and her sister were educated entirely at home by their learned father and through correspondence courses. Their long summer vacations were spent on the Continent; and all the time Lucy was absorbing the great amount of learning with which her mind was stored. Later, the sisters with two friends went to Heidelberg to continue their studies for two or three years. On their return Lucy studied music and obtained a musical degree. The father was a brilliant scholar, rather "advanced" theologically; a saintly man, with the keen sense of humor which Lucy inherited. It seems as if she had more in common with him than with her mother. They lived a happy self-contained home life; and Lucy once went so far as to volunteer the information that if young men ever showed signs of interest "they received no encouragement."

Her conversion to Anglicanism was certainly assisted if not inspired by the influence of Evelyn Underhill; and she first heard of her through an almost casual remark by the parish minister of Innellan on the Clyde where her family had a holiday house, which led her to borrow *Mysticism*. This, to Lucy's mind was the turning point. Correspondence brought them into touch, and everything followed from that.

Discerning readers of Evelyn Underhill's *Letters* will probably have guessed that the last section of the book is composed of those written to Lucy Menzies, and through them have gained deep insight into her spiritual development. There is a difference of opinion as to the date of her Confirmation, some thinking that

she deferred it until after her parents' death, and others saying that
"dear old Professor Menzies would do nothing but help her on
her way." One of her oldest and most intimate friends writing of
that time makes an interesting remark on the "cast" of Lucy's mind
in matters of the spirit: "My one hope at that time was through
Transcendence, whereas Lucy's was through Immanence."

An unforced sense of humble gratitude was an endearing fea-
ture of Lucy's character. It was among the few things that made
her vocal. And to the very end of her life she never ceased speaking of what she owed to Evelyn Underhill. She begins a letter to
a new correspondent in 1946 with the words, "How glad I am to
hear from anyone who reads Evelyn Underhill. She was, and is, my
greatest friend. To me, too, her writings opened a new world. No
one else ever made me conscious of God as she did. Everything
she wrote somehow helped me on." And again, "No one else's
writings ever spoke to me so clearly."

Through Evelyn Underhill, Lucy was led into the sphere where
she had the fullest scope for exercising her special gifts, and which
hundreds of persons will always associate with her name. "She sent
me to Pleshey where I was for ten years, till my eyes made it
impossible." There she left a lasting heritage in the spiritual atmosphere and way of life which she established, and, more obviously,
in the lovely chapel which might almost be called her creation.
One of her colleagues and most intimate friends recalls how she
spent herself unsparingly on the retreat work, unmindful of her
physical limitations; "and some of us found it difficult to keep the
pace she set us. The high pressure of the work—and pressure of
retreat work in the absolute silence demanded could be very
high—made it unthinkable that she would relax. Indeed to the
end she never acquired the art of doing that. An hour, or less, after
luncheon on her bed was all the 'time off' she gave herself; and this
after being up very often at six o'clock or earlier for an early
morning Celebration for departing retreatants, and with a day
before her that would not end till nearly midnight.... She was
never a conversationalist. Rather she spoke to the heart, and was a
Presence.... At Pleshey she burned herself out, as she did to the
end for any she could serve; and would wish so to be burnt

out....What she most wanted to do and the people she most
wanted to see were always put last."

2

Her literary career began early, though none of her books were
published in her father's lifetime. The first three were translations
from the French. With her fourth, issued in 1920, she enters her
own proper field with her life of Saint Columba. Two years later
came her anthology of canine friendship; and after that, every year
or two, there appeared some evidence of her unflagging
diligence—*Saint Margaret* in 1925, *Mirrors of the Holy* in 1928;
Malavel in 1931. During her time at Pleshey she was otherwise
occupied, but on returning to St. Andrews, despite her failing sight,
she was constantly at work with her typewriter. Though only a
meager reference is made to her in the preface to Evelyn
Underhill's *Letters* by far the greatest part of the editing was done
by her. She provided all the material from which Charles Williams
made his selection, and this meant countless hours of typing and
re-typing. During the last eight years she produced her biography
of Father Wainwright, living for some time in his slum parish to get
the "atmosphere" right; re-wrote her life of Saint Columba for the
Iona Community; devoted immense labor to the very difficult task
of translating the long and obscure *Revelations of Mechthild of
Magdeburg,* living in Germany to obtain the best MSS. and spending days in the British Museum poring over others, and at the
same time uncertain whether any publisher would risk the production of so expensive a book for so limited a public. That last
venture was an act of piety to Evelyn Underhill who had first suggested it to her; and other tokens of her undying sense of obligation are seen in her editorship of the *Collected Papers,* of *The Light
of Christ,* of *The Anthology of the Love of God,* and of the little book-
let of *Meditations and Prayers,* which last she had printed privately.
This was followed by her editorship of Father Talbot's *Retreat
Addresses,* a bulky book which came out in 1954. His friends and
the members of his Community were insistent that she should do
this; and boxes of notes, some nearly illegible, were landed on her
to cope with, regardless of her increasing disabilities. And finally

came the urgent request that she should do what no one else could do with such insight, knowledge, and love, write the "Official" life of Evelyn Underhill, on which she spent the last months of her life and remnants of her energy.

3

There was nothing conspicuous in her appearance to the eyes of strangers. What they saw was a slight, self-effacing person with wistful eyes looking out through tinted glasses, a forehead with a tiny wrinkle as she strained to hear; and the loveliest of friendly smiles. When she spoke there was the hint of a lilt in her soft husky voice (a heritage from her highland forebears?) and a curiously suggestive plaintiveness that (to use a Scots expression) "came up round your heart," signifying that here was another fellow mortal who would understand and sympathize. She might easily have been overlooked in a crowd (indeed, as one smart young thing asked: "There isn't anything very special about her, is there?"), but when you found her you discovered something very rare—a heart at leisure from itself, which is the essence of the rarest of all virtues, that of humility, not thinking badly about yourself but not thinking about yourself at all. Everything was immediately referred to God. "Anything you think you found in my letters was probably put there by yourself or by God. I don't feel I have had anything to do with it, just prosing on things I have been taught." She seemed to be immediately ready to become *en rapport* with you, and without explanations to see your point of view and be completely at your service. This characteristic is what all her friends emphasize. Like Christina Rossetti, of whom this remark was made, "she was replete with a spirit of self-postponement"; and she might truly have made her own the words of Sir Thomas Browne: "There is no man that apprehends his own miseries less than myself and no man that so nearly apprehends another's."

Similarly her self-effacement had hidden her remarkable efficiency in the arts and in practical life. She got things done because she did not mind who got the credit for doing them. Thus she was an expert in architecture, as was shown in the building of the lovely chapel at Pleshey, where she inspired the workmen to get it finished in time in spite of great odds. And her own charming houses and

gardens in St. Andrews. Few knew of her musical distinction, or
the extent of her learning, enabling her to speak several European
languages and to read others with ease, and to be entirely at home
in mystical and abstruse theological literature. Her Doctorate of
Divinity, which embarrassed her modesty and delighted her
friends, was no empty honor. Scottish universities are not lavish
with their honorary degrees, and her learning amply justified the
one she received. She wore all this lightly with her inimitable
charm. The quiet humor which glinted in her eye and suddenly
flashed out in an unexpected phrase of disconcerting penetration;
the old-fashioned courtesy which made her so acceptable a warden
at Pleshey and delightful hostess to children and grown-ups in her
home were the shining colors on the veil of her self-effacement.

This rare quality concealed (as she would have wished) some of
her other characteristics, such as the iron and unremitting discipline
with which her integrity was guarded that others might be spared
the knowledge of her conflict and suffering. From a letter written
in 1946: "I don't know what you think I am! I must tell you plainly
that all my life I have found very great difficulty in prayer: it is really
a matter of blood and tears.... I do want you to realize that though
I know Prayer is everything I find it almost impossible." She habit-
ually wore a shining veil of cheerfulness; and though she seldom
laughed aloud her sense of humor was acute. No one would have
known of "the extreme irritability" which she confesses to a
friend, or believe her when she says to the same friend, "I'm a lazy
creature by nature." If she could not entirely hide her physical suffering she would at any rate make light of it, and at all costs she
would disguise her periods of depression and inward distress. Only
after her death do we discover how uphill and exacting was her
road. These glimpses come to us through letters written to encourage other pilgrims in like case; for their sakes she forced herself to
break through her sacred reserve. And as she was distressed when
she recovered the "lost" letters of Evelyn Underhill to von Hügel,
to find out the "dark nights" which she had so carefully concealed,
and yet was comforted in the sense of her companionship in this
trial, so it may be that to some readers the revelation of what both
these women suffered may bring just the reassurance they need.

4

The last decade of her life became increasingly difficult. Though she believed that Evelyn Underhill still continued to help her, nevertheless her bodily presence had been withdrawn.

> For this alone on death I wreak
> > The wrath that garners in my heart:
> > He put our lives so far apart
> We cannot hear each other speak.

And it was that insuperable silence that made her conscious of her loneliness. It was to be increased when her dearly-loved sister died, after a long illness, in 1947, and by the death of the Reverend Mother at Burnham in 1949. Lucy's own health was deteriorating, though she made as little of this as possible. From 1946 onwards we hear of visits to oculists, with more than one operation. Every year until her death she has a bout of 'flu; in 1947 she has a "bad knee," and later on a microbe, both of which keep her in bed, and then throat and glands are affected. In 1946 begin the recurrent series of carbuncles, some of them lasting several weeks at a time, which are acutely painful and debilitating, necessitating the use of morphia. From these she suffered periodically for years. We hear of laryngitis, and then of "a bad ear." She speaks of "feeling the cold" and of being "old and weary" and of "only having half an eye for some time," and of becoming so deaf as "to hear practically nothing in church." She can seldom have been out of pain, but it is rarely that she lets slip a reference to it, and she refuses to permit it to subdue her spirit. To another sufferer, Mrs. Mackenzie, she wrote: "It's no use, really to try to fathom why there is suffering. But we've got to accept it, gladly. Don't try to understand: just *be* in God." And again: "Yes, I'm sure redemptive suffering is the answer to it; and it's a grand vocation really." And again, to the same sufferer: "God gives us our circumstances and environment to make something of. It is within these circumstances that we are to achieve sanctity.... The Lord's way for you is just where you are; and—if I may say so—a jolly good way, too." This expressed her attitude to her own suffering.

When foreign travel became possible again after the war she resumed it, visiting her friends in Florence and the holy women in the Eremo near Assisi on more than one occasion. Twice at least she is staying at Einsiedeln while translating *Mechthild,* and she made several journeys to Austria, one so shortly before her death.

But though she refused to speak of it she wrote to a very intimate friend: "You don't fear death, I'm sure. I find myself longing for it, longing to go home, really." And again: "But then, I am old; and if you ever hear that I am going or gone, hoist the flag at once. Not that I'm not perfectly happy to stay on, but it would be *wonderful* to be allowed to go." And to another friend, speaking about a case of sudden death she wrote: "There is something very awe-inspiring about death. . . . After the distress and weakness all seems full of peace and tranquillity. I am glad for her that it was so swift and merciful."

Those words she wrote about another she would have liked us to use about her. We can only rejoice that she has entered into rest, and that for her the end "was so swift and merciful." We can also, for our comfort, lay to heart other words she wrote: "The penalty of getting older means that we lose our friends—but how lovely to think of them a stage nearer to God—and I feel sure helping us on, so that we can follow them."

Lumsden Barkway, Bishop

Evelyn at fifteen

Evelyn on the yacht *Amoretta* with her father and mother

1

CHILDHOOD AND GIRLHOOD

Evelyn Underhill's friends seem to agree that she never talked about her childhood. That may have been because she was an only child without brother or sister to share in her memories, or perhaps neither her father nor her mother treasured up stories. They may not have been small-child–lovers; indeed, one gets the impression that Sir Arthur Underhill really discovered his daughter in her late teens, and became aware then of her good brain and penetrating ability.

When she was born in 1875, her parents were just about to leave Wolverhampton and move to London. Arthur Underhill, who had been trained in his father's office as a solicitor, had determined to leave that side of the legal profession and practise as a barrister. It was a risky decision, and in his memoirs he discloses the struggles of his first ten years. Such time as he could spare from the law he gave to his absorbing passion for sailing, which was shared by his wife. A small child does not fit very well into a yachting holiday, so perhaps the little girl was sent to relations on dry land, or to some seaside lodging where the yacht could make an occasional call. Miss Menzies records that she went to a not particularly good boarding school at ten years old, and was away at school until the end of her sixteenth year. Still, family life, if rather under-emphasized, was secure and affectionate. Evelyn remained through their whole lives very much at her parents' call, and very sure of their value. At sixteen she wrote of her mother as coming nearer to her ideal of what a woman should be than anyone else that she knew; she shared her father's interest in the law, and above all she went many a cruise with them in the various boats purchased and sailed by Sir Arthur, and many a journey in Europe with her mother or both parents.

Our earliest look at her is in a photograph which survives of the family on board the *Amoretta,* Arthur Underhill's first yacht of any size. Evelyn is twelve, and has rather the look of a visitor to the nautical scene. Father and mother are wearing yachting caps, Mrs. Underhill carries the ship's mascot, and Sir Arthur has his hand on the tiller, the two bearded sailors have the name of the yacht woven into their jerseys, but the little Evelyn has a book in her hand, and sits loosely to the party, a shy child with an interesting rather than a beautiful face, more like her father than her mother, not wishing to make the most of her inclusion in the company, not quite part of the close circle of those who have sailed together and love their boat with an almost personal affection.

What had this father and mother got to hand on as a heritage to their little girl? What stock did they come of? What history lay behind the family group on the yacht?

Both father and mother were from the Midlands and both were born and brought up in Wolverhampton. Neither aspired to belong to county families, but they came of sound professional stock, with a stake in their borough. The Underhill family tree, which Arthur Underhill took pains to discover, goes back to a William Underhill in the fifteenth century, who was qualified to bear arms and took for his motto *Vive et Ama,* a motto which Arthur Underhill revived and used. In Tudor times there was one Underhill who was a hot-gospeller, and another who was a member of the Inner Temple, and yet another who sold New Place to William Shakespeare. Later in the eighteenth century a certain John Underhill was a stout Nonconformist divine, but the family seem to have veered back to the Established Church, and Evelyn's father was educated at one of the Woodard schools. There he wearied of constant school chapels, and put down his later mistrust of orthodoxy to too many services at school. These seem to have had an opposite effect on his younger brother, who became an Anglican priest. Evelyn's father was a clever child, a great reader, carrying out books from his father's library to read in his house among the tree-tops. His devotion to sailing dates from his childhood, which was partly spent in the country, though never within hail of the sea; but the boy who made a boat, with the help of a young uncle, out of a packing case, with a torn sheet for a sail to voyage on a neighbour's pond, grew into the man who founded the first Cruising Club and became its secretary and later its Commodore. When he married Lucy Ironmonger in 1874, it pleased him to discover that one of her ancestors, Goodwife Underhill of Boscobel, helped John Ironmonger of Wolverhampton to assist Charles II in his escape after Worcester.

There was, as we have seen, a strain of religion running through the Underhill family history, but Evelyn's father and mother had drifted away from it and neither were practising Anglicans. Perhaps when the uncle who was a priest came to stay with them there would be talk of a religious nature, and where it was linked with legal custom, as in the Warburton Lectures, Arthur Underhill was observant of his duties. Still, Evelyn could write later: "I was not brought up to religion."

But in reading Sir Arthur's own account of his life one feels that she might have said more accurately that she was not brought up to Churchmanship, for her father was a convinced Deist, and argues against the sufficiency of science to produce a satisfying view of life with a cogency which might almost belong to his daughter. But the Underhills didn't go to church, and Evelyn was to find her way to the worship she so much loved by paths of her own making.

After the twelve-year-old portrait we get no further sight of Evelyn until she was fifteen years old. A charming photograph by Mendelsohn shows us a serious, gracious girl with a thinking face, and there are one or two links that remain that show us what she was making of the two things which were to become most important to her—praying and writing.

They are contained in two books which she must have preserved herself and therefore felt to be in some way part of her growing. The first is a solid black notebook, entrusted to me by Miss Clara Smith to whom it was given by Hubert Stuart Moore. It was her notebook which she used during her preparation for Confirmation with that orderliness and thoroughness which were even then part of her make-up. (I think it was a private book, for it contains private prayers.) Apt for religion she seems, wanting to write a prayer and hymn of her own to say before her Confirmation as well as whatever else Mr. Russell Wakefield[1] might provide. A girl one would say deeply impressed by what she is learning, not "scimping," as she wrote herself, her work of preparation, and ready to meet its demands. A girl who makes an impressive and rather amazing effort to order her life according to God's Will. Lucy Menzies had recorded only the presentation of a rather deplorable little manual to the growing child, but I have wondered, looking at this careful preparation, whether something of it did not emerge to influence, perhaps subconsciously, the woman who became a practising Anglican in later life. But at the time it seems to have been too regulated for her enquiring spirit. The next two years which have produced the second entries in the black book, show us someone who has made a leap in growth. One wonders if her father began to talk philosophy, which he loved, to his daughter, or if her introduction to popular science shook her spirit. (She was reading Huxley at the time.) The document at the other end of the black book is so complete a picture made by herself of the adolescent Evelyn that it must be quoted as it stands:

Dec. 5 1892:

I am going to write down this short account of my own feelings and opinions because I think that tomorrow will close a period of my life, and I want to preserve some memory of it before it quite goes away. [I imagine that the great change coming must have been her leaving school, and coming home as a grown up young lady.]

First as to ideals. My ideal of a man is that he should be true, strong, intellectual, and considerate; not an adherent of any extreme party, but always ready to help the poor and oppressed. It does not matter if he is not good-looking or is shy or brusque, for those are outside things. I have never read or seen a man who comes up to my ideal. In real life I most admire Mahomet, because he was sincere, Giordano Bruno, because he was strong for the truth, and Jesus Christ because ethically He was perfect, and always thought of the weak ones first.

In fiction, I admire Milton's Satan for his strength, Tennyson's King Arthur for his goodness, and Shakespeare's Romeo for his personal charms.

My ideal of a woman is that she should be clever, vivacious, accurately but not priggishly informed, gentle, truthful, tactful and tolerant, and should have a due sense of proportion. I have never met or read of anyone exactly like this, but in real life my own mother comes nearest to it. I think in fiction, Angela Messenger in *All Sorts and Conditions of Men*.

My favourite heroines in real life are Joan of Arc for her sincerity, and Caroline Herschel for her unselfish love of knowledge. In fiction I like Hypatia, Portia, and Princess Ida, for their mental qualities, Milton's Eve for her womanliness, and Angela Messenger for herself.

My favourite prose writers are Matthew Arnold, Hallam, and Huxley for their style, Carlyle for his Philosophy, Besant for his characters. Amongst the poets I prefer Shakespeare for general excellence, Milton for majesty, Tennyson and Keats for beautiful thoughts, musically set, and Calverley and Austin Dobson for *vers de société*.

Amongst animals I prefer the cat, because when off duty in a zoological capacity it makes an excellent muff.

In politics I am a Socialist [this rather startling document goes on]. I think it is the only fair form of government, and it gives every class an equal status, and does away with the incentive to many sorts of crime.

As to religion, I don't quite know, except that I believe in a God, and think it is better to love and help the poor people round me than to go on saying that I love an abstract Spirit whom I have never seen. If I can do both, all the better, but it is best to begin with the nearest. I do not think anything is gained by being orthodox, and a great deal of the beauty and sweetness of things is lost by being bigoted and dogmatic. If we are to see God at all it must be through nature and our fellow men. Science holds a lamp up to heaven, not down to the Churches.

I don't believe in worrying God with prayers for

things we want. If He is omnipotent He knows we want them, and if He isn't, He can't give them to us. I think it is an insult to Him to repeat the same prayers every day. It is as much as to say He is deaf, or very slow of comprehension.

I do not believe the Bible is inspired, but I think nevertheless that it is one of the best and wisest books the world has ever seen.

My favourite occupations are literature and art, though I do not think I have much taste for the latter. When I grow up I should like to be an author because you can influence people more widely by books than by pictures. If I had been a rich man, I would have been a doctor, and lived among the poor, and attended them for nothing. I think that would be one of the noblest careers open to any man. My motto at the present time:

Be noble men of noble deeds,
For love is holier than creeds.

Goodbye sixteen years old. I hope my mind will not grow tall to look down on things, but wide to embrace all sorts of things in the coming year.

It is an interesting self-portrait, because it was written just for herself. She has grown up a good deal in the year or so that separates it from the careful preparation, the resolutions, the very simple prayers of her fifteenth year. It was probably not at all easy to be the only practising Anglican at home, to go to church by oneself, to stand up against the atmosphere of tolerant agnosticism, to have no Christian company. She admired her parents, especially her mother. What was she living by? What inspired her father, whose interest in the philosophers she was beginning to share? What books came into the house and lay about? Did the Anglican-priest uncle seem to her to be less valuable as a person than her non-professing parents? What made her think that to be dogmatic was a mistake, and that it was to science, the study of Nature and man, that one must look for light? She had now a long, strange way to go before she came to realize that there is something in the dogma and structure of the Church, which the mystic needs almost as much as the less adventurous Christian, a channel cut in the rock where the water of life may flow deep. If she had come home to an orthodox Church family, we should not have had Evelyn Underhill, who had to be a path-finder for so many searching souls. It is a rather great document, so free from many of the things that are vital to most seventeen-year-olds— clothes, pleasures, parties. It is an early declaration of a dedicated spirit who had shaken herself free from an orthodoxy that could not quite match with what her honest soul was trying to discover. There was another influence in her life which would not make it easy to hold on to the Confirmation teaching. In her prayers, among intercessions for various relations and school-fellows, we find that at fifteen she prayed every day for two boys who had become her close companions, Jeff and Hubert Stuart Moore. Their father was a fellow bencher of Arthur Underhill's, and as their mother died when they were still quite young, Mrs. Underhill took them under her wing. They shared some of the yachting holidays, for their father was almost as keen on his boat, the *Wild Wave,* as Arthur Underhill was on his *Amoretta.* They were to be near neighbours when the Underhills moved to Campden Hill Place. Hubert was rather older than Evelyn, and Jeff a little younger. They drew, they took snapshots, they explored old castles and churches together. They shared an interest in Nature. Hubert had clever hands, he liked making things, and this must have endeared him to Evelyn who also liked making things, and always respected a good craftsman. But something of the boy's indifference to the spiritual side of life may have made this girl, who mothered and admired him, wonder at this point whether these things really counted as much as she had been taught that they did, counted as much as this companionship which became more and more central to her as she grew out of her teens.

She came at least to a home where serious things were encouraged. She was helped to develop her mind, and began her connection with King's College, London, which was to continue all her life. As a student there she first studied botany, a lifelong preoccupation, and languages; but later, probably encouraged by her father, philosophy and social science.

She was also mastering there the art of expressing herself. Evelyn, as we see in the seventeen-year-old document, had always loved writing. At first she tried out her skill in the rather prim little essays written for the competitions in *Hearth and Home* and *The Lady*. But she was never indifferent to her own powers in this line. She cherished whatever *Hearth and Home* successes she had, and cut them out and pasted them in the second book where she collected newspaper cuttings on subjects that interested her. But her own collection was importantly described as "Works of Evelyn Underhill." They were not very remarkable works except that they show a girl learning to express herself, with a leaning towards fantasy, a love of books and poetry, and a certain amount of adolescent wit, for she always liked to be amusing. Just how she came to establish a style so distinctive as the one she uses in her first novel is rather a mystery, unless she had some tutor at King's who fostered her writing as well as giving her a sound education.

Another pursuit which meant a great deal to her was occupying her in these daughter-at-home years. She became an expert bookbinder. There is no record of her going to work in a bindery, but the description of the bindery in her first novel is so fresh and first-hand that probably she did work in such a place, and perhaps also had a press at home. This bookbinding satisfied something in her that was important to her make-up. Something of what it meant to her is reproduced in the character of Carter, the working bookbinder in her novel; the precision, and the satisfaction of good workmanship fascinated her: "There was a sincere and beautiful relation between Carter and his work. With him it was a manual religion, faithfully followed, without a sordid thought. He felt slovenly work to be a sin against his material."

It was Carter who said: "It ain't effect you're here for, it's good tooling; and that work's not sound. Look at them corners, you haven't mitred them neat. You don't want to do your finishing shop-window style, you wants to do it so as it looks right when it's held in the hand after it's bought."

Did she also experience the sense which she gives to her bookbinder hero? "He learnt here for the first time in his life the meaning of his hands and discovered their use. They gave his soul inexplicable pleasure."

Evelyn had used her hands for drawing, she had books full of rather indifferent little drawings, but the bookbinding asked for something further. It made a demand which her eager hands longed to answer.

She reached a high standard as a binder, and exhibited her work. "In the days when I was still too timid and reverential to dare handle the English language," she wrote to a friend, "I was almost a professional bookbinder, and even once had a pupil who used to put me into agonies of impatience by her finicky amateurish ways."

She had no use for finicky amateurish ways in other and deeper crafts later in life.

The bookbinding interest she shared with Hubert, who sharpened her knives for her. He was always a man of his hands. It was one of the things which they understood very well about each other. "Nothing fosters helplessness so much as an education which gives all its attention to the brain, but utterly neglects the hands" she had written in one of her essays for *The Lady*.

But however absorbing the bookbinding might be it was not in Evelyn Underhill to neglect her mind. Her father had a good library and encouraged her to read. Perhaps she discovered Dante in these late teens. Plotinus comes early in her studies of philosophy. She once told a friend that when she went to King's she decided that she need not bother any more about religion, and set it aside with almost a sigh of relief. But she should not have studied philosophy if she wanted to be quit of those "obstinate questionings" which she shut away in the secret places of her mind.

Her father found her apt to pick up his lawyers' jargon and to help him in the work that he brought home. Hubert was also destined for the law, and between them they primed her with the amusing side of legal dilemmas which emerged later in her *Bar-Lamb's Ballad Book*.

She was not altogether either a binder or a bookworm. She was an early bicyclist, and when at last we come to some hard news about her in the first letter which we possess to Hubert in 1895, there is not a word about books in it. It is the sort of letter which any jolly outdoor girl with a taste for craftsmanship might have written to her boy-friend. She wants his company, that is clear

enough, and depends on his sympathy with her over the things
that she is doing and seeing. Her letters to Hubert are rather puz-
zling. They are all on this sort of level as if she had already erected
"that bulkhead, carefully fixed to prevent undue exploration" of
which she wrote to him when at last it was necessary to her to talk
to him about the things which were so vital to her. Did she deliberately, even when she was twenty years old, keep their relationship at a level on which she knew they could always find each
other without the incursion of things that might have troubled
them? That they belong to each other and need each other on that
level is clear enough, and it is not just a brother and sister relationship; that becomes clearer in every letter; but Evelyn was perhaps already aware of the Mystic's device "my secret to myself."
Did she perhaps cling all the closer to the staunch affection which
claimed no entry into her inner life because that life was to be so
cloudy and tempested, so dizzying in its snow-bound heights, so
sudden in its ascents and descents that even from the first she felt
the need of a plain domestic path to counterbalance the other?

The first letter dates from home after a visit to cousins at St.
Albans, and if one had been told that it was the letter of a girl of
sixteen, and not twenty, one would not have been surprised, but
in 1895 people did not grow up so quickly as they do now. We are
introduced to Hubert as "My darling laddie," and to herself as
"Your little girl, Nursie," which suggests that she had spoilt and
mothered the boy who had no mother of his own:

> My Darling Laddie,
>
> I was so sorry to have to write such a short scrap yesterday,
> but really I hadn't a minute of time. We really had a very nice
> day. St. Albans is a sweet old fashioned little place quite coun-
> trified, with an open market place in the middle, full of
> lovely cattle and pigs. The Cathedral is simply lovely and the
> roads round seem very good. They have persuaded me to go
> down with Diavolo [her bicycle] from Tuesday to Thursday
> next week. I thought I had better get it over whilst the
> weather was good for cycling. I'm *so* glad you are having
> such a good time; mind you stay as long as you can, it will

quite set you up for the winter. I am as busy as I can be with books and bazaar work. Miss Birkenruth has been ill so I can't have my lesson from her till next week. On Monday I am probably going to a lecture by Cobden Saunderson on Arts and Crafts for women at Grosvenor Crescent. I think it ought to be rather good. There will be such a lot to talk about when you come home. Aunt Emily gave the Missis [her mother] an old Bristol jug yesterday, so she is in high favour and the Missis came home purring. I have been mounting some of the photos we took this summer; it improves them muchly, and the clouds and Rostrevor Church really look quite grand. I've been for a ride round this morning—eight miles only as there was such a thick fog over the Thames that I did not go to Battersea as I intended; and this afternoon we have got a rather paltry lot of people coming in. We are making a list of little things we want you to do for the bazaar, so I am afraid there are hard times ahead for you. However my boy shan't be worried if I can help it. I am feeling splendidly well and hungry like yourself, so you need have no anxieties. I am afraid there is no more news today, dearest. You see I haven't got so many fresh things happening as you have. The photo of the calf I sent in for the *Gentlewoman* competition came out next to the prizewinners—rather an annoying position, wasn't it?... Now goodbye, darling with all the love of your little girl, Nursie. [And some kisses follow.]

There it is, in all its simplicity and lovingness; and there is the girl with her concern over her mother's bazaar for which she loyally worked, and the bicycle ride, and the bookbinding, and the lecture, and her love for the young man whom she was going to protect from boredom, and over whose health she had established a right by her nickname to concern herself. Not a hint of her vocation though she probably felt some pricks of its growing. She knew how to love, she was what the old Friends used to call tender in her approach to life, a delicate keen instrument, like the little bookbinder's knives that Hubert kept sharp for her.

There is another letter belonging to this year. It had evidently followed one that contained a scolding, for Hubert's letters had been getting scrappier and scrappier. She is with the St. Albans cousins again and planning a Sunday visit to them, with Hubert, on bicycles. But her chief concern is with Hubert's homecoming, when is she to see him again? Will he be home on Saturday to relieve the boredom of the day which is "worse even than Sunday I think"? He was coming home to set up his name on a door in Chambers. She ends rather wickedly: "The parrot here is most embarrassing. It has just said: 'Kiss, kiss, kiss Clifford, you're very naughty!' What a good thing we don't keep a parrot."

2

"I ENTERED ITALY"

In 1898, when Evelyn was twenty-three, her parents decided to forgo one of the yachting holidays and to go abroad with their daughter, to Switzerland and Italy. None of the three had made this venture before, and it was a choice that affected Evelyn very deeply. After all there had not been much at home to call out her particular spiritual capacity. The dry atmosphere of the law, her mother's kindly but rather uninspiring hospitality and philanthropy were arid soil for her to grow on, reading and bookbinding probably brought her nearest to the Creator Spirit, and her love for Hubert kept her heart warm. But she was just at the stage when she was ready to be called out by some quite new experience into new apprehensions of Reality.

Now she was to see the Alps, and I never remember her speaking at a retreat without some mention of those fiery snowfields which symbolized so much to her of spiritual beauty. And beyond the Alps lay Italy, of which she wrote later: "Italy, the holy land of Europe, the only place left, I suppose, that is really medicinal to the soul....There is a type of mind which must go there to find itself."

Certainly Evelyn had that type of mind, and did to a great extent find herself during the next few years when the Underhills went abroad every spring. I wonder how much she had really looked at pictures or thought about them before she went to Italy. There is a wonderful description of Italian pictures at the National Gallery in her first novel, but she may have acquainted herself with them after her visit to Italy.

It was her first long journey away from Hubert, for he nearly always took part in the yachting holidays. Her very loving heart could not bear to think that he might be lonely, and her letters show how generously she loved him. Apparently before she left him they had had a rather tormenting talk about their future. They knew very well by now how much they needed each other, but Hubert was making one of those long protracted struggles to succeed at the Bar, and he may have felt that he ought not to commit her to an uncertain and long period of waiting until they could become officially engaged.

> I read my boy's letter several times when the others were out of the way [she writes to him]. New scenes haven't yet made me forget the last face I saw at Charing Cross. I feel a brute to cause you pain by leaving you, dearest; but you have promised that if it really hurts to be without me, you will ask me to come home won't you?.... Our Saturday talk gave me plenty to think of…whatever happens I must not desert you, or put my fads before your real interests. Don't you think that is the best solution?

(*Vive et ama* was a good family motto for Evelyn.)

The rest of the letter is full of the usual mishaps and tiny adventures which befall travellers. They did not have a very propitious start. Lucerne was cold and cloudy, so she missed her first possible mountains, but she enjoyed poking about in the town, and admiring the painted houses, and wrought iron door knockers, and Thorvaldsen's lion.

But the parents decided to go forward into the Italian lakes. Evelyn marked the date in her Dante birthday book with a little rather stiff sentence: "I entered Italy."

She got her Alps and pictures and churches altogether on one blissful day: "We went first to the church at Lugano to see the Luini frescoes. They are superb, simply, but I won't bore you with rhapsodies. I spent all my odd minutes in that church while we were at Lugano." (Pushing the door open, I hope one of those heavy leather ones, and seeing something that makes her want to rhapsodize, but she can't tell Hubert about it…he might mock.)

> Then we went up a small mountain by funicular railway. There were Christmas roses and hepaticas growing wild all the way up, and the view from the top was simply grand

> ...we saw Monte Rosa, and the Matterhorn and all the great
> Alps spread out all around us. It was the most glorious thing
> you can imagine, and such a blue sky....

All the doings of the little town she can recount to Hubert, and because he is a keen craftsman, and perhaps already beginning to work in enamel, she is sure that he would like "a most lovely cross" which the sacristan showed her in the church at Gravedena, about three feet high, made of gold, and blue enamel work, and set with turquoises. "You would have loved it. All around the base were beautifully modelled little saints and enamelled figures." "I have come to the conclusion," she ends her letter, "that the Italian lakes would be the proper place for you and I and the White Angel" [was it a cat?] "to retire to in our old age. Lots of nice lazy sailing and good air and walks." But she is still preoccupied with the Saturday talk, and its repercussions in Hubert's letters.

> You are not to blame yourself. You were quite right to put
> the probabilities before me, and I mean to stick to what I
> wrote to you. Nothing is a sacrifice that is or might become
> essential for your health or happiness. Your Nurse is going
> to give up principles, and always try to do her best for her
> boy...so we will end the discussion with that.

She will not be outdone in generosity.

Hitherto Evelyn had gone about with her parents, but her real initiation began when they turned home and she was left to go on to Florence by herself. The Underhill parents always seem to have allowed her a good measure of freedom. And though she was carefully put into a coach *for ladies only,* she was able in the fortnight that she had in Florence to wander to her heart's content, and generally alone, through churches and galleries.

She had seldom been alone, and that in itself is an experience which leads to thought, and searching. Hubert had written in good spirits, so she was not worrying immediately about him. All was set for a step forward in perception and understanding.

There is nothing in her diary which expresses the effect that the pictures had upon her; it is mainly a record of what she had seen.

It is obvious that the San Marco frescoes touched her deeply, so did the Spanish chapel in Sta. Maria Novella: "I could have lingered there for hours. It was so peaceful, so filled with the best mediaeval spirit, learned yet pious, stern but loving."

Since first novels are nearly always autobiographical we get a moving estimate of what she was feeling when she writes about her hero, coming face to face with great pictures for the first time.

> He sat down presently before that lovely panel which is called "The Madonna adoring the infant Christ." Its ceremonious beauty caught his eye; the ardour of its emotion held him fast. The peculiar fascinations of Florentine piety, at once so mystical, reasonable, and austere come together in this picture, in its joyous purity of outline, the intimate holiness of its atmosphere, the strange majesty of the rapt Madonna who sits with her hands folded in prayer, and looks gently down on her Son. The wistful angels who lean against the side of her throne are hushed by her intense stillness. They are spiritual persons who cannot understand the earthly love which blends Mother and worshipper in one. She dreams of her Child, lying very helplessly and gladly upon its mother's knee, as all that is holy lies upon the lap of perfect beauty.
>
> As he watched her something unearthly, something remote from life laid its quieting hand upon him. These things had not been conceived in the petty agitations of ordinary life. The Beyond had been at their birth, and left a token of its presence.

In this way perhaps did Evelyn Underhill sit and look at the pictures in the Florentine galleries and churches, taking her time over the things that she loved. It was a seed time for her, only writing to Hubert she found that she could not say much about the pictures:

> Of course I will tell you about them if you really care to know, only I can't promise that you will like them just at first, because it takes time to get the feeling of them into your mind. But you always used to mock at such things, so I

didn't try to talk about them. This place has taught me more than I can tell you [she ends passionately]: a sort of gradual unconscious growing into an understanding of things.

She came home longing to penetrate into that Beyond which had been at the birth of those pictures. In these years she was learning to love Blake who was evidently a citizen of the Beyond, and yet free from all that her spirit shied at in Institution and Dogma. When she wanted an introductory sentence for her novel she found it in his writings.

How I wish that we knew who first brought the mediaeval mystics into her ken. She was making in these early twenties a set of friends of her own, rather different from the legal society of her parents' circle; J. H. Herbert and his wife Alice, May Sinclair, Mrs. Belloc Lowndes, Sylvia Townsend Warner. Arthur Machen was another close friend with whom she shared at this time an interest in the occult. It may have been Herbert who was then keeper of MSS at the British Museum who set her to study the mediaeval stories of the Virgin which she afterwards collected. The Herberts were devout Roman Catholics, and perhaps encouraged the habit she had learned in Italy of pushing open the door of a Roman Church, and exploring the Beyond which it enshrined. The Carmelite Church in Kensington Church St., now in ruins, had a very potent atmosphere, and was not far from her home in Campden Hill Place. Other writers whom she knew well were Maurice Hewlett, Arthur Symons, and Mrs. Ernest Dowson.

There was another journey to Italy in the spring of '99. This time Evelyn took her mother to Florence. They were good fellow travellers, she enjoyed playing showman, and Mrs. Underhill was very happy in Florence. "It is very jolly," wrote Evelyn to Hubert, "showing it all to her, much more interesting than going round by oneself." Much more interesting, but perhaps not so important.

Hubert gets scolded for scrappy letters. I don't suppose he was ever much of a correspondent, but Evelyn's love flows out even when she scolds. He had taken a fearfully independent step in her absence by shaving off a small beard that he wore.

> Oh, it's dreadful to think you really have shaved, so that I shall
> come back to quite a different boy, and never see the one I
> learnt to love any more. Please don't meet me at the station.
> I don't want to see you in public for the first time.... It's sure
> to be horrible at first.

But she must have liked it in the end, for he never grew it again.

Some time in these years before 1904 she joined a little company of people who were interested in occult experiments and experiences. But she probably found it as unsatisfying as the Society of the Searchers of the Soul was to her hero in *The Grey World*. "The first meeting astonished him, the second disgusted him but he persevered...."

So perhaps did Evelyn till she had learnt enough to serve her when she needed material for her novels.

She was also studying social conditions, as were so many of her generation. How much she came into actual contact with people living in those conditions it is hard to discover, but she writes in *The Grey World* with a certain authority about the life of a slum child which makes one think that she must have made some expeditions into the back streets of Notting Hill.

The holidays were divided between the yacht and Europe. There was a journey to France, which included Chartres where she found—in the Portail Royal "a miracle of beauty, which does really exhale a strange spiritual force—The Three Queens—one by vocation a nun, one the Christian Cocotte who was sister to the Prodigal Son, and one who was haughty and *difficile* before she became a saint—these should be friends of a lifetime...."

Evelyn became a competent hand in a sailing boat, but the sailing never gripped her as it did her father and Hubert. She liked best the lazy days when the yacht drifted up some estuary, and she could watch the birds, and perhaps sketch a little, or go on land to see some castle or church. But she did write one poem full of the swiftness and joy of sailing which must have delighted Hubert and her father.

Ten Tonner Song

Dancing down the Channel 'long the summer day,
Dancing down the Channel with the breeze;
Dwelling in a dreamland built of sun and spray,
Dancing down the Channel with the breeze.

Peace upon the cross trees, Hope upon the prow,
Love to be our pilot through the seas;
Need we ask for Heaven, we who have it now?
Dancing down the Channel with the breeze.

Sweet to lie in harbour 'long the summer night,
Sweet to lie in harbour when it's still;
List the lapping waters, watch the flashing light:
Sweet to be in harbour when it's still.
Whisper in the moonbeams; while the luggers creep
Slowly to the shelter of the hill;
Days of happy roaming bring the night for sleep
Sweet to lie in harbour when it's still.

I find that I have left out the cats, so dear to both Evelyn and
her mother, who once turned back when actually on the yacht on
a report that one of the precious creatures was ill. To Evelyn the
cats were definitely part of the household, as important and as
interesting as anybody else. They assisted at the making of her
books; things that pleased her were "purry," it was a specially cosy
adjective that she uses a good deal in her letters to Hubert who
also loved cats. She took a serious view of her friends' cats; and
wrote them letters as from her own. Cats were decidedly part of
the fun and delight of life with their unexpected loves and hates,
their enchanting play, and their passion for comfort.

Then in 1902, in the spring of the year, she went another journey to Italy with Mrs. Underhill, this time to Umbria, which
thereafter had a special claim on her spirit. Perugia, Arezzo, and at
the end Assisi. We have to go again to her novel rather than to her
diary for her real feelings about Umbria.

In Umbria, where the little hills reach up towards the kiss of God, bearing her small white cities nearer heaven: In Umbria, clothed with olive woods where Francis walked... there is a Peace of God eternally established. In this country, long beloved of the dreamy arts, spirits wearied by dark journeyings may still feel the quieting touch of Immanent Peace.

Of Assisi she writes in her diary:

Assisi is well called La Beata for its soul is more manifest than any other city that I have ever known. There is something in the quiet spaces of her streets, in the wonderful way in which she hangs on the slope of the mountain, and turns a sheer face to look out over the valley, in the contrast of her pale but warm stones with the prevailing blues and greens of Umbria, which very perfectly expresses the heart of Italy. I think after careful consideration that St. Francis must rank with Our Lady of Chartres as one of the two most beautiful churches that I have seen.

3

Years of Discovery

Some years stand out as being years of discovery in every life, and 1902 seems to have been one of these for Evelyn. According to Lucy Menzies, Mrs. Underhill about this time seems to have accepted the fact that Evelyn and Hubert would eventually marry, and this must have made it easier for them, though they were still to wait five years longer for their marriage. It was a familiar enough situation in Victorian times, but it meant such an exercise of self-control as might have stopped the sap from rising in any spirit that had not a secret well of life. It did not hinder Evelyn's growing in the way that was most essential to her, but perhaps it made it necessary for her to keep her relationship with Hubert on an undisturbing level, a level that they knew and would share; loving enough, but not penetrating into a deeper state.

The years 1902 to 1904 were years of literary achievement for Evelyn; 1902 saw her first small venture, a book of little satirical poems on the funny side of legal dilemmas which she called *The Bar-Lamb's Ballad Book,* a little paper-covered book with a linocut by Hubert on the cover. These verses are too technical for the ordinary layman to find them very funny, but they do show how she had mastered her father's craft. The book was dedicated to the cat of the moment, it may be said to represent the side that she was showing to the circle of friends in Campden Hill Place and it probably entertained them considerably, as she meant that it should, for she loved to be entertaining. It shows us that verse forms came easy to her; one imagines that she had scribbled verses to amuse herself before.

The *Bar-Lamb* had quite a little welcome from the sort of papers that concern the Law, and one rather pert one from *The Isis,* which ends: "Miss Underhill is to be congratulated on her clever verses. What a treasure she must be to her 'Pa!'" *The St. James's Gazette* refers to her as "The learned daughter of a learned father."

Hubert and Evelyn bought a book labelled *Press Paragraphs,* and began by pasting in this little handful of reviews, but they needed all the space the book could provide when in 1904 she published her first novel, *The Grey World.*

The reception of this first book must have made her feel that her sixteen-year-old aspiration to authorship was justified at last. She had tried the bookbinder's craftsmanship, and succeeded so well in her craft that one of her books had been bought by the Hungarian Government for its national museum. But now she was to be launched on her own chosen way.

The book was published by Heinemann as a novel, but some wise reviewers saw it as it really was: "Quite different from the ordinary novel," said the *Arena* from Boston, "an extremely interesting psychological study." "We read her book," says Leonard Courtney in the *Daily Telegraph,* "not because it is a good novel but because it suggests an attitude." There was scarcely one adverse review, the unusual theme, the vivid style with its flashes of wit, all caught the imagination. Evelyn's friend, May Sinclair, published her *Divine Fire* about the same time, and the two together made a considerable impact on the reading public. They were two original forms of fiction, the one the history of a poet, and the other of a mystic.

Evelyn's hero, who for some reason, perhaps connected with her ironic quality, bore the most unheroic name of Willie Hopkinson, first meets us as a little slum child, dying in a London hospital; then after a baffling interval as one of the dead who inhabit the grey world of the loneliness of the material creature with no spiritual affinities, he is reincarnated in a suburban household, a philistine and unreligious ménage. This household, a little warmed by the honest love of his mother, is where he battles his way from point to point on the mystic's journey to a stage which many of her reviewers found disappointing, but which serves to show the place where Evelyn had found herself at this point in her soul's journey. The book is full of her own discoveries. She leaves

her hero deciding to find the holy thing that he needs in the simple life of a country craftsman, devoted to beauty encouraged by
the companionship of another who has discovered a country
beyond the grey world and its terrors. They two will be hermits,
with the works of their hands as their *opus Dei*. "It's difficult isn't
it?" says his anchoress. "It seems so much easier in these days to live
morally than to live beautifully. Lots of us manage to exist for years
without ever sinning against society, but we sin against loveliness
every hour of the day."

He emerges from his talk with the anchoress and on his walk
home receives the certainty that his choice of life in the wild has
been right for him:

> The Silence was benevolent; there was at once an entire
> loneliness and a very intimate sense of consolation. Earth
> undisturbed took up her maternal rights, showed him in a
> flash of vivid insight the Imaginative Universe shining dimly
> through the Vegetative World [the phrases are Blake's]. The
> mesh of time had broken. Eternity was here and now: and he
> wondrous, immortal, saw through the glassy symbol which is
> Nature the glory of the spiritual flame.

This I think we may take as a part of her own experience, as it has
been so often with the mystics, an early stage, but a curiously con-
vincing moment.

That she makes her hero a very simple-minded creature and not
an intellectual like herself, severs them from each other and makes
the book perhaps less of an autobiography than I have suggested.
Willie Hopkinson is her creation, not herself; but many of his
experiences are drawn from things that she was gradually coming
to see, and know, through the great painters, the holy land of
Umbria, and his visit to the Roman Catholic church in the dark
alleyway. To her, every move was more acutely difficult because her
keen mind accepted reluctantly what her ardent spirit longed for
so eagerly. It was the dilemma of her personality. She is content to
leave her hero as a Nature mystic, asking no more for him than a
country place where he may do his bookbinding, and shake himself free from the material values of his old surroundings praying at

the little shrine set up by the Anchoress, but owning no allegiance to creed or company of believers.

This was, I think, her own position at the time. She had, like Willie Hopkinson, pushed open the door of Roman Catholic churches, both in Italy and in London, and found there something that held her, something that told her that "this place where invocation of the invisible never ceased had an existence in Eternity not granted to the hurrying City streets."

Since the more religious of her friends were Roman Catholics, she learned to class the Anglican Communion, as the Romans do to this day, with the Protestant communions whose churches she found so destitute of joy. "I've often been in Protestant Churches," says Willie, "and they never feel like this. They have the same atmosphere as the rest of the world."

Yet there were Anglican churches at the turn of the century where she might have found that sense of Eternity, but she did not know the people who were going there to worship. Lucy Menzies wrote: "For some strange reason, as a young woman, she seems to have had few friends belonging to the Church of England.... She experienced the best of the Church of Rome but never the best of the Church of England." The churches that most corresponded to the summons that was calling and claiming her were the churches where her friends who were religious worshipped, where she sometimes went with them or alone, and where, especially in Italy, she found offerings of beauty from painters and craftsmen who were trying to give a body to the heavenly beauty. The thing that she was sure of at this point was that Beauty and Truth had an intimate and perpetual harmony. What she was not sure of was whether that harmony was integrated in any creed. But she felt that there were people who could tell her. They were not primarily theologians, though some of them were theologians, but they were people who had experienced God. And she must about this time have begun to collect all that she could about their life histories, and their confessions, their stumbling efforts to express the inexpressible, and above all their love for the One whom they had found and followed. She began to plan her book on Mysticism, to gather together what she would need for it. I think she did not actually attempt to write it until some years later, but she read for it all through the years before her marriage.

One of the significant things that resulted from the publication of *The Grey World* was that she received a letter from a lady who had read the book, and felt that Evelyn had made her see "what Reality really is." Evelyn's reply, published in her Letters, gives us a glimpse into her first effort to do what she did so supremely well later, her direction of souls.

> As you say the finding of Reality is the one thing that matters, and that always has mattered, though it has been called by many different names.
>
> You say in one place that the more urgent the want of Reality grows, the less you see how to effect it. Now this state of spiritual unrest can never bring you to a state of vision, of which the essential is peace. And struggling to see does not help one to see. The light comes when it does come, rather suddenly and strangely, I think. It is just like falling in love; a thing that never happens to those who are always trying to do it.
>
> When once it has happened to you to perceive that beauty is the outward and visible sign of the greatest of Sacraments, I don't think you can ever again get hopelessly entangled by its merely visible side. The real difficulty seems to me to come from the squalor and ugliness with which man seems to overlay the world in which he lives.
>
> Perhaps you will write to me again when you are in the mood. Those who are on the same road can sometimes help each other.

The mixture of authority and companionship, so reassuring and yet always so humble, is there in this early letter, the forerunner of so many others.

She pursued her novel writing after an interval and wrote two more novels, neither of them with such a clear-cut shape and style as *The Grey World,* and neither of them so full of the witty and neat phrase which gives to her first book real entertainment value as well as its deeper claim. The later books are more involved,

more turgid and this may mean two things: first that her own spiritual life was passing through a confused period which she could
not very well master, and second that the main stream of her creative ability was going into her big book on Mysticism. After a
very successful first novel her readers and friends, and probably her
publisher, demanded more, but she stepped aside first from the
novel to produce a little work of religious scholarship and
romance, *The Miracles of Our Lady St. Mary.* It was a bit of work
which called for some things which she had a mind to give; a
really striking amount of exact scholarship, a style which without
being mock archaic suited these fairy-tales of mediaeval faith, and
a reverence which saw through the fairy-tale disguise into the real
love of Our Lady which was part of the faith of the Middle Ages.
The stories were translated from the Latin and the old French ver-
sions, where they had lain hidden. It was a gentle piece of work,
and by all accounts beautifully done. Perhaps it was a sop thrown
to her spiritual hunger, committing her to nothing but beauty,
while the great questions battled on in her spirit. It was very well
reviewed, and her handling of her material came in for much
praise: "'We doubt if any living English writer could have recon-
structed these beautiful and touching prose poems with more
grace and feeling than Miss Underhill has proved herself to possess'; says the reviewer in the *Illustrated London News.*"

The introduction to the book came in for its share of praise, and
Evelyn must have felt the thrill of the antiquary who restores a
beautiful possession to its place in the esteem of the discerning. But
there was more, she was entering into her own country like a shy
child. This was a position from which she could retreat or simply
play the antiquary, and yet it was an offering into which she might
pour some of the revealed beauty which she already felt compelled
to offer to a world in bonds of ugliness and materialism.

4

VOCATION AND MARRIAGE

Mrs. Belloc Lowndes, a friend who met her first about this time, gives a picture of her which shows her to us as she seemed to those who met her. She wrote of her friendship:

> With a delightful being who stands out fondly in the memories of my youth. She was gentle, quiet and unassuming; her name was Evelyn Underhill, and when I first met her she had just written *The Grey World*, soon to be followed by *The Column of Dust*. Both novels had about them a quality of poetic beauty no writer has since attained. Evelyn was exceedingly modest, and never spoke of herself or of her writing.

Evelyn made a great friend, soon after her book was published, perhaps the greatest friend of her lifetime, and one who could understand the things which were more and more absorbing to her. Ethel Barker was the daughter of Prebendary Barker of St. Paul's. She was a woman of some intellectual standing, had been a student at Girton, was at the moment an extra-mural lecturer for the University of London, and had published her first book, *Buried Herculaneum,* her subject being ancient history and archaeology. Ethel was probably a simpler nature than Evelyn. Mrs. Salter told me that it was through knowing Evelyn that Ethel Barker was drawn back to religion from a period of agnosticism. I have not been able to discover where they met, but I believe they came to know each other as both being friends of Mrs. Salter. At this time she, like Evelyn, was turning to the Church of Rome; and they made a plan to spend a week at a convent of French Franciscan Nuns, St. Mary of the Angels, Southampton. How they came to choose this house we do not know, but Evelyn was probably

attracted by the fact that it was a convent of Perpetual Adoration.
She had never before gone aside in a deliberate effort to "make
her soul" though she had opened her heart to all that had been
given to her through beauty, and spiritual learning. I think it was
before this that she had "found out," as she writes, "exalted and
indescribable beauty in the most squalid places." "I still remember
walking down the Notting Hill main road, observing the
extremely sordid landscape with joy and astonishment. Even the
movement of the traffic had something universal and sublime in
it." Her poem "The Uxbridge Road" is evidently a picture of this
moment.

> The Western Road goes streaming out to seek the cleanly
>   wild,
> It pours the city's dim desires towards the undefiled,
> It sweeps betwixt the huddled homes about its eddies
>   grown
> To smear the little space between the city and the sown.
> The torrents of that seething tide who is there that can see?
> There's One who walked with starry feet the Western
>   Road by me.
>
> Behold He lent me as we went the vision of the seer,
> Behold I saw the life of men, the life of God shine clear.
> I saw the hidden Spirit's thrust; I saw the race fulfil
> The spiral of its steep Ascent predestined of the Will.
> Yet not unled, but shepherded by One they may not see,
> The One who walked with starry feet the Western Road
>   by me.

The expedition to the convent must have been a secret affair as
neither family would have smiled upon it. Some years later she
wrote to a friend: "In those days I used to frequent both English
and Roman churches and wished I knew what their secret was.
Finally I went to stay for a few days at a convent of Perpetual
Adoration."

The quiet and peace, and the affectionate welcome of the nuns
must have been very pleasing to Evelyn's hungry heart, but the

atmosphere of perpetual prayer was almost too heady for her. She wrote later to Father Robert Hugh Benson:[2] "I fled after the fourth day, otherwise I should have submitted there and then, as it was it gave me a 'push on' from the effects of which I have not yet recovered."

It probably opened a way for her to receive one of the major experiences of her life. Her own account of it was: "The day after I came away, a good deal shaken but unconvinced I was 'converted' quite suddenly once and for all by an overpowering vision which had really no specific Christian element but yet convinced me that the Catholic religion was true. It was so tightly bound up with Roman Catholicism that I had no doubt...that that Church was my ultimate home."

Both friends were obedient to the heavenly Vision received in what Evelyn called "that wonderful week." Ethel Barker seems to have gone quietly ahead, and was received into the Roman Church about nine months later, but Evelyn had a more chequered course to follow. She mistrusted for herself anything that could be the result of a sudden upsurge of emotion, though she never returned to the agnostic's position after this converting vision. Something had happened that she could not go back upon. She still went on frequenting her favourite Roman Catholic churches and seems to have attended some Lenten services at the Carmelite Church in Kensington where Father Benson was preaching. She had met him before at her friend Mary Cholmondely's house. Now she wrote to him:

> I have got half-way from agnosticism to Catholicism, and seem unable to get any farther.... I feel that you know all that there is to be known about this border land, and the helpless sensations of those who are caught in it. I want to get out, but without sacrificing intellectual honesty, and each struggle only sends me back again with renewed sensations of unreality.
>
> As I understand the matter, before one can become a Catholic, and for me Catholicism is the only possible organized faith, one must get into the state of mind which ignores

all the results of the study of Comparative religions, and accepts, for instance the Ascension, in as literal and concrete a spirit as the Spanish Armada. Is this really so?

Of course innumerable bad motives are mixed up with this muddle and indecision…at the same time the border-land position is horrible morally because it means losing the old idea that it was natural and justifiable to be self-centered without gaining the power of not being self-centered. Also the alternative fits of mystical fervor and critical examination lead nowhere except to complete self-contempt, and a mis-erable sense of the unreality of all things, and the incalcula-ble dangers of self suggestion.

What ought I to do? It would I am sure be many months before I could take any definite step—but if you would help me, and tell me where I have gone wrong, I should be truly and deeply grateful.

Father Benson replied with a good deal of wisdom; several letters passed between them, and they had at least one interview and after a few weeks she wrote: "After Holy week, and much time given to considering the question, I felt practically certain that I must eventually become a Catholic if I was to be true to my convictions."

She had been advised by Father Benson to tell Hubert exactly where she stood. They had never talked of such things, and Evelyn was quite unprepared for the passionate "storm of grief, rage, and misery" on Hubert's part. It was the confessional that worried him so desperately. "He insists," she wrote to Father Benson, "that all hope of our happiness is at an end, that he could never again trust me, no more mutual confidence possible, that there will always be a priest between us."

Father Benson had met this trouble before: "One doesn't in the least wonder, considering the industrious lying that goes on about the confessional, that people who have never come across it, are absolutely at sea as to what it means." But he agreed that it would be wise to wait, and Evelyn conceded to Hubert that she would wait for a year before taking any steps to become a Roman. "He is so heartbroken and has so little but this one thing in his life," she wrote. She was so used to putting his plans before hers, that she felt that she could not satisfy her own personal longings at the expense of her love for him, and their long, long awaited marriage. "The cruelty one would commit seems a negation of half the spirit of Christianity for the sake of one's personal beliefs and tendencies. The sacrifice of oneself is really nothing compared with this."

It seemed to Father Benson that Hubert might be reassured especially as, apart from the confessional, he had a real respect for the Roman Church, and he offered to see Hubert, and did in fact write to him.

So Evelyn deprived herself of the Sacraments in the name of charity, knowing quite well that she was risking much. "I feel," she wrote to Father Benson, "the real point is not so much whether one is inside or outside the visible Church, as whether one can keep 'the flame of adoration' burning bright without the Sacraments when one is living under strong personal influence which sets the other way."

She went abroad with her mother to Italy, making no fuss about this reversal of her hopes, and there Hubert seems to have written a comforting letter, for she replied to him:

> I only hope you are telling me the truth, and are really feel-
> ing purry and closer to one another in spite of the depres-
> sion. After all...if it was to separate us you ought to have felt
> it coming on long ago, and as the chief result has been to
> force us to talk to each other openly about all the real things
> which we sedulously kept from each other before, the final
> effect, in spite of difference of opinion, ought to be to make
> us much more real companions than in the past, when we
> each had a watertight bulkhead carefully fixed to prevent
> undue exploration. Also I think it must be a real gain for you
> if I can make you see the real beauty of Catholicism, as well
> as the merely superficial corruptions on which you had been
> led to concentrate yourself.

A brave letter, and one which made it possible for them to go forward to their marriage with a complete sense of openness. Evelyn's concession to Hubert's desperate request altered her life more completely than she could ever have expected at the time

when she made it. She thought it was a question of delay, until
Hubert's suspicions of the confessional could be allayed, but the
selfless decision on her part gave her in the end the great chances
of her vocation.

They were now set on preparing 50 Campden Hill Square
which Hubert's father had left to him, to be their future home.
They lived there until the last year or two of her life, making it a
house to which all sorts of friends came to their great delight and
comfort. Evelyn wrote to Hubert from abroad about its furnish-
ings: "I have written to C. and told her that we should probably
want a pair of purple curtains for the dining-room.... I'm sure it
won't be worth while to have anything but fast dyed pure stuff....
I think very few draperies but very good ones is the right line to
go on, don't you? and first class linen in preference to cheap silk."

Somehow this little direction is so typical of her, and the
unshoddy preferences show how integrated she was, and how
much the same person all through. The house had a good deal
of charm, and possessed quite a big garden for London. It had a
blue, purple and silver quality which gave it a rather rarefied
feeling. Evelyn had a writing-room which she called her study,
on the first floor, on the ground floor the drawing-room and
dining-room opened into each other, and somewhere in the
basement Hubert had a workshop full of the materials for his
own crafts. He was handy in the house, and it must have been
fun planning a home with someone who could turn his hand to
making shelves or smaller gadgets. The house was just the right
size for the sort of hospitality that Evelyn delighted in.

The passionate talk and truth telling do seem to have battered
down the bulkheads, for we find her writing to Hubert from
Sienna, where she was attending St. Catherine's *fiesta,* with a freedom, and an assurance that he will care for what she is feeling and
thinking about one of her favourite saints, which is new.

M. R., the lady who had written to her to ask for spiritual advice
after reading *The Grey World,* comes to the surface again at this
point, and Evelyn's letters to her form a series which show her
learning her own great office of direction of souls. She entered into
it, as her letter to Hubert shows, with some misgiving: "———

writes a rather pathetic letter asking me to help her out of her spiritual tangles. I think this sort of thing is a most horrible responsibility, and rather ridiculous when the person applied to is still in just
as much of a tangle as anyone else. A. has also been shying her rather
shallow doubts at my head. I wish I could make them see that I am
not an authority. Suppose I tell them all wrong."

But she writes, even in this early correspondence with
M. R., with a very certain note. She speaks as one having authority, the authority in her case of religious genius. "You may also take
it for granted, of course, that so long as you want peace and illumination for your own sake you will not get them.... I think no
one really finds the Great Companion till their love is of that kind
that they long only to give and not to get."

In this letter is a list of books which tells us quite a lot about
her own reading standbys, that she felt sure of recommending to a
kindred spirit. She always expected people to want to read, and
very often lent her own books, even the newest, with reckless generosity.

Here was the list she gave for a start to M. R.

Of the Classics:

The Confessions of St. Augustine
L'Ornement des Noces Spirituelles, Ruysbroeck
Theologia Germanica
Revelations of Divine Love, Lady Julian

Of the Modern Books:

The Soul of a Christian, Granger
The Soul's Orbit, M. Petre
Oil and Wine, Tyrrell
Lex Credendi, Tyrrell
A Modern Mystic's Way
The Rod, The Root, and the Flower, Coventry Patmore

The fact that she was reading and recommending Tyrrell and
Maud Petre is rather significant of what was to follow.

Before her stipulated months were up the Papal Encyclical
condemning even a moderate "Modernism" was published, and

Evelyn did not feel free to make her submission. As she put it in a
later letter to a friend: "Unfortunately I allowed myself to wait a
year before being received, and meanwhile the Modernist storm
broke. Being myself Modernist on many points, I can't get in
without suppressions and evasions to which I can't bring myself."

At the time when she was writing in 1911, she felt this to be a
grave deprivation. She now had to face years of spiritual home-
lessness, before she could contemplate any other home than
Rome. "To have any dealings with Anglicanism seems to me a
kind of treachery," she wrote in the same letter.

But at the time of her wedding she probably felt quite sure that
she would be received when her year was up. She had written to
Father Benson asking him to say a Mass for her intention on her
wedding day, which he did. There is a picture of Evelyn with three
little bridesmaids all wearing the circlets on their heads which
Hubert had made for them. She was hardly ever a good subject for
the camera, and it is hard to know whether the rather weary face
that looks out of her wedding photograph is due to a hatred of
being photographed or expresses her real frame of mind. "You
look very serious," wrote Sister Eucharistie from the convent, to
whom Evelyn sent one of her photographs. She was still in loving
touch with them, and they had told Ethel Barker that she and her
husband were part of the family, and evidently confidently
expected her reception into the Church.

Ethel Barker was received that autumn and wrote to Evelyn
from the convent: "I assure you inside is much more comfortable
than outside. I feel you are out of it, and I am rather a brute to be
in." But this made no difference to their friendship, and she and
Evelyn went on Sundays together to Mass at Westminster
Cathedral whenever they were both in London. They lived so
close to each other that there are few letters to tell us about this
friendship, which meant so much in spiritual companionship to
Evelyn.

Life at 50 Campden Hill Square took on its ordered routine.
Evelyn worked at her writing all the morning, ordering, collecting
and translating material for her big book on Mysticism. M. R.
was offered, and most joyfully accepted, a share in typing and

translating. She was a good German scholar, and Evelyn, who had no German, sent her passages from the German Mystics, and even asked her to choose and select some.

> If I sent the books would you read them leisurely through, check any passages I sent you and extract and translate for me any bits you thought specially good.
>
> It is a study of mystical methods and doctrine, *not* of specific Mystics: so that bits bearing on my points are more useful than bits showing their peculiar Characteristics.

It was a complicated book to write, and as she had never written anything but novels and translations, it was a considerable venture and demanded real scholarship. "I have not any MS. to send; it is all in little bits, being added to and corrected, and won't settle down." She was finding rewarding treasures, and sent M. R. scraps from Richard Rolle, whom she had just discovered.

Each working day had a considerable break, for Evelyn generally lunched with her mother, both of their lawyer husbands being in Chambers all day. "I seem to go out to tea a terrible lot, and gardening takes most of my play hours in London, and I do a little Health Society and Poor Law visiting," she wrote to another friend. She and Hubert were good guests and hosts. Evelyn was an enchanting talker, delightedly but not unkindly amused by the small ridiculous things in life. Here is her description of the Women Writers' dinner:

> My opposite neighbour was a lady who has made herself a religion of Conic Sections and Curves which were the Key to the Universe and an infallible corrective of Pantheism.... Next her sat Mrs. Tay Pay O'Connor who interrupted the discourse on curves to ask her if she knew Mrs. Cecil Raleigh who had done so much in Drury Lane melodrama. Add to this a large chorus of Suffragettes full of Saturday's demonstration and the usual hare and hounds business of anxious admirers chasing successful authors in order to have the pleasure of saying "I *do* so like your book" and it's not surprising if every scribbler in London is feeling weak and light-headed to-day.

She was a quick worker, and a really diligent one; in the four years after her marriage as well as all the writing and research involved in her big book, she wrote her third novel, and a little devotional book, *The Path of Eternal Wisdom*. This was her first venture into writing a completely religious book. "It was really my own attempt to make something of that particular devotion *[The Way of the Cross]*—and then a great friend suggested it might be worth while perhaps to print it," she writes later to Mrs. Meyrick Heath. When she sent it to M. R. to type she wrote, "As it is a specially private document would you please take particular precautions to avoid any human eye falling on it while it is in your charge.... I don't know yet whether I shall print it.... I'm afraid it is scrappy and sentimental, and full of vain repetitions, altogether quite different from what I intended it to be." It was published under the pseudonym of "John Cordelier," and though Evelyn later did not care for it, it did represent her first step on that long road of teaching people to pray which she was to tread so steadfastly. *The Column of Dust* had a tremendous subject, and some very good observation, but I think she was only giving it the over-plus of her powers. "Don't look on reading *The Column of Dust* as a solemn and saddening ceremonial!" she wrote to M. R. "It has not been written in that spirit I assure you, nor am I the pious and pain enduring invalid you seem to suppose.... *No,* everybody does not 'find my works painful.' Some find them dull, and some eccentric, and others read their own prepossessions into them. They don't tear themselves to ribbons over them anyhow, and neither do I. I just write what comes into my head and leave the result to luck."

But the big book was more costing. "The book gets more and more difficult. I am past all the stages at which scraps of experience could guide one, and can only rely on sympathetic imagination which is not always safe."

They must have been strange years for her as she found herself as Charles Williams wrote "face to face with an impossibility...something she could not be and yet was." Ethel Barker stood by her, and does not seem to have made the "impossible" more bitter by urging her to come into the Roman Communion, as some of the pious Roman ladies did—"I wonder how many Protestants they make in a year"—she wrote bitterly to Father Benson.

Meanwhile God had given her books to write, and one or two people to direct. M. R. was Evelyn's initiation in Direction, and the series of letters to her published in *The Letters of Evelyn Underhill* are astonishingly definite and clear considering her own troubled course at the time. But she never let her own questionings confuse the clear directions which she gave to her disciples. Even on holidays she carried this responsibility seriously and she writes to M. R. from Vézelay: "I have been thinking you over a lot since we were here."

M. R. was a shy, introspective and rather scrupulous Christian, and the first thing that Evelyn had to help her about was a worrying concern over her spiritual state:

> My first impulse was to send you a line begging you to let yourself alone. Don't keep pulling yourself to pieces. Let yourself go more, and trust more, you will get in the end what you are meant to have. [A piece of advice which must have come from the heart of her own experience.] Every minute you are thinking of evil you might have been thinking of good instead. Refuse to pander to a morbid interest in your own misdeeds. Pick yourself up, be sorry, shake yourself, and go on again.

She was anxious to help M. R. out of the *tête-à-tête* of spiritual life, to give her God and her neighbour in the right relation.

> It seems to me that your immediate job must be to make love active and operative right through your life, to live in the light of it all the while, and act by it all the while, to make it light up all your relations with other people, with nature, with life, with your work, just as much as it lights up immediate communion with our Lord. Try to see people by His Light, then they become real. Nothing helps one so much as that. Prayerful and direct intercourse is only half one's job;

the other half is to love everything for and in God. Remember that you are to be a companion in arms, a fellow worker as well as a lover and secret friend, that you are to further the coming of the Kingdom by your outer as well as your inner life.

5

EARLY MARRIED YEARS

Evelyn continued the custom of taking her mother abroad, and in the spring of 1908 they were at Carcassonne and also made an expedition into Italy. Hubert had gone on a sailing holiday but, with a flash of real imagination, he remembered to send flowers to the convent for Easter.

> You were a darling [Evelyn wrote] to send flowers to the Convent for Easter—nothing you could have done would have pleased me more, as you know. Sister Eucharistie wrote a delightful letter saying how beautiful they were, and that she put them on the High Altar, near the Blessed Sacrament. I do love you for having done that. It's lovely to think there was something of ours there then....

It was the holy place to her still, the place that had led her to vision, and so, I think, were the Florentine galleries and churches. She writes in a letter to Hubert: "I'm now quite raving mad about Italian pictures and you will find me a horrid nuisance on the subject. I thought I knew how to appreciate them before I left England, but I know that I knew less than nothing. The Botticellis here are entrancing; after a bit they cast a sort of spell over you."

Into these early married days it would be right to put a good deal of her poetry, though "Immanence" was not published till 1912. Poetry was a transitory form with her, belonging rather to the Evelyn who produced the Cordelier books, and sometimes falling into the same snare of over-weighted sentences and too many "purple patches." But when she is restrained and simple her poems are very lovely and have a great sense of line and shape, and she probably "eased her breast of melodies" using the discipline of verse to steady her troubled spirit. The poems rather than her prose at this date give a real sense of the joy that she was finding.

"Immanence" is well known and in many anthologies, but this *Missa Cantata* one does not very often see:

> Once in an abbey-church, the while we prayed,
>   All silent at the lifting of the Host,
> A little bird through some high window strayed;
>   And to and fro
>   Like a wee angel lost
> That on a sudden finds its heaven below,
>   It went the morning long
> And made our Eucharist more glad with song.
>
> It sang, it sang! and as the quiet priest
>   Far off about the lighted altar moved,
> The awful substance of the mystic feast
>   All hushed before
>   It like a thing that loved,
> Yet loved in liberty, would plunge and soar
>   Beneath the vault in play
> And thence toss down the oblation of its lay.
>
> The walls that went our sanctuary around
>   Did as of old, to that sweet summons yield.
> New scents and sounds within our gates were found,
>   The cry of kine,
>   The fragrance of the field,
> All woodland whispers, hastened to the shrine,
>   The country side was come
> Eager and joyful, to its spirit's home.
>
> Far stretched I saw the cornfield and the plough,
>   The scudding cloud, the cleanly running brook,
> The humble kindly turf, the tossing bough,
>   That all their light
>   From Love's own furnace took;
> This altar, where one angel brownly bright
>   Proclaimed the sylvan creed,
> And sang the Benedictus of the mead.

All earth was lifted to communion then,
    All lovely life was there to meet its King;
Ah, not the little arid souls of men
        But sun and wind
      And all desirous thing
The ground of their beseeching here did find;
     All with one self same bread,
And all by one eternal priest were fed.

She had a double holiday abroad that year, for she and Hubert went in the late summer to Vézelay and other Burgundian towns. Evelyn and Hubert were good travellers, and immensely enjoyed going about together. They had enough of common interest in their love of good architecture and craftsmanship and in their delight in the countryside. Evelyn might slip away to Mass while Hubert made a contact with some crony in the town or village, for he was a friendly man. They attracted all sorts of acquaintance:

> The company has been very amusing [wrote Evelyn to
> M. R. from Vézelay]. Two French lady artists, and the
> Director of the Bibliotèque des Arts Décoratifs at Paris, a
> delightful person, both cheerful and brilliant, who became
> very friendly and is going to take us round the Musée in per-
> son when we return to Paris. We walked over together to
> Herre Perthuis yesterday afternoon. What a perfectly lovely
> place! It was very clear after a rainy morning, and the view
> from the high bridge was marvellous. The old gentleman
> whose garden contains the ruins of the cloister, dorter, and
> refectory, and the monks' garden and vineyard here asked us
> in yesterday and showed us round: gave Hubert a local fossil
> from the "grotte" and me a bunch of roses.

Yes, they were friendly travellers: "It was quite affecting saying goodbye to all our friends, particularly Madame Bobelin, who for some unknown reason loved me dearly and kissed me fervently (to my great amazement)."

That journey wound up in Paris with a "little of everything, with the Sainte Chapelle at one end of the scale and new autumn hats at the other."

The year 1909 saw the publishing of *The Column of Dust,* her last novel. It seems to have had a mixed reception. "Wasn't *Punch's* review of *The Column of Dust* beastly?" she wrote to M. R. "Quite the nastiest I have had. There have been about forty now, representing all possible shades of opinion."

In the spring she had another short correspondence with Father Benson, after sending a letter of introduction to him for her friend Mrs. Herbert. The letters from her show that her struggle to know what was right as to submitting herself to Rome was not over. She makes no mention this time of any opposition from her husband, so perhaps that point had been resolved between them. It is that other crux of the giving up of intellectual honesty. She confesses the loneliness and the perils of isolation from other Christians. "I wish the invisible Church had a little more substance in it; it has many conspicuous advantages over the visible one, especially in that matter of intellectual liberty, as to which I'm afraid I still disagree with you. I would like to talk to you very much, or rather let you talk. I simply cannot talk about religion, and get shy or snappy at once, sometimes both...but it's merely wasting your time. I'm afraid I'm destined to go on fidgeting away and trying to square the spiritual circle." "At present," she writes in a later letter, "really I want to do God's will and my own both at once." She breaks off the correspondence on a rather despairing note: "The general result of allowing me to argue with you is to provide a state of internal uproar, in which I more often feel hard, bitter, contentious and irreligious than the opposite." It needed a greater man than Father Benson to set this troubled soul on the way that she desired so much, and she still had to wait for two years before she came into contact with Baron von Hügel.

In 1910 her spring journey with her mother took her to Rome for the first time. St. Peter's disappointed her: "It is frankly hideous and not a bit more religious than St. Paul's," she wrote to Hubert, and to Mr. Herbert: "St. Peter's is mostly hopelessly un-Petrine. He is about the last person one can think of in connection with that horrid monstrosity." But the older basilicas, Sta. Maria Maggiore and Sta. Pudenziana, and above all the lovely little Sta. Maria in Cosmedin fascinated her: "It is a little jewel on the banks of the Tiber. It is marvellous to be in the centre of the Western tradition and see it all spread before one from the earliest catacombs right through the basilica period...and Oh! such marvellous mosaics, from the fourth century to the fifteenth," she wrote to M. R.

Father Benson and J. H. Herbert secured her an audience with Pope Pius X. To J. H. Herbert she writes: "I'm deeply grateful to you and R. H. B., as I don't think I should have got an audience without you; as it was, I went down to San Silvestro this morning and Robert Hugh's name acted like a charm."

She was tremendously impressed by her audience. "The Pope came in in his white things," she wrote to Hubert, "and ascended the throne so quietly and simply that he was there before one had noticed him. He has a beautiful voice, and gives one an intense impression of great holiness, kindness and simplicity." "I never received such an impression of sanctity before," she wrote to M. R. "Whatever muddles he may make intellectually or politically, spiritually he is equal to his position. I do not think anyone who had been in his atmosphere could doubt it."

Her mother fell ill in Rome, tiresomely but not dangerously, and as they had secured a nursing sister for her, Evelyn had extra time for roaming about the Forum, the Catacombs, St. Cecilia's house and St. Lorenzo-outside-the-walls. Of one such walk she writes to Hubert:

> I had rather a nice solitary prowl on the Coelian Hill...in fact very nice.... I think I most enjoyed San Gregorio. It has been rather done up and rebuilt, but there were lots of nice things in it, and as there was a sudden downpour of rain just then, I was there some time and saw it at my case. Tell Dickums [her cat Richard] that it was built on the site of the house to which Gregory the Great retired from the world in the 6th century, taking with him nothing but his favourite cat, so I was very pleased to see on one of the front chairs of the nave a very nice black and white cat sleeping soundly.

The old woman who was bossing about told me it always
slept there, and during mass was often curled up in the
Sanctuary.... I felt as if I was stroking quite a reverend piece
of Church Furniture.

She herself fell ill and was detained in Rome for a week or so,
but was soon home again, "well and strong and walking 10 to 12
miles a day, and anxious to get back to the vast amount of work I
have waiting for me."

6

HER BOOK CALLED *MYSTICISM*

The big book was finished in the autumn of 1910 and came out in the spring of 1911. I could not find any reviews of it among her papers, but some letters are mentioned. The most important thing for Evelyn was that her book was read and appreciated and commented on by Baron von Hügel, and because of this they became known to each other. "I forgot whether I told you," writes Evelyn to J. H. Herbert, "that I have become the friend (or rather disciple and adorer) of von Hügel. He is the most wonderful personality I have ever known, so saintly, so truthful, sane and tolerant. I feel very safe and happy sitting in his shadow, and he has been most awfully kind to me." He was perhaps the only living authority who had studied the Mystics from the same viewpoint and with greater depth of experience than his new disciple. Some things in her book had made him a little anxious for its author, but he recognized her quality and her teachableness. Evelyn also had another letter which gave her great pleasure: "I've had a perfectly charming letter from the Abbot of Downside, who wrote to say how absolutely he agrees with my book. Wasn't it sweet of him, and such a surprise. It came yesterday and made me feel so warm and comfy and ready to tolerate the ever growing crowd of bores, who have had visions and want me to tell them what they are like."

Reviews she mentions were one in the *Record:* "Most generous in its language…great book, classic work, etc.," and "A long and splendid review signed C. E. Laurence from the *Daily Graphic.* So I am purring."

We must now take a look at the book which brought her into the forefront of religious writers.

She divided her great subject into two parts. The first "is intended to provide an introduction to the general subject of

Mysticism. The second, the longer part, contains a somewhat detailed study of the nature and development of man's spiritual consciousness."

In her first part, in order to free her great subject from confusion and misapprehension, and to establish it in its true place, she looked at it from the point of view of the psychologist, the symbolist and the theologian. To clear it from its most dubious connection she also wrote a chapter on Mysticism and Magic. For mysticism at the time when she wrote was suspect. It appeared occult, erotic, unsound. "One could not hear it spoken of," wrote Maritain, "without immediately being on one's guard against an eventual invasion of fanaticism and hysteria." But to Evelyn Underhill: "The mystics are the pioneers of the spiritual world, and we have no right to deny validity to their claims merely because we lack the courage necessary to those who would prosecute such explorations for themselves. A certain type of mind has always discerned three strait and narrow ways going out towards the Absolute: in religion, in pain, in beauty with the ecstasy of artistic satisfaction. Down these three paths as well as by many another secret way, they claim that news comes to the self-concerning levels of reality, which in their wholeness are inaccessible to the senses: worlds wondrous and immortal whose existence is not conditioned by the 'given' world which those senses report."

The second part of *Mysticism* she called *The Mystic Way* and she illustrated it by record after record of mystical experience. *Mysticism* "was a great book precisely not because of its originality, but because of its immediate sense of authenticity," wrote Charles Williams in his introduction to her *Letters*. "She knew her men and women; she could choose the utterances which best conveyed them, and the mighty truths they stood for to the seeker of today. To the reader, Evelyn Underhill, as the author, was altogether occulted by the dark and shining fierceness of the sayings which she had collected."

She divides her map of the way into five sections, preferring these to the well-known three of Purgation, Illumination and Union. Her first section is The Awakening of Self, which she illustrates, among other quotations, from a passage by Suso: "That which the Servitor saw had no form neither any manner of being; yet he had of it a joy such as he might have known in the seeing of shapes and substances of all joyful things. His heart was hungry, yet satisfied, his soul was full of contentment and joy: his prayers and his hopes were fulfilled."

Her second stage is The Purgation of Self. "Behold, says the *Theologia Germanica,* on this sort must we cast all things from us and strip ourselves of them; we must refrain from claiming anything for our own. Poverty, wrote Jacopone da Todi, has so ample a bosom that Death itself may lodge therein."

And the next stage is the Illumination. "Everything in temporal nature," says William Law, "is descended out of that which is eternal, and stands as a palpable visible outbirth of it, so when we know how to separate the grossness, death, and darkness of time from it, we find what it is in its eternal state."

The fourth state is the Dark Night, when the soul is deprived of all sense of the presence of God, the "Education in selfless constancy" of which Mechthild of Magdeburg wrote: "Lord, since Thou hast taken from me all that I had of Thee, yet of Thy grace leave me the gift which every dog has by nature: that of being true to Thee in my distress, when I am deprived of all consolation. This I desire more fervently than Thy heavenly Kingdom."

And last she devotes a chapter to the Unitive Life, the end and sum of the Mystic Way, and I have chosen a quotation from her favourite Ruysbroeck, from the many lovely writings which she collected: "When love has carried us above all things into the Divine Dark, there we are transformed by the Eternal Word Who is the image of the Father; and as the air is penetrated by the sun, thus we receive in peace the incomprehensible Light, enfolding us, and penetrating us."

Where she perhaps struck new ground was in her insistence that this state of union produced a glorious and fruitful creativeness, so that the mystic who attains this final perfectness is the most active doer for the Kingdom of Heaven, and not the hidden and secluded dreaming lover of God.

After the Way has been traced with all its august sufferings and surprising joys, Evelyn Underhill gives herself a final chapter in

which to link these tremendous experiences to the life of the
ordinary Christian man and woman, busy with the five-
finger exercises of his faith.

> We are all the kindred of the mystics [she urges].... Strange
> and far away from us though they seem, they are not cut off
> from us by some impassable abyss. They belong to us; they are
> our brethren, the giants, the heroes of our race. As the
> achievement of genius belongs not to itself only but also to
> the society that brought it forth; as theology declares that the
> merits of the saints avail for us all, so because of the solidar-
> ity of the human family, the supernal accomplishment of the
> mystics is ours also, their attainment is the earnest money of
> our eternal life.
>
> The Mystics on their part are our guarantee of the end
> to which the Immanent Love, the hidden steersman which
> dwells in our midst, is moving: our lovely forerunners on the
> path towards the Real. They come back to us from an
> encounter with life's most august secret, as Mary came run-
> ning from the tomb; filled with amazing tidings which they
> can hardly tell. We, longing for some assurance, and seeing
> their radiant faces, urge them to pass on their revelation if
> they can. It is the old demand of the dim-sighted and incred-
> ulous.
>
> *Dic nobis, Maria*
> *Quid vidisti in via?*
>
> But they cannot say: can only report fragments of the
> Symbolic Vision.
>
> According to the manner of their strength and of their
> passion, these true lovers of the Absolute have conformed
> here and now to the utmost tests of divine sonship, and the
> final demands of life. They have not shrunk from the suffer-
> ings of the Cross. They have faced the darkness of the tomb.
> Beauty and agony alike have called them, all have awakened
> a heroic response. For them the winter is over, the time of
> the singing of birds has come. From the depth of the dewy

garden, Life new, unquenchable and ever lovely comes to meet them with the dawn.

The book ends with an extremely valuable Appendix, a kind of *Who's Who* of mysticism, which also shows its persistence and interconnection from century to century.

7

The Years before the War

Mrs. Meyrick Heath was one of Evelyn's most intimate friends in 1911–12, though there seem to be no later letters to her. She was one of the readers of *Mysticism* who wrote to Evelyn about it. The correspondence begins with a grateful letter from Evelyn after a sympathetic one from Mrs. Heath about the book. Evelyn was not prepared as the result of writing her big book to be considered as a prophet by her friends. "Please don't ever talk of 'sitting at my feet' or any nonsense like that. If you knew the real animal you would be provoked to either tears or laughter at the absurdity of the idea…. I am not 'far on' but at the very bottom. So there!" She gives this friend a history of her spiritual state, the Agnosticism, the Philosophical Theism, the visit to the convent and her vision, her decision to wait before joining the Roman Church, and her subsequent feeling that she was now exiled from it by the Papal Encyclical: "I no more like the tone of contemporary Romanism than you do," she writes, "it is really horrible. But with all her muddles she has kept her mysteries intact."

> Oh that dreadful limiting of salvation! [she breaks out in another letter]…. You are right, we are all too narrow for God…. I cling to St. Paul—and seem to find his inmost teaching over and over again in all one's experience, and in everyone who cares for Christ—Catholic or Protestant or whatsoever he may be.
>
> I wonder what you'll think of "The Everlasting Mercy."… I think the last twelve pages the most wonderfully exact and yet highly poetic description of that sort of vision that has ever been written. Every time I read it, it makes me live the first fine careless rapture over again.

She shares with this friend "a truly divine week at Storrington" where "as on many previous Easters I found nature a good deal more spiritually suggestive than Ecclesiasticism! Everything seems then to surge in on you with new life, doesn't it? It is too much to be pinned down to any rites or symbols however august, isn't it? It's only after the glory and madness have worn off a bit that one can bear them."

She brings this friend into a new venture that she has adopted herself, I think rather reluctantly: "Did I tell you about a thing called The Religious Thought Society which has been started lately. It is supposed to be going to get hold of the modern mind, and deepen its spiritual life." I think this is the first religious group that Evelyn belonged to, and she found herself co-opted on to its committee "amidst earnest and orthodox females" but was rather reassured by "one nice open-airey man with the proper Christian twinkle in his eye," and by the fact that Dean Inge was chairman. Though she is convinced in her mind that the Society is good, "sound Missionary work really worth doing if it can be done in the right way," she gives us an illuminating glimpse into her own special way of helping people at that time. "I feel that the ideal thing—and for me the only possible way—is to get people individually, bit by bit, one by one, when a door is opened to one. The idea of talking generally about anything that really matters makes me squirm."

Another thing that she shared with this friend in the same year of 1913 was a wonderful Italian holiday in Umbria. "We drove back by moonlight—so wonderful. It was full moon, and we drove in full sight of La Verna. I felt as if the original night must have been like that. There were sheets of lightning, too, playing round the tops of the mountains. Do you remember how the peasants reported that on the night of the Miracle they saw a mystical fire lighting up the summit of the Mount?"

Then there was a set of lectures by Bergson: "I'm still drunk with Bergson, who sharpened one's mind and swept one off one's feet both at once. Those lectures have been a real great experience: direct contact with the personality of a profound intuitive thinker of the first rank."

That year saw the publication of the book that she had been

writing as a much shorter and simpler exposition of *Mysticism,
The Mystic Way*. Some of her friends (especially J. H. Herbert)
thought it dangerously Modernist. It was written very much
with the unorthodox seeker in her mind. Publishing the big
book, and noting its repercussions, had shown her that there
would be readers waiting for a shorter study, and that many people were turning to the testimony of experience, and were
becoming aware of a science of prayer. It had not been an easy
book to write: "I'm immersed in my book, which is very difficult, but enthralling," she had written to Mrs. Heath. "I write all
morning and read all evening, at least as long as I can, but I generally collapse with dimness of mind about nine o'clock."

She defended herself against the charge of Modernism to J. H.
Herbert in a long letter which shows that she had suffered from
his criticism. "Far from going further on the path of destruction,
the last thing I want to do is to destroy the one thing that gives
meaning and beauty to me: but what seems to you, to my great
grief, to be blasphemy, seems to make the things I love best more
real and more sacred."

She was evidently seeing enough of von Hügel at that time for
him to enter into her position in the book: "As to the critical side
of the book, I simply took the least common measure of what
seems to me practically established beyond reasonable doubt, and
did not in most particulars even go as far as Baron von Hügel
thought I should have done."

About this book the Baron had written to her: "I see how fine
the structure of the book is, and how carefully you seem to have
borne in mind the all important place and function in religion of
liturgical acts, of the Sacrament, of the Visible, of History. You will
remember that I was not quite sure about this side of the question
in your *Mysticism*. I am so very pleased, too, that the structure of
your book proclaims the three stages of the New Testament: The
Synoptists, St. Paul, the Fourth Gospel."

She ends her second letter to Herbert with a passionate sentence: "Personally, if I didn't think the *whole* of life was the work
of the Holy Spirit, I should give everything up. It is the centre of
my creed: so vivid that the things which seem to us disgusting,

cruel, unjust—and I don't deny them—can do nothing against it."

She had the comfort of talking it all over with the Baron: "Much about your letter which had disturbed him considerably— a firm but gentle lecture on my own Quakerish leanings! His main point seems to be that such interior religion is all very well for our exalted moments, but will fail us in the ordinary jog trot of daily life, and is therefore not a whole religion for men who are not pure spirit."

One other experience came to her in 1913, the chance of working with another great man, the Indian Mystic, Rabindranath Tagore, who was recovering from an operation in London. "He likes me to go to him every afternoon to work out some transla- tions of old Indian Mystical lyrics. It is fascinating work, and a real joy and education to be with him—but it does not leave much spare time."

The book of Kabir's poems which they compiled and translated together came out in a limited edition to which Evelyn wrote the Introduction. The form which they chose was the same that Tagore had used in translating his own *Gitanjali*. It is a sort of rhythmic free line which left the translators free to express the original without distorting it. It was a great and delicate piece of work which these two, the Indian and the Englishwoman, achieved between them, and it is rather sad that the edition was so small, for they had made a beautiful thing. To Evelyn at this moment of her own pilgrimage, when she stood outside any alle- giance to Church or sect, Kabir's position as he shook himself free of the ritual and shape of both Mohammedanism and Hinduism was probably very satisfying.

> "I am neither in Temple or Mosque. I am neither in Kaaba
> or Kailash.
> Neither am I in rites or ceremonies, nor in Yoga and
> renunciation.
> If thou art a true seeker thou shalt at once see Me: thou
> shalt meet Me in a moment of time.
> Kabir says, O Sadhu! God is the breath of all breath."

8

THE WAR YEARS

She was aboard her father's yacht when the war broke out on 4 August 1914. The yacht was confined to harbour, and lights on board were forbidden. Those were the days when the rumours of the Russian Army arriving in England went abroad; the days when the war was bound to be over before Christmas. Evelyn had a book in the press, the short volume, *Practical Mysticism,* in which she was addressing herself especially to those who had no allegiance to any Church, to the religious man in the street. But still she wondered if it were right to publish such a book. "Many will feel," she wrote in its preface, "that in such a time of conflict and horror, when only the most ignorant, disloyal or apathetic can hope for quietness of mind, a book which deals with that which is called the Contemplative attitude to existence is wholly out of place."

The terrible German advance, the desperate stand of the little Expeditionary Force, the glorious muddle of the committees dealing with the Prince of Wales Fund, and the hopeless struggles of the Soldiers' and Sailors' Families Association to deal with a situation beyond the capacity of their staff: all these were battering at her spirit, for she almost certainly was plunged into a certain amount of social work in the first months of the war.

An article in the *Westminster Gazette* must be her own experience as a visitor to Mrs. White, "the respectable reservist's wife ...greatly troubled by the contrast between her own conduct and character and that of her neighbours," but just as anxious as they are to get her share of the Prince of Wales Fund. Her neighbour Mrs. Miller has received her ring paper. Mrs. Miller when taxed with this produces "an expression of astonishment and horror: 'Does Kitchener let yer know when he sends it?' she asks. Mr.

Morgan next door has an unfortunate absence of marriage lines. "E mayn't be me 'usband but he's behaved to me like an Englishman,' says his lady companion. In the next house they have a letter from camp: 'They tells us we're serving our country, but from what I sees of it it's worse than hopping.' 'This unfavourable view, however, is not common [she concludes]. Those of our recruits who have come back for a day's leave are already proud of themselves.... Their language abounds in technical terms, and their attitude to the neighbourhood is friendly but very condescending.'" So wittily and shrewdly does she size up her neighbours in Notting Hill.

But the taxing of the spirit which underlay the courageous gaiety is shown in other writings in the early war years.

She decided that the publication of her *Practical Mysticism* should go forward. There was need for spiritual sustenance, and, as she wrote in her Preface: "It becomes a part of true patriotism to keep the spiritual life, both of the individual citizen, and of the group, active and vigorous; its vision of realities unsullied by the entangled interests and passions of the time." She was writing now, not for the expert but for the "Average man"..."my business being confined to the description of a faculty which all men possess in a greater or less degree." What the book meant to one reader, Bishop Barkway records: "By the mercy of God, *Practical Mysticism* came into my hands at a time of great need. It was given to me at the first Christmas of the Great War in 1914. I had been prepared for its message by many years of searching without finding, and it spoke straight to the heart of my condition...it is the book to which I owe more than to any other theological book I have ever had."

To her, as to many sensitive Christians, the agonizing question raised by a major war had to be faced. It had seemed to her, as it had to many alive Christians in the first twelve years of the century, that there was a real hope of spiritual renaissance, there was a new hopeful stretching out of eager hands for spiritual life. Those who remember the early days of the Girls' Diocesan Association, of the Student Christian Movement, or the revolution in Sunday religious teaching, or the group that she herself belonged to, The

Religious Thought Society, will recollect the sudden realization of
the possibilities of the prayer life. All this she saw perishing in the
"sudden onset of brute force."

In the spring of 1915 she was writing in the *Hibbert Journal,* trying to estimate the values and results of Peace and War. At that
time she was not a pacifist, and wrote of the pacifist position as
perverse. She was trying to hope that

> the demand which the war has made on us is just that
> demand of an unselfing, a mergence of that small thin per-
> sonal existence in the rich whole of a larger life, which
> coarsely and harshly evoked by the necessities of race con-
> flict, is at bottom the demand which religion makes under
> more beautiful and subtle forms.... Perhaps for some of those
> who struggle, believing their cause to be just and high, and
> for those of the warring nations who strive for truly ideal
> ends, the violence and folly of war may yet be justified, and
> the purpose of Creative Love made plain.

Some time in those early months of 1915 she wrote a lovely
appreciation of the French poet Charles Péguy, who was killed in
the first weeks of the war; and all through the war years she continued her vocation as a writer on prayer. We find her one of a
group of writers upon prayer, in a series instigated by *The
Challenge,* that inspired weekly which kept up the spiritual
courage of so many baffled Christians in the war years. Evelyn's
contribution was a paper on the prayer of Silence:

> In the prayer of Silence the child ceases to chatter, and waits
> for the Father to speak; and thus staying quietly in His
> Presence at once gains in intimacy and trustfulness.
>
> The prayer of silence has an active and social as well as a
> religious and personal value. In it the soul feeds upon God,
> draws new vitality from the source of all life. The citizen who
> is so strengthened is worth more to the state than the man
> whose roots do not strike deep into Eternity.

During the war years she wrote most of the essays which were
later published in a collection called *The Essentials of Mysticism,* but

the work that must have given her the most satisfaction was a short study of Ruysbroeck, which she wrote for a series called *The Quest*. If she had a favourite among the mystics it was this quiet monk from the Low Countries who loved his flowers, and birds and all the country things and found them paths into Eternity, as she did herself. He was to her the most satisfying of all the Mediaeval Mystics, and she found herself very much at one with him in the years when he was working as an almost unknown priest in Brussels, for she herself at this time had also a hidden side.

> His Career [she writes] which covers the greater part of the fourteenth century, that golden age of Christian Mysticism, seems to exhibit within the circle of a single personality, and carry up to a higher term than ever before, all the best attainments of the Middle Ages in the realm of Eternal life.
>
> The central Christian doctrine of the Divine Fatherhood, and of the soul's "power to become the Son of God," it is this raised to the nth degree of intensity experienced in all its depth and fullness, and demonstrated with the exactitude of the mathematician, and the passion of a poet, which Ruysbroeck gives us.
>
> I regard the ninth and tenth chapters of *The Sparkling Stone* as the high water mark of mystical literature. Nowhere else do we find such a marvellous combination of wide and soaring vision with the most delicate and intimate psychological analysis. The old Mystic, sitting under his friendly tree, seems here to be gazing at, and reporting to us the final secrets of that Eternal World, where the "Incomprehensible Light enfolds and penetrates us, as the air is penetrated by the light of the sun."

The Life is a small book, but the bibliography at the end is formidable and gives us some idea of her standard of study, and her wide steadfast reading.

Meanwhile the chances of war came rather near home. The house next to her father's was destroyed by a bomb, and part of the Law Courts where his chambers were situated shared the like fate.

Hubert was busy in his spare time working on hospital boards. His practical inventive mind helped him to devise a special sort of splint which was called after him. But one gets the impression that life went on in straightforward hard-working lines for the two of them. Evelyn was still seeing Ethel Barker often, and they kept up their plan of going together to Westminster Cathedral on Sundays. She probably also saw von Hügel from time to time.

In 1916 she began to do war work proper at the Admiralty, translating guide books, where her languages were valuable. In the room where she and her friend Emma Gurney Salter worked, a young brother and sister, Robin and Barbara Collingwood (now Mrs. Gnospelius), were also employed—artistic people with good brains; the sort of company that Evelyn delighted in. Robin Collingwood was already making himself a name as a philosopher. The room where they worked was a gay one, but time sometimes hung on their hands. It was on one of these afternoons when Evelyn invented a county, complete with flora and fauna, and sent it up to the proper authorities—it nearly found its way to the printer. We are not told how the Head of the Department dealt with Evelyn. Barbara Gnospelius sent me a wonderfully clear impression of Evelyn as she was in those mid-war years:

> The astonishing thing about Evelyn in 1916 when I first met her, and when she was already a very well-known and respected poet and writer, was her gaiety. She was not certainly an impressive or even a striking object at first sight. She was smallish, stooping, and round-shouldered, her clothes definitely dowdy and her hair most unsatisfactory, though even in those days she wore her little lace caplet, which while giving her a cachet seemed less appropriate than in later years. But her creased little face, full of animation and very mobile, was an instant attraction; and as I remember it her face was always creased with laughter and twinkling with fun. She had a way of laughing up at you…which, while endearing was, to the young and shy, just a trifle daunting. I had expected to meet a lady rather exquisitely withdrawn, but no one could have seemed less lofty and remote than Evelyn or more ready

to meet everything and everyone with a bit of a grin, and a splutter of laughter and a naughty irreverent joke. It was most refreshing.

She was terribly nice with Robin and me, and from the first we were on the easiest and happiest terms. We visited her often at Campden Hill Square, met Nick [Hubert] and had great fun; and they both dined with us in our big basement kitchen, when we moved to 30 Bedford Gardens, and we talked about everything, not so much as I recollect War and Politics, as Philosophy, Psychology and Religion.

Her second book of poems was published in 1916 and named *Theophanies;* this, with *Immanence,* contains all her output as a poet. Poetry was a medium that she laid aside in later life. Most poets even if they are diverted into other forms of writing occasionally turn back to that dearest and most enthralling of ways of writing. But Evelyn laid it aside altogether. "It is too easy," she is reported to have said about writing poetry, which seems to indicate that she could not put her deepest self into her poems, or that she did not consider it worth while to purge them as true poems must be purged. If one compares them with the work of her contemporary Alice Meynell one sees that she has said too much, and withheld too little. Still, her work was deeply appreciated, and was reproduced in the *Augustan Poets* in the 1930s, which gave her great pleasure; and she must be counted among the first religious poets of her generation. This poem, "Continuous Voyage," links up the seafaring holidays with her venturing spiritual life.

At twilight, when I lean the gunwale o'er
And watch the water turning from the bow,
I sometimes think the best is here and now—
The voyage all, and nought the hidden shore.
Is there no help? and must we make the land?
Shall every sailing in some haven cease?
And must the chain rush out, the anchor strike the sand,
And is there from its fetters no release?
And shall the steersman's voice say, "Nevermore
The ravening gale, the soft and sullen fog,

No more the cunning shoal, the changeful ebb and flow.
Put up the charts, and take the lead below,
And close the vessel's log"?

Adventure is a seaman's life, the port
Calls but the weary, and the tempest driven:
Perhaps its safety were too dearly bought
If that for this our freedom must be given.
For lo! our Steersman is forever young
And with much gladness sails beneath the stars;
Our ship is old, yet still her sails are hung
Like eager wings upon the steady spars.
Then tell me not of havens for the soul
Where tides can never come, nor storms molest;
My sailing spirit seeks no sheltered goal,
Nought is more sad than safety—life is best
When every day brings danger for delight,
And each new solemn night
Engulfs our whitening wake within the whole.

Beyond the bent horizon oceans are
Where every star
Lies like an isle upon Eternity.
There would I be
Given to his rushing wind,
No prudent course to find
For some snug corner of Infinity;
But evermore to sail
Close reefed before the gale,
And see the steep
Great billow of his love, with threatening foam
Come roaring home
And lift my counter in its mighty sweep.

She was probably easing her heart in the war years by such
poems as the one from which these lines are quoted:

Never of us be it said
We had no war to wage,

Because of our womanhood,
Because the weight of age
Held us in servitude.
None sees us fight,
Yet we in the long night
Battle to give release
To all whom we must send to seek and die for peace.
When they have gone, we in a twilit place
Meet terror face to face,
And strive
With him, that we may keep our fortitude alive.
Theirs be the hard, but ours the lonely bed.
Nought were we spared—of us, this word shall not be said.

She kept in her poems that word that she had spoken in *Immanance,* it was the first poem in her first book, and here is part of the last poem in her second book, her final word as a poet.

I too have heard Thy ceaseless song,
   I have discerned Thy radiant feet
That flash in rhythmic dance among
    The squalors of the city street:
      And in its gutters every day
      Have seen Thy ragged angels play.

For deep the secret world within,
   I feel Thy stirrings soft and strange
And know all growing things my kin
    In this Thy nursery of change:
      In every kitten's fluffy dress
      Our Father's cunning I confess.

The poems on the whole belong to the "John Cordelier" Evelyn and not to the one that she became when she had found herself at last, and her truest vocation, and her loveliest use of words.

Now at the end of the war she had a great grief to face in Ethel Barker's death after a long illness. When Lucy Menzies

first wrote to her in 1917 she was going every day to see Ethel
Barker who was then very seriously ill. It was the earthly end of a
very intimate friendship; perhaps there was no one except Ethel
Barker who knew the stress of the position she felt herself bound
to take up. She wrote later of this friend: "near to sanctity as anyone I ever knew," and also remembered years afterwards how, as
she lay dying, she kept saying: "Such music! Such Light!"

It was some time in the lonely period between Ethel Barker's
death and her own decision to put herself under von Hügel's
direction that she took the step that at one time seemed so impossible to her, and she decided that she would commit herself to the
Anglican Communion. There was no need to take any dramatic
step, it was the Church of her baptism and confirmation. There is
very little to show just what made her feel that it was right to do
this. Perhaps Ethel Barker's death loosened her nearest tie with the
Roman Church. She was writing in this year the lectures which
Manchester College had asked her to deliver in the inaugural
course of lectures on religion established under the will of
Professor Upton. These lectures were published later in book form
in a volume which she called *The Life of the Spirit and the Life of
Today.* Some of her statements in the chapter on institutional reli-
gion show that she had come to regard the membership of a
Church as essential to the fullest Christian life.

> A Church has something to give to and something to
> demand from each of its members, and there is a genuine loss
> for man in being unchurched…when once the historical
> character of reality is fully grasped by us, we see that some
> such organization through which achieved values are con-
> served and carried forward, useful habits are learned and prac-
> tised, the direct intuitions of genius, the prophet's revelation
> of reality are interpreted and handed on, is essential to the
> spiritual continuity of the race: and that definite churchman-
> ship of some sort or its equivalent, must be a factor in the
> spiritual reconstruction of society.

One remembers the little stout black book, and Russell
Wakefield's solid teaching, and one wonders if she remembered

it, too, when she writes: "A church may often seem to lose her children, as human parents do; but in spite of themselves they retain her invisible seal, and are her children still…a large part is undoubtedly played by forgotten childish memories and early religious discipline surging up and contributing their part to the self's new apprehensions of Reality." In the last resort, she writes, criticism of the Church, of Christian institutionalism, is really criticism of ourselves. Were we more spiritually alive our spiritual homes would be the real nesting-places of new life.

Lucy Menzies writes: "To Evelyn the Church always meant the one undivided Church, the Body of Christ yet she not only found her own nesting place in the Church of England but showed many others the way there."

She had been coming into contact with the most living spirits in the Church of England by her work for *The Challenge,* and that may have altered her view-point. There seems no evidence at the moment to tell us exactly when her decision was made; but I think it must have been before the Oxford lectures were delivered. She was the first woman to be chosen by any Oxford college as an outside lecturer. The fact that she was chosen for this lectureship shows that she was considered to have a vital message about religion to deliver to the younger men and women of her day. She was alive to the view of the ordinary person, in England, often a little anti-clerical, her articles written during the war had shown her as a person with a width of sympathy, and a foundation of sound scholarship.

The Essentials of Mysticism, collecting up her various articles which she had published in the war years, was the last book which had the word "mysticism" in its title. She had done her definite work as an author for that great approach to religion, making its profound exponents known by their own confessions, and declarations, bringing them into the ken of those who were ready to follow them. She had mapped out their path; she had freed that great Way from the clutter and haze with which the pseudo-wayfarers had masked it. Its stern and adventurous attraction lay open, the hazards were not minimized, but the glory was revealed. Her later books rest on a wider basis. She was often to write about

the mystics again, but she saw them as part of the Church
Universal to which she was soon going to dedicate her powers.

The titles of the two books, *The Essentials of Mysticism,* and *The
Life of the Spirit and the Life of Today,* seem to symbolize this change
in her emphasis.

Evelyn had many women friends, some literary, some who
came to her through religion. She had an easy and encouraging
approach to other women, and a very generous attitude towards
her friends. Two life-long friends came on the scene in 1919: one
was Lucy Menzies, to whom this book owes so much, and the
other was an Italian Franciscan Nun, Sorella Maria.

Lucy Menzies was introduced to Evelyn by her publisher,
J. M. Dent, during the war, but did not know her well till Evelyn
reviewed her life of St. Columba and they began to write to each
other. She was at that time a Scottish Presbyterian, but later found
her place in the Anglican Communion. She was undoubtedly the
most intimate of all Evelyn's family whom she directed. Evelyn
wrote to her constantly, generally exercising a quietening and
restraining influence on this ardent follower. The group of letters at
the end of *The Letters of Evelyn Underhill* was addressed to Lucy
Menzies, and shows how deep and understanding and confidential
a friendship there was here; a friendship which was constant until
her death.

Sorella Maria became known to Evelyn through her friend
Miss Turton. She was an Italian religious, "inspired," writes Miss
Menzies, "with such charity to all men, such love for Christ, that
she was specially permitted after a private audience with the Pope
to leave the convent in which she had been trained, to found a
small Franciscan Community of her own." Evelyn's first description of this convent in a letter to Lucy Menzies was: "A house
where you will find an Italian lady who feels she has a call to
poverty and prayer living with six poor women by the Primitive
[Franciscan] rule."

From this group emerged a little society of praying people from
many Communions called the Confraternity of the Spiritual
Entente, with a concern to pray for unity while remaining loyal to
their own branches of the Church. It was to work invisibly. The

fellowship spread, and Evelyn was one of its early members and later, with Miss Turton, one of its secretaries. It was one of the things that sprang up after the first war, when in the early 1920s people had a sudden vision of peace. They did issue in all the ecumenical understanding and wisdom which has blessed the Christian Faith since then; and this hidden group may have been one of the mainsprings.

Maria was a sustaining and loving friend through Evelyn's working life; perhaps she took her back to the old dreams of simple living that she had written of in *The Grey World*. She confided to her, I know, much of the pain that came from her own periods of darkness. Later they saw each other face to face, one of those creative meetings that need not be repeated to bear their own fruit.

At the very end of the war Evelyn had started work on an appreciation and life of Jacopone da Todi, one of the second generation of St. Francis's followers, who held to the primitive rule. He was the outstanding poet of the movement, and it was the publication in 1910 of the first collection of his *Laude* that made it possible for him to become known to lovers of the Franciscans. Evelyn's friend Mrs. Theodore Beck made some translations of the *Laude* for this book of Evelyn's. Jacopone the lawyer, the quick-brained intellectual who became the singer of the Love of God, and the anguish and joy of the Mystic who experiences it, was a congenial subject for her writing. He may have been one of the voices that called to her in the war years of whom she writes to von Hügel.

The war years had been progressive for her as a writer, and at the end of them her place as a religious writer and teacher was assured, but she herself had felt them to be spiritually years of personal confusion, and also years of deprivation. This is shown by her short word to von Hügel: "During the war I went to pieces"; and her letter to M. R. in 1917, "The present abnormal conditions are as bad for the spiritual life as for every other kind of life. We are all finding it frightfully difficult and most of us are failing badly." She needed some great resetting if all her gifts were to be made available in their highest degree.

9

CHOICE OF A DIRECTOR

Evelyn in 1921 was to all outward appearances in an assured and enviable position. She had been asked by the University of Oxford to give the first of a new series of lectures on Religion, and she was the first woman to have such an honour. She was an authority on her own subject of Mysticism, and respected for her research and scholarship. She had published her two books of poems, and had enough *réclame* as a poet to be included later in the *Augustan Poets;* she was writing for a good many distinguished periodicals. She was, in fact, as she wrote to von Hügel, "professionally very prosperous and petted." She had an interesting and notable set of friends, and many readers who were devoted to her. Her marriage was a happy one, and her relation with her parents affectionate and loyal.

But we find her asking the old gospel question: "What lack I yet?" She seems to have felt that her foundations were insecure, that her zeal for Reality was resting on a basis that was too fragile. She may have been almost overwhelmed by her own knowledge of the achievements of the Mystics and of the One who called them to such perilous heights of prayer. She had recovered in her personal religion much that she felt herself to have almost rejected in the war years, and she found herself strangely overwhelmed by the forgiveness of God after what seemed to her some rather serious refusals of His call: "Now I have got back," she wrote to von Hügel, "but what seems to me so strange, and makes me nervous is that I should have expected to have to fight my way back inch by inch. Instead of that everything has been given back to me that I ever had, and more.... Is this sort of experience what is meant by forgiveness? Because that is what it feels like, final and complete reharmonizing and secure."

She was in the forties when she made what was to seem to her the major decision of her life. When, ten years before, *Mysticism* had been published, this had led to a friendship with von Hügel, which was at once stimulating and humbling to her spirit. In her life up till then she had never found a living master to whom she could confidently turn. Father Hugh Benson had satisfied her up to a point, but he was not a giant, and in her studies of spiritual life she had been keeping company with giants.

The woman who had been exploring the inmost souls of Ruysbroeck, of St. John of the Cross, of St. Teresa, and Meister Eckhart, knew a good deal about the height and depth, the length and breadth of the Love of God, as it was mirrored in these stupendous Christians. She would not be easily satisfied if ever she were to seek for direction. She seems to have had a certain amount of teaching from von Hügel before the war, she had been "sitting at his feet," and he had been both critical and appreciative of the books that she had written. This brilliant unyoked creature who loved God had impressed him and yet made him anxious.

Records of war years are rather scanty but I do not think they met often. Evelyn had had something rather like a standstill in religion. Only one thing seems to have persisted, people still came to her for advice and spiritual counsel, the simpler books published after *Mysticism* brought her enquirers, and she had given them all she had to give, perhaps more than she had to give. However chaotic she felt her own religious life to be she did not pass on her own questionings and doubts, but what she had made her own of the experience of the saints, whatever she had that was constructive in her own experience. Thus, Lucy Menzies, who corresponded with her in 1917, had no idea until she read Evelyn's letters to von Hügel that the war years and early 1920s had been years of stress for Evelyn. Only one person perhaps knew, Ethel Barker, and it was probably her death that left her friend bereft of spiritual companionship, and made her turn to von Hügel not merely for advice but for direction.

Though in the course of making her Oxford lectures, she had begun her Anglican practice, it may not have been an absolutely settled question in her mind when she first wrote to von Hügel.

It was obviously not a foregone conclusion in his mind; but it is a measure of his wisdom, and also of his own difficulties at the moment, that he never pressed her to come into the Roman Communion. He was at the time in close touch with many non–Roman Catholic Christians whom he admired greatly: the Bishop of Winchester (Talbot) and his two sons Edward and Neville, Tissington Tatlow of the Student Christian Movement. His own niece, Mrs. Plunket Greene, then an Anglican, was also coming to him for spiritual help.

Evelyn writing later to Dom John Chapman said: "When I put myself under Baron von Hügel's direction, five years before his death…he said I must never think of moving on account of my own religious preferences, comfort or advantages, but only if so decisively called by God that I felt it was wrong to resist. Under God, I owe him my whole spiritual life, and there would have been more of it than there is, if I had been more courageous and stern with myself, and followed his directions more thoroughly."

In her article on von Hügel in *Mixed Pasture* she wrote: "In the advice and training which he gave so generously to many outside his own Communion, he showed the fullest willingness to use, discriminate, take seriously the institutional practices of all branches of the Church."

It was certainly a formidable decision on her part; writing later of von Hügel she says: "There is the memory of an immense spiritual transcendence, a personality at once daunting and attractive, an Alpine quality. Those who cherish memories of him may even be inclined to think first of a volcanic mountain; for he combined a rock-like faith, a massive and lofty intellect with the incandescent fervour, the hidden fire of an intense interior life. The piercing black eyes which compelled truth and obtained it, the awe and passion which were felt when the Baron uttered the name of his God, these will not be forgotten by any soul which came under the sphere of his influence."

So, in the autumn of 1921 she wrote to him, to make this request for direction. Her letter to him has not survived, but in his reply, which she kept, a good deal of it may be traced. His letter is dated 29 October.

It has been quite a pain to me not to be able to thank you most gratefully at once for the great joy your long letter has given me. It was indeed good of you to be so frank and so full in your self expression to me on those points which I so deeply care about. You evidently realized why and where I was hoping and praying for a development in you. Such development did not—at least directly—concern Rome at all. I quite realize how difficult (how dangerous unless definitely called) such a change to the Roman Catholic Obedience has become for many educated minds. And though I certainly should love to see you simply and completely one of us; and though again I am not going to be sure that you will never be given that special call, I mean *that* was not what so far made me wistful at the thought of you. No! what I directly and clearly wanted for you was just what you now tell me you have gained and won! *Deo gratias!* I congratulate you and beg you to persevere most faithfully in all that is positive in this your new and, I pray, confirmed outlook. Of course you will have dryness, disgusts, strong inclinations to revert to the more or less pure "mysticism." But it is excellent news that, preparing one of these addresses for Manchester College, Oxford, you found you had really come out strongly and self committingly for Traditional, Institutional, Religion.

With some souls I might well have the fear that the latter type of religion would appear in them too exclusively, either because this kind of exclusiveness was congenial to them, or for the opposite reason, because convert like, they felt that if they adopted such an uncongenial attitude at all, they must silence within themselves what continued to push and grumble against this new guest in their souls. You will, please God, not belong to this latter sort; but your visible religion will safeguard your invisible religion, and your invisible religion will give freshness and variety to your visible religion. Of course, the perfection of such a combination remains an ideal for even the most advanced of us. Yet it can be, and with yourself also will be, an ideal considerably and growingly realized to your own profound profit, and to the rendering truly safe and entirely beneficent your great influence as a writer. With this growth of yours I cease to have any misgivings within my pleasure at your popularity. May you indeed still grow much in influence, so long as you remain firm and grow in these your new lights, adding to and penetrating the old.

One little word more. Do not I pray you, if ever you feel at all clearly that I could help you in any way—even if by only silently listening to such troubles and complications as God may send you—do not, because I am busy, shrink from coming to me, or letting me come to you. We are *both* very busy, so we have each the guarantee that we will not take up each other's time without good cause. But, such good cause arising, it would, it will be, nothing but consolation to me, if you let me help as much as ever you feel the need. I will pray my little best for you, that God may bless and keep you along this path—so safe and so sound—and which (at least in time) will bring you consolations of a depth and richness far surpassing the old ones.

And do not forget me before God.

It was an inspiring letter to receive, it showed so clearly his belief in her, and his affection for her, and his sureness that the step she had taken towards accepting a Church was the way of God for her.

Two years later she was writing herself to one of her correspondents: "I am not a bit unpleasant about sins and penances …but apt to be disagreeable on the Church question. I stood out against it myself for so long and have been so thoroughly convinced of my own error that I do not want other people to waste time in the same way…. I do not mean that perpetual churchgoing and sermons are necessary, but some participation in the common religious life and some sacramental practice."

Evelyn must have written to him as soon as she received his encouraging letter, for he is writing to her again on 5 November in reply to a letter of hers which has not survived.

Your last very kind and very interesting letter has been running in my head, especially because one half questioning remark in it really raises a point I should love to think you understood me about. As a matter of fact I fear as much for you the overdoing of institutionalism as the ignoring or even flying from it: indeed these two extremes are assuredly twin sisters in such a soul as yours. What I do pray for, for you, is that you should in a time of peace and light, fix upon a certain minimum, a nucleus of institutional practice, to which you will then adhere with a patient perseverance, carefully not adding—not much adding—to it when in consolation; and not detracting—not much detracting—from it when in desolation. And this minimum, this nucleus should not be fixed as for a naturally institutional soul, or even as for an average soul, but for your soul, which to the end will find the institutional more or less difficult, but will none the less greatly require some little of it faithfully performed.

I think of Church of some kind—preferably Holy Communion, every Sunday; at most that and, say, one weekday Mass, once a week at the Carmelites. Perhaps even these two practices are too much for the minimum, since, of course, not the resolution alone but the execution matters really, and I should wish to save you *above all things,* from any real overburdening. Also I should like you to continue or to develop in yourself, some non-religious interest—Music? or Painting? or Gardening? If you have to choose (about Church going) you would choose the early Holy Communion.

Evelyn wrote to the Baron again before Christmas, and this letter we have, with its revealing opening concerning the thing that always at intervals racked her.

Charles Williams wrote in his introduction to her *Letters:* "The equal (or all but equal) swaying level of devotion and scepticism which is, for some souls, as much the Way as continuous simple faith is to others, was a distress to her.... She wanted to be *sure.*"

She wrote to a friend later who had the same distress: "I'm glad you feel dark, and doubtful, and shaky sometimes. I do too, and I believe it's much safer for people who get things to say, and have to do jobs. The alternative is something plump and satisfied."

But for her it was always a Way of deep joy and obscure pain. Here she pours it out to von Hügel:

> The chief point is, am I simply living on illusion? It seems impossible but all the same I felt I must be sure. I don't mean by this any unwillingness to make a venture, or any demand for impossible clearness of faith but simply to be certain my own experiences are not imaginary. The points in favour of their reality seem to be,
>
> (1) What you call givenness, unexpectedness, entire non-earnedness.
> (2) Overwhelming sense of certitude, objective reality, and of obligation.
> (3) That I have never tried either to obtain or to retain them, and know that such effort would be useless.
>
> I leave out the merely emotional side, as that is said to be no guarantee of genuineness. All the same it is difficult to conceive that a construction of one's mind can produce such feeling. I have had this sort of experience on and off for over sixteen years, since a sort of conversion experience of a quite definite sort, which put a final end to a (very uncomfortable) period of agnosticism. This had happened before you first knew me, and I then very nearly became a Catholic, but didn't quite. However, I went on for a long time going to Mass on Sundays as a sort of free lance and outsider: but gradually this faded out in favour of what I vainly imagined to be inwardness, and an increasing anti-institutional bias.
>
> Then, during the war, I went to pieces as I told you: though with several vivid calls back which I did not respond to. Now I have got back, but what seems to me so strange and makes me nervous is that I should have expected to have to fight my way back inch by inch. Instead of that everything has been given back to me that I ever had—and more. I can't go

into this but I do just want to know whether such completely undeserved restitution is normal and all right, and whether the process of behaving like a rebellious and hardened beast: mind getting into utter blackness; then realizing it, however bitterly—can be an actual way of development? Is this sort of experience what is meant by *forgiveness?* Because that is what it felt like—final and complete, reharmonizing and secure.

Of course I know all the arguments and could explain it all quite neatly to myself on psychological lines; but that sort of thing seems very unreal when you are faced by reality, and does not allow for the strange sense of being personally dealt with, which must, I suppose, be part illusion.

Of course the door will shut again, is indeed shut now, but that does not particularly matter. So the first point is: Is all the above real? and can I trust it? or am I living in a dream? or still obsessed by *pure mysticism.*

What ought I to do? I am having too easy a time and ought to do something hard—some modern equivalent of the hair shirt that would keep on reminding one. And being naturally self-indulgent and at present unfortunately professionally very prosperous and petted, nothing will get done unless I make a Rule. Neither intellectual work nor religion give me any real discipline because I have a strong attachment to both. So anything practical you will tell me about that will be a great help. But it is useless advising anything people could notice or that would look pious. That is beyond me. In my lucid moments I see only too clearly that the only possible end of this road is complete, unconditional self-consecration, and for this I have not the nerve, the character or the depth. There has been some sort of mistake. My soul is too small for it and yet it is at bottom the only thing that I really want. It feels sometimes as if, whilst still a jumble of conflicting impulses and violent faults, I were being pushed from behind towards an edge *I dare not* jump over.

(3) In your second letter you emphasized that whatever one's rule about institutionalism, it should be constant, not added to much in time of light, nor reduced in times of

darkness. Does this apply all round? e.g. should there be an average rule about times given to prayer, etc.? not to add or reduce this? That seems fearfully difficult. It seems much more waste of time when you are shut off to say over verbal prayers that have no meaning for one and perpetually try to capture a wandering attention; five minutes then seem like an hour. And it seems an equally hard saying that one may not add on time when one has a strong impulse to and can manage without neglecting necessary work.

However, if you will say what I ought to do about this, I shall try to do it. My tendency has been to very wide variations; scamping everything in dark times, which in these last years have, of course, been pretty constant: and anyhow I don't give a great deal of definitely set apart time—not more than an hour every day, as a rule, and often less. Probably I ought to try to make time to increase this.

(4) Christo-centric devotion. This is still a difficulty. I can't do it. And yet the average Christian appears by declaration to do it naturally and instinctively. It seems to me to involve the fusion of two incompatible conceptions. Yet I really am a Christian—at least I believe so—though in the modernist rather than strict orthodox sense. But God seems to me the only and inevitable Object of adoration and, anyhow, all that I know at first hand. *Is* this all right? It is very far from the negative unconditioned sort of apprehension which I understand is what you condemn, but is on the contrary, more coloured, vivid, real and personal than anything else.

All this seems hard to reconcile with the Evelyn who tells Mrs. Heath that she clings to St. Paul, who seems so clearly Christocentric, but it was never her most natural way to come to God through Christ, and years afterwards she was saying some of the same things, though after her teaching from von Hügel she began as never before to "experience Christ" (her own words) and to speak and write of Him, and to pray to Him with increasing light.

Christmas seems to have intervened before the Baron's next letter, and Christmas to Evelyn always meant a very loving and often rather lavish giving to her friends. She was a generous giver; Barbara Gnospelius recalls how she once lent her house with staff complete for a week.

But after Christmas sometime—the letter is undated—she received the Baron's next letter.

I

I believe the Invisible religious experience you have described to me, to have been and to be essentially genuine. I think so because of the three peculiarities you describe confirming and supplementing each other as they do: and still more a fourth reason because of the concomitant and subsequent disposition it evokes in you as you define it later on.

I believe this decision to be very important, for thus you acquire a touchstone (to be used, of course, with sobriety and only in the long run) for the wisdom and appropriateness, or the reverse of the following counsels. Such practices as in the long run feed and steady that experience you can treat as truly meant for you, and such practices as, again in the long run, starve and disturb that experience, are not for you, at least at this stage of your growth.

II

I believe you ought to get yourself, gently and gradually, interested *in the poor;* that you should visit them, very quietly and unostentatiously, with as little incorporation as possible into Visiting Societies, etc. You badly want de-intellectualizing, or at least developing homely, human sense and spirit dispositions and activities. Gradually you may be able to draw out, perhaps even to help some of these poor religiously. But the good *you yourself* will gain, long before this, and quite apart from this, will be very great. For it will, if properly entered into and persevered with, discipline, mortify, soften, deepen and quiet you; it will, as it were, distribute your blood—some of your blood—away from the brain, where too much of it is lodged at present. And if and when religion does appear on the scene you will find how homely, how much of sense as well as spirit it has and had to be. Again, how excellent for you! For what is a religion which cannot mean anything to the uneducated poor? So in the case of Unitarianism, and in some forms of Anglican Modernism. I shall be quite satisfied with two afternoons a week given to such visiting. But pray strive to spread the spirit derived from these two days over the other five days.

I think you should aim at, and should gently practise, a moderate amount and kind of devotedness as well as devotion; both so practised as to contain a reasonable variety, but no vehemence, no feverishness, and much, much self oblivion—dropping all unnecessary thoughts of self, and even of the improvement of self, and gently turning instead to thoughts and acts for others, and, above all, to humble aspirations towards God.

I would carefully give the preference to the two weekly visitations of the poor against everything else, except any definite home and family duties, or any express wishes of your husband—in each case as distinct from your own likes and dislikes.

III

As to helping educated people—Direction work. I believe this (practised only on the unsolicited invitation of the persons concerned and in the spirit and way that you describe) is distinctly good for you, and that you should be able more than ever to help such souls. But I should like you to evade or postpone any new cases till after Easter. Old cases where you can postpone further help to the same date, do so postpone; otherwise help without hesitation, but more soberly even than you have done already.

IV

[This section probably refers to something Evelyn had written in the letters which we do not possess. Later in life she was to prove herself the most unexacting of friends. Her affection for her friends was quite certain and most sustaining to them, but it had become the most undemanding relationship, and if she made a demand it was always with a sense of humble apology, most humbling also to her friends. It was one of the remarkable things about her, and shows how far it had been possible for her to travel under direction that she trusted and understood.]

As to *Detachment and Particular Friendships.* I am particularly glad that you have brought up the vehemence and exactingness of your nature and the way in which you have tried to master it. I believe this great vehemence and its offshoots to spring, not only from the ardour of your natural temperament but also (perhaps very largely) from the too intellectual character of your religion. Religious sentimentality "makes you sick": Yes! But if you can get a greater variety of homely emotions and activities into your religion, you very possibly will lose the hunger for the ardour of human affection. However this may eventually turn out, I want you carefully to discriminate between your affections and your giving them to particular persons, and the claimfulness, distractions, vehemence, etc., which arises within or on occasion of these affections. I would have you not directly check those affections, though you should be slow and deliberate as far as you can without great strain—in letting such affections begin and get established with any new person. But I would wish you ever more faithfully to drop, to escape from the vehemence, etc. This you should do, not by a direct fighting of these passions, but by a gentle turning to God, or to the thought of serenely loving saints. In this way you will practise detachment within attachment; you will keep material and occasions going for your detachment. You will thus grow more fully than by concentrating upon attempts to keep out such material and occasions.

V

Yes! I should like certain definite time given each day for *deliberate prayer,* not much added to in times of consolation, nor much detracted from in times of desolation. But such fixed times for prayer—as over and above your Church doings—should not be long. What you propose will do very well indeed. Of course, we are talking simply of deliberate prayer—whatever kind and degree suits you best: i.e. most strengthens you to love, to work, to suffer, and most humbles and braces you. For as to the spirit of prayer, the prayerful disposition: this should more and more penetrate all your waking hours.

VI

As to being or becoming a Catholic, I very certainly see your first difficulty—your first impossibility. You assuredly must not declare the opposite of what you really believe. And I cannot, and do not profess for one moment to know whether this will ever change. But my direct motive for bringing up the point remains, I think in full force. For if you cannot be a complete and formally received Catholic, you can gain more and more of certain most really Catholic dispositions and general outlooks. And in that case you can safely be given much more latitude in the matter of Theocentric devotion than would, I still feel quite clear, be safe otherwise. The less of an Individualist, the less of a judge of the worth of the Christocentric devotion you become, the less also will be the danger and the starving which will accompany and follow sheer Theocentricism as practised by yourself. For you will then practise it as *for you,* as a devotional way, not simply as the norm for all, as *the* Devotional Way. And surely you are not far from that already: or else ought you not to join the Unitarians?

VII

There is another, a more direct and explicit way, in which I think you already can and hence ought to practise the Catholic mind. You tell me that you could not truthfully profess belief in certain supposed Historical Facts. I suppose these to be the Virgin Birth, the bodily Resurrection, the

Johannine Miracles, at least primarily. But pray note that even so you can still retain the more general and the bed rock principle of the Catholic mind.

I should feel that you were not clear as to your own deepest instincts or were being unfaithful to them if you could not or did not, humbly set about the full definite development of the principle I have in view. Now and then it shows in your acts, works, temper of mind; and then it disappears for a while, overlaid by thoughts or moods of another, a quite contrary provenance. Let us work gently but wholeheartedly, at getting this principle to become one of the chief beams of your spiritual edifice, *part of the rock,* known and willed at all times *of your faith.*

There are two possible positions with regard to Historical Happenings. (Two positions over and above the ordinary orthodox position that the Church not only holds a list of Spiritual Truths, but knows which of these Spiritual Truths is also a Factual Happening, and that this knowledge is infallible, unchanging, and binding upon all men to the end of time. I am not asking this of you.)

You can hold that Historical Happenings *generally, some* Historical Happenings are necessary; that belief in them is necessary to every at all powerful religion, hence especially so to Christianity. Or you can hold that Historical Happenings even quite generally and in Christianity in particular, can flourish after every single supposed Historical Fact has been demonstrated non-historical, and after all men have come to recognize this complete defactualizing of religion.

Now I am very sure that the position which holds that *some* Historical Happenings—that the non-refusedness of their historical character and the definite belief in this genuine Historicalness, *are essential* ingredients of every at all powerful and at all perfect religion—is true. And I am quite sure that the opposite position—the reduction of religion to a system of mere ideas, principles, etc., is *profoundly* false.

But when I come to watch your mind and soul, I find certain volcanic eruptions in favour of position 1: yet also

whole tracts of intervening as it were slowly accumulating
aqueous formations, which really imply, or even spring from,
position 2. If you could or would, gradually but most thoroughly, drop and eliminate all the position 2, you would be
left (even without adding one item to the list of historical
happenings held by yourself to be such) with an outlook
possessing the fundamental Christian quality.

I note that you do not "at present understand in the least
the religious feeling of the need of a half-way house between
oneself and God." I note too that the "human historical values" appear to you as of secondary importance. [These must
be quotations from the first letters which we do not possess.]
Now here I cannot help feeling a serious weakness, a *lacuna*
indeed an inconsistency, in your psychology, your analysis of
the religious temper, and in your own, at least implied, attitude on other occasions. As you probably know as well as I
do, all the finest recent psychology, indeed all the deepest
epistemology, shows us and insists upon how we, poor
human beings, at least in this life, never begin (or in the long
run keep up) the apprehension of things spiritual except on
occasion of the awakening and stimulation of the senses. That
is, there is no such thing as an exclusively spiritual, entirely
mystical, quite non-historical, quite non-successive religion.

Next, religiously, the human soul upon the whole, in the
long run, in its richest developments, certainly I think, requires
not a half-way house for it on its way to God, *but God
Himself to come down to it* not half-way, but the whole way. To
put it in the most homely way, surely the infant feels that
breast as the self-giving of that mother, as a self-compression,
a touching condescension, for bringing the mother's own life
to the infant and thus gradually to raise this infant to the
mother's strength and stature.

St. Augustine surely has got this point right, in spite of
the great attractions which quite evidently a purely spiritual
religion possessed for wide stretches of his mind. He felt that
it was this condescension, *this coming down to us of God,* this
appearing to us in human forms and ways, which "nourished

love and ousted inflation." Quite, quite right! *That* alone at least in some form or degree, will ever give us a religion sufficiently lowly, homely, humbling.

And finally, I again fail to make sense of your frequentation of Holy Communion, even of Benediction, unless at the bottom of your mind there were an instinct, stronger than all *pure mystical* inclinations, that God does dwell in, and manifest Himself by, historical happenings—here more than there, now more than then. But this speaks of grades of Self-Revelation. And since, in the higher and highest reaches of spiritual reality, the differences of degree issue more and more in differences of kind, we reach at last an apex of spirituality which is, at bottom, the deepest fullest self abasement of God—Jesus Christ, in the manger, on the Cross; you lose an infinity of concrete, fullest religion by not seeing this, or seeing it so fitfully.

You could gain this Incarnational, which is also the only completely creaturely temper of mind, without forcing yourself on any of those (to your mind) hopelessly non-historical supposed facts. For the great Fact of God's general self-revelation would remain; and also the supreme fulness of such revelation in the person and life of Jesus Christ.

VIII

You ask me how on earth you can manage to "slip in" some bit of Christocentric devotion into your hopelessly Theocentric mind and practice. I certainly did not mean that you could or should slip in something you do not at all believe—should bamboozle yourself. I meant and mean that two interhostile currents actually exist in your mind as it is, and that you should and could (in ways and degrees too special and subtle to be easily described, but which with your goodwill grown more alert you yourself will be able to discover) gradually learn to practise the thought and the expression to yourself of one or other of the several catholicizing general facts and principles which I have been putting before you.

The tremendous—the appearance of tremendous logicality of mind and of unbending principle which you give— I fancy sometimes even yourself to yourself—is, I am confident very largely the result of oscillations, the doubleness in you which I have tried to lay bare. For when (as is usual) the alternative of pure spirit going to Pure Spirit straight and only is uppermost, you can for the moment be very intense upon *that*. What I want, on the contrary, is the gradual interworking of both currents, with special care given to sensible, contingent, historical, incarnational current, since this current has been specially starved. If you cannot, alas, as yet pray to Jesus, the heavenly Christ, as now living as much as ever, and as Himself bringing God Incarnate into your soul, try at least to pray to God Unincarnate with thought and affections as to Nazareth, the Lake of Galilee, and/or Calvary, where so much love was shown, was it not? for God and by God. I am sure that the term "slip in" or perhaps better the words "slipping away from" the reasoner, and the person in you that says "I could not do this" and "I could not do that" into the deeper depth of your soul, stand for real facts.

Evelyn had given two reasons to Baron von Hügel why she had felt it especially difficult to become a practising Roman Catholic: the first he had answered as we have seen in these letters, treating her possible reception as a Catholic as not the major issue at the moment, a thing to depend on the unfolding of God's will after she had gained what he considered a deeper standpoint in her approach to Faith. His answer to her second reason is along the same lines. Evelyn had told him in her letters that she still felt that it would be a bitter blow to Hubert if she joined the Roman Communion.

"You give me as your second, and as much the most decisive reason for your inability ever to become Catholic," writes von Hügel, "the fact that your husband, a most Christian minded man, is an intense anti-clerical, that he would feel sure you had committed yourself to the ruin of your mind and that you love him too much to inflict such pain." One wonders if Evelyn and Hubert had discussed the question again, or whether she still had in her mind the stormy interview before their marriage. As far as one can tell, Hubert had made no objection to her direction by von Hügel, as he would have done earlier if she had placed herself under the direction of a Roman Catholic priest. Possibly he never knew of this correspondence at the time.

How delicately the Baron proceeds:

> I am then deeply touched and delighted in thinking of your husband's goodness, and of your determination to save him all avoidable great pain. [He infers that Evelyn has never felt this antipathy of Hubert's herself.] His attitude leaves your interior attractions and obstacles untouched. [He reminds her that there were wives among the early Christians who must have wounded their husbands deeply when they embraced Christianity.] To my mind [he ends his letter] the only quite satisfactory, just and balanced, definitely supernatural position is to hold most firmly that all who in any way depend upon you—hence above all your husband—possess an inalienable right to be as much sustained and consoled by you, and as little pained by you as is ever possible; that no mere preference, or greater helps, and consolations, religious or otherwise, can justify you in inflicting pain upon your husband; but that if and when your conscience came to make you, after waiting and testing to feel bound to move, you ought to do so, trusting to the same God, who is determining you to make it less of a pain and in some way of a material gain for your husband also; whilst you would yourself, of course, do everything possible to minimize that pain for him.

He does not, I think, feel that this crisis is upon her at the moment, but that if it came she "must however slowly and indirectly resolve this bit of amiable naturalism in the ocean of the supernal love of and waiting upon God."

His long letter is coming to an end. Evelyn, so he directs, should test his advice for six months and then report at midsummer how she is getting on; after that he proposes a yearly report.

There is a P.S., characteristic of both of them:

> I much like your love for your cats. I deeply love my little
> dog, and the Abbé Huvelin was devoted to his cat. We all
> three can and will become dearer to God for this love of our
> little relations, the smaller creatures of God. Again it was God
> incarnate, it was Jesus of Nazareth, of Gethsemane and
> Calvary, and not pure Theism that taught this. De-
> Unitarianizing, if you please!

Lucy Menzies notes that though no further direction or report
in writing was to be given for six months, Evelyn still went quite
often to see the Baron. His "Alpine quality" must have made these
visits steep spiritual climbing, though his affection for her and his
belief in her must have given her new heart. She had had on the
whole so little affectionate care in her search for God; none over
a long period, such as she was to experience with the Baron. He
was severe sometimes. "You should see my old man dusting me
down!" she said once to Lucy Menzies. He could also laugh at her
and with her. Someone overhearing their laughter on the occasion
of one of her interviews thought that religion must be the most
amusing thing in the world.

But one superlative thing he did for her, which she recorded
later:

> I had from time to time vivid experiences of God. This posi-
> tion I thought to be that of a broad-minded and intelligent
> Christian; but when I went to the Baron he said I wasn't
> much better than a Unitarian. Somehow by his prayers he
> compelled me to experience Christ. He never said anything
> more about it, but I know that humanly speaking he did it.
> It took about four months. It was like watching the sun ris-
> ing very slowly. And then suddenly one knew what it was.

She summed up his letters in a document which she called *My
Rule.* It is a masterly précis of his advice, which his German habit
of thought made sometimes rather discursive and obscure. It is
dated Christmas 1921.

My Rule

1. Invisible religion shall be the touchstone for all external practices, which should in the long run steady and feed it. Those that disturb it to be discarded.

2. *Active work.* Get gently interested in the poor. Two afternoons weekly to be given to this and take priority of everything else except strict family duties. This work must be entered into and persevered with, with the object of developing more homely and human religious dispositions: and the spirit derived from it spread over the whole week. Aim at a reasonable devotedness as well as devotion with sufficient variety and no feverishness: above all much self-oblivion: dropping introspection and thoughts of self and turning to thoughts and acts for others; humble aspirations to God.

3. *Direction.* No new cases to be taken before Easter if avoidable.

4. *Detachment.* Affection for particular persons not to be directly checked but new relationships to be entered on very slowly and deliberately. Claimfulness, passion, to be dealt with and dropped *not* by direct fighting, but by gently turning to God or serenely loving saints. Thus detachment will be practised within attachment, and material and occasion for detachment kept going.

5. *Prayer.* A fixed time must be given daily to deliberate prayer: but it must not be long or very much altered, as to time, whether in consolation or desolation. The kind and degree shall be that which most helps to love, work and suffer, and both humbles and braces. But the spirit of inarticulate prayer should more and more penetrate all working hours.

6. *Mental Dispositions.* Seek to acquire the Catholic Mind. Become less of a judge of the worth of Christocentric devotion, practising Theocentric devotion as a way, not *the* way, and trying to balance it by Incarnational thoughts and sympathies.

7. Try to set about humble, full, definite development of

principle of God found in history, here and now, not by sheer ascents, and make this part of the rock of personal faith. Realize that all powerful and personal religion requires some historical happenings as essential to its completeness. Strive to eliminate a merely philosophically based Theism in favour of real Incarnationalism.

8. Keep in mind that since spiritual perception without *some* sense stimulation is a psychological impossibility, there is no exclusively spiritual apprehension of spiritual reality. Human and historical contacts are essential to its fulness. Entirely mystical and purely nonsuccessive religion is a dangerous abstraction from reality. Further, religiously, the soul requires God's own descent into it—the whole way—in human and homely forms and ways, rather than its ascent to Him. This alone gives a religion sufficiently homely and humbling. This means God manifested in history; grades of Divine self-revelation. At the apex, difference of degree issuing in difference of kind, we reach the deepest fullest self-abasement of God as expressed in the Incarnation and the Cross. Full religion demands a temper of mind able to grasp and assimilate this.

9. *Spiritual Dispositions.* Two hostile currents of feeling at present exist in my soul: namely the purely mystical and philosophic, and the Catholic Incarnational. Must try in various degrees and ways to practise and encourage thought and expression of the second current. The oscillation and doubleness at present weakening my religious life must be resolved, the two currents being gradually interwoven with special care given to the Incarnational and Sacramental, because it has been specially starved. Accustom myself to retreat from levels of merely theological reasoning into the deeper levels of the soul, and hold as much as possible in prayer thoughts and affections as to God found in Christ.

10. Everyone dependent on me, and especially H., have an inalienable right to my consideration and to be as much sustained and as little pained by me as possible. No mere religious preferences, or getting greater help or spiritual comfort

can justify inflicting pain on them. On the other hand, conscience takes priority of all such obligations. Must hold myself ready to obey with real inward pressure, whatever it demands. "Amiable naturalism" must be resolved in the "Ocean of the supernatural love of, and waiting upon God."

These rules and discriminations to be tested and practised for six months, quietly and steadily, with a disposition to find them true, even where uncongenial.

Perhaps this last sentence lets us into a deep secret of sanctity. It is willing to be taught by uncongenial things, to find uncongenial things true. Evelyn was always telling her retreatants later to beware of any fastidiousness in religion. Here she took the tremendous step of "slipping away," as von Hügel put it, from the person in her that said "I could not do this" and "I could not do that."

And this is what Evelyn wrote to the Baron at the end of her first six months, in the summer of 1922:

(1) *Invisible religion.* Inwardly, till the last few weeks, I have had rather a rough time. When I came to you I was frantic and feverish, and afterwards that got worse, and got altogether too near the psychophysical danger zone. I had to stop it, with resulting dimness, great restlessness, and not knowing what to be at. Then, by the beginning of Lent, I got into a state of vague, increasing inward suffering and struggle, as if one were fighting shadows and more and more obsessed by the feeling of sin. I could not think of anything else, and lost my spiritual world view. It was just as if one's soul were being scorched. Useless to tell myself I had got to practise self oblivion—impossible to forget it except when with my poor people. I was beginning to be faintly Christocentric then, but it spoilt my communions, and I dreaded my times of prayer—they meant dimness, incapacity, pain and horrible remorse. By Holy Week I was so tortured I decided to go and make a general confession; first because I had always loathed the idea, so it would be something definite to do, and second, I thought perhaps it would be like a spring cleaning, and

I would be all right afterwards. Probably I ought not to have done it without your permission, but I felt I must.

It was not a bit like a spring cleaning, and I did not feel a scrap absolved; but as a humiliation it left absolutely nothing to be desired. It is one thing to make voluntary acts of abjection to God and quite another thing when a human being forces you to recognize your own beastliness. You were much too kind to do this, but the man I went to devoted his time to smashing me up...when he had finished I felt utterly degraded, hopeless and smirched all over. The very next day I found two horrible insects kissing one of my slum children. Of course you will laugh at this or feel I should not bother you with such trifles. But the point is on the top of all the rest it seemed to complete the ruin of my self-respect and filled me with horror and self-loathing. I felt vile through and through, body and soul, just rubbed in the mud.

And the queer thing is, it was then—when I could not look at or think of transcending holiness, that I realized what the agonizing need is that only Christianity *can* meet by coming right down to one in the dust. *St. Augustine was a thousand times right!* Plotinus can never have had to face his own beastliness. Neo-Platonism goes to bits when one gets really to the bottom and knows oneself unmendably displeasing to God.

I stayed at the bottom for weeks with occasional moments of peace, but mostly suffocated by the unescapable sense of sin and utter loneliness. I confess I had times of the blackest depression, when it seemed the strain could not be borne, or the utter loneliness. Religion seemed suddenly to have become savage and unrelenting. Gradually it wore off a bit and I crept out, but miserably conscious I should never be any good.

Then at Ascension tide I went into retreat at Pleshey. This was not another case of taking the law into my own hands—the Warden is a friend of mine, and I had promised to go, before you took charge of me. I went with a lot of Elementary School Teachers from the East End. It helped me a good deal. [I think this was probably only the second time that Evelyn had definitely gone to a religious house to learn and to pray; the first, of course, being her visit to the convent. This visit to Pleshey, when she was in such great need, was the beginning of the long connection between her soul and that place which became so dear to her, and which she made so lovely and strengthening to others. One ought to mark it in this book with the white stone which the first Christians used to single out any specially sacred day.]

The intense silence seemed to slow down one's far too quick mental time and give one's soul a chance. To my surprise a régime of daily communion and four services a day with silence between was the most easy unstrained and natural life I had ever lived. One sank down into it, and doing it always with the same people, all meaning it intensely, and the general attitude of deep devotion—for the whole house seems soaked in love and prayer—cured solitude and gave me at last the feeling of belonging to the Christian family and not counting except as that. I lost there my last bit of separateness and wish for anything of my own, and gained a wholly new sense of the realness and almost unbearable beauty of the Christian life. I came away quite tranquil and determined on entire surrender and so far have not wavered from that—though again and again I have fallen far below it and done and said things inconsistent with it. Anyhow I know now what I ought to be like, if my love were of a better quality.

The general result of these adventures, as far as one can make them out is: I have lost the violent and overwhelming sort of consciousness I had six months ago; and also lost, alas! (for many months now) the prayer of quiet which seems a real set back. But I have a dimmer, but on the whole steadier sense; varying a good deal in character and intensity and often only a vague background feeling—but seldom past recall—though there are utterly blank days. Much gentler than it was, and yet more penetrating and spreading in a way.

My old religious life now looks too thin and solitary: this

is more various—contemplating, Holy Communion, the felt presence of God, struggles to behave properly, and love for my poor people—all seem articulated points of it. All sense of contact departs abruptly the minute I become critical or horrid or fail in love and patience, or otherwise fall below my none too high standard.

As to practices: what help and feed me most are Holy Communion and short, constant bits of recollection and prayer (when I am not too rushed to forget them). The Retreat was like a week on the glaciers—bracing, purifying and calming. I should like to do this several times a year—it would be time well spent. On the other hand I think regular confession would wreck me altogether. It tears me to bits, leaves me in a state of nervous illness, and encourages my hateful and unconquerable habit of introspection. Apart from Holy Communion I cannot honestly say church-going attracts me much, and I seldom go to Benediction now. Silent prayer seems as easy and fruitful at home as in church.

It is valuable to know that Evelyn found later confessors who were a real standby to her. Possibly it was not this first priest who laid this strange burden of sin upon her, and left her unconvinced of absolution, but a sudden long deferred identification with the sin of the world, which our Lord gave her to share with Him so that she might experience the world's need of Him, in its terrible and heartbreaking intensity.

She goes on with her report:

(2) *Visiting the poor.* This prescription has been a complete success. I realize now I was starving for something of the kind. It is an immense source of interest, often of a heart-breaking kind; for they are always in some trouble and misery, poor darlings, often actually hungry—and it is little one can do to rescue them. I got eight families from a friend who had wrecked her health by devoted work for them and others, and as they adored her I come in quite second best (although all are great friends with me) so there is no food

for vanity. On the contrary one comes away feeling an utter worm: comparing one's own secure life with their incessant struggles and anxieties and the amazing courage and sweetness with which they bear it. The women are perfectly wonderful. If I were like a particular friend, living in a basement with six restless children, poor health, endless difficulties, and a drunken cruel beast of a man to whom she is not even married, I should go completely to bits. It all makes one feel, religiously, as well as physically, rather pampered. I think more and more unless one can stretch out one's own devotional life to make it avail for them (for they have not any, and how can they have?), it remains more or less a spiritual luxury. But I do not see how to do this in any real way at present. Nor, except for getting one baby baptized, have I yet found any outlet for religion. It is mostly a case of being a family friend and cheerer-up—not at all a spiritual job! Of course, sometimes it is taxing and a bit of an effort, but on the whole a source of real happiness, not mortification, so the screw will have to be put on somewhere else. The queer thing is the tranquillizing effect they have. However jangled one may be when one goes to them, one always comes away mysteriously filled with peace and nearer God. You were absolutely right; they give one far more than one can ever give them, and I feel I ought to give them a much greater love and compassion than I do. Of course, the temptation is to concentrate on the most attractive, but I try not to do that. I'm afraid a great deal of time is spent simply consorting with the little kiddies and feeding them with chocolate. This is not a very elevated occupation, I know, but it means a lot to me. You see when you have none of your own it does rather freeze you up; and I am too shy and awkward to get on with educated kids. But these are such nice friendly appealing little creatures, like tiny flowers in those grimy places; and one can enjoy them without self-consciousness or anyone knowing. I can't tell you what a sense of expansion and liberation I have got from this.

There seems to be a note of real regret here, the only one I
know of, over her own childlessness. I think she did feel cut off
from children in general, though she loved these little back-street
toddlers. She also gained from her visits to the poor street one very
great woman friend, Laura Rose, an invalid living in very poor circumstances. Evelyn discovered that she was a reader, and offered
to lend her books. To her surprise Mrs. Rose asked for books by
St. John of the Cross, and Evelyn found her deeply interested in
the mystical writers. She was a real support to Evelyn, who often
confided to her difficulties about work and people. Evelyn felt
herself involved in the fortunes of all the Rose family, and helped
them in many ways.

She kept up this visiting of the poor families mentioned here
all her life till her health made it impossible. It was an engagement
she seldom broke.

> (3) *Direction work*. I have not had much to do in this
> except keeping one or two old cases going: but am now
> doing more than before in the way of instructions, addresses
> to guilds, collections of clergymen etc. (!), I think I had bet-
> ter take all this sort of work that offers as it is direct and
> inconspicuous and seems really to be needed.
>
> (4) *Detachment and general behaviour*. (*a*) Really, because I
> have been so absorbed in religious interest and struggles, I
> have not felt the old temptation to exactingness, etc., in per-
> sonal relations, but expect it is only dozing and not killed. I
> still find people attractive but can now take friendships less
> intensely. All the same, in many ways I am still absurdly over-
> sensitive, and easily tipped off my spiritual balance by wor-
> ries and vexations, though I do stamp down this sort of
> thing, and refuse to luxuriate in it and so scramble back,
> rather more quickly than before. It is a struggle to leave all
> one's professional vanity at the foot of the Cross—but unless
> I can do this, I may as well give up altogether.
>
> (*b*) Even although I manage to stifle a good bit of my
> boundless impatience, capacity for exasperation, and snappy
> temper (formerly written off as due to nerves and over-

work), still, some pops out if I am off my guard and the rest seethes inside for a bit. All the same one *can* win these battles if not at the moment, at least next day.

(*c*) All the strains and conflicts come in with ordinary active life, professional and social intercourse, family duties, perpetual scrimmage to adjust rival claims and fit everything in: opportunities of accepting boring things, etc. Here I don't think I improve. I pick out objects of devotion instead of taking obvious and unattractive ones. Though except when nervous and cross, I do find people in general far more lovable, and feel more tolerant and less critical towards them; still I fail perpetually in gentleness, love, and abnegation. One trues oneself up on Sunday, but it peters out very soon.

(*d*) I am also very cowardly (I like to call it reserve) about my mostly pagan friends, and entirely non-church-going family, suspecting how much I care for religion: and descend to almost any evasions and concealment to avoid this. I live in nervous terror of discovery, make elaborate plans to get to Holy Communion unobserved, and let my rule lapse when staying with people rather than seem pious. This is despicable from one point of view but all the same there is a horribleness in letting one's treasure be seen.

(*e*) As for self-oblivion, it seems *hopeless*. Incessant introspection and eternal self-communings seem to possess me: I hate it but can't get away from it. It ruins my prayers very often, and is, I know, altogether wrong. Now and then one gets away from it and all tangles into the depths and is nothing—but this is very seldom and only for a bit.

(5) *Prayer.* (*a*) You told me to practise the kind and degree that "most humbled yet braced." But I can't stick to one kind or degree: I range from complete self-absorption or mixed silence and aspiration (which I think suit me best really) to mere chatterings, vague considerations, and wandering attention. Orderly Three Point Meditations seem impossible and a good deal of the (very short) time you allowed is wasted on distractions. I wish I could have a bit more latitude about this. You see, if one has to scurry round

one's house, order meals, etc., just before, it does not put
one in the most favourable state for recollection; and often
most of that half-hour is spent trying to get recollected. On
the other hand, when the states of real absorption, which
alone are really worth while, happen they take time to get
established and then the time is up and I have to break off
forcibly. I have been really very obedient about this, but
would like to feel freer, and would not, I promise, make it
an excuse for religious daydreaming. I would like a minimum of one hour and a maximum of one and a half hours
to include morning and night prayers, but not odd five
minutes during the day. Also when I can't get to the
Carmelites in the afternoon, or only at the price of over-
fatigue, to take that quarter of an hour at home instead.

(*b*) I feel I ought to spend more time in Intercession, and
would, if I could feel it did real work. But it is so unreal to
me that I forget all about it. Yet I know, when you pray for
me, you do somehow bring a tremendous force to bear! And
even in my tiny way I ought to be able to do something,
especially for the souls I have got to try to help. In general I
forget all specific requests—after all why should one ask for
things? To bring one's deepest desires and intentions and
moral difficulties into the presence of God and hold them
there is, of course, tremendously effective, but trying to affect
other people's lives in this way seems to me at present to
belong more to the realm of idea than to that of concrete
fact. I am almost certainly wrong about this, and blinded here
as I was in other directions, and I want to get it right.
Because I must give my devotional life some redemptive and
social character and prevent it getting too thin and vertical.

(*c*) You said further, my aim must be to keep as continu-
ally as possible in the spirit of prayer. Well! I made an awful
struggle for this; but if by it you mean *conscious* constant ten-
dance and aspiration of God, it is beyond me. When working it splits my attention hopelessly: and when with other
people it vanishes. Although there are whole days in the
country when I am much alone, I can do it, there are more

when I forget for hours. If, however, you mean only a sort of background awareness, a vertical orientation to God, and now and then a short and very simple recollection for a minute or two, I can more or less do this. But it is too easy and too superficial to be what you really mean, I feel sure.

(6) *Christocentric devotion.* I take back with shame every word I said against this. This does not, however, mean a devotional *volte-face.* I am still mainly Theocentric; but the two attitudes are no longer in opposition in my mind; they are two aspects of one thing. Something you said showed me how to bridge the gap between theism and Christian devotion, which had worried me for years, and latterly had been driving me steadily in a direction not *much* removed from Unitarianism, as you perceived (though I did not at all like it when you said so!). Now I have got my universe all in one piece again. This has meant throwing overboard some Nicene language about pre-existence, eternal generation, etc., and Platonic conceptions of the Logos Christ. But perhaps you will allow me a little latitude here.

(7) *Historical values in religion.* Yes! I now fully and solidly accept your position, with no reserves at all; and with a growing feeling in favour of such historical realism, and dislike of fluffy and notional, instead of factual religion. You forced me thoroughly to reconsider my own foundations and realize that a mere philosophy of value, however sublime, has no power to redeem unless these values have been incarnated in human life. The main historical happenings as given by reasonable N.T. criticism—and especially the Passion—are absolutely necessary to Christianity as I understand it. I never doubted their occurrence but they now mean a great deal more to me. Also as regards Holy Communion, the historical link comes in strongly, and at least part of what it seems to me (putting aside the purely spiritual and quite undiscussable aspect) is the feeling of being linked with, and doing the same thing as all the others who have really cared, right from the beginning—and through them, stretching back to the beginning, too; a sort of spiritual time stream.

You may say as a non-Catholic I do nothing of the kind, but I do not think you will—anyhow that is how I feel it.

(8) *Human and historical contacts necessary.* This is really a continuation and development of the preceding. I feel I do not yet fully understand all you said under this head: but sometimes for a bit I do. Anyhow I thoroughly accept and trust it.

(9) *Spiritual dispositions.* Here again, while fully accepting what you say, I have only been able very partially to practise it. The transcendental and incarnational currents are woven together now and there is no opposition between them in my mind. But the incarnational current is still the weakest. If my soul is left to itself, it moves off in the non-spatial, theocentric direction at once. I do try by persistent N.T. reading and meditation to strengthen the strictly Christian side and it is never quite out of my mind—but the other is most vividly and factually present.

(10) *Possible change of obedience.* I accept this in theory, though whether I am yet equal to performing it in practice is more doubtful. Frankly I cannot at present conceive the question of submission to Rome, as to which this point first came up, ever becoming a case of conscience. In fact I feel now quite satisfied as an Anglican; having discovered a corner I can fit into, and people with whom I can sympathize and work. Still it might happen, and if it did I hope I should not draw back.

So by the summer of 1922 she feels herself a settled Anglican. My own feeling is that the retreat at Pleshey and the Warden Mrs. Harvey's friendship and understanding may have had a great deal to do with this. She does not mention anyone else who is helping her to understand the genius of Anglicanism. She always wore her Anglicanism with a difference. It was tremendously enriched by her having companied so long with saints and thinkers from every century. She gave us our Church made beautiful by a garment of praise which she made for it from her own deep instinct for worship. There was nothing stodgy about belonging to the Church of England in her company.

The Baron gave his advice in what he himself called "a bulky affair," giving unsparingly time, prayer, and affectionate care. He was not happy about her having made a general confession without consulting him, but he approves of her motive in going to Confession, and tells her that God will have over-ruled it for her good. But he was glad that she had gone to Pleshey.

> As to the retreat at Pleshey, your frequenting it was a very wise decision, and by all means go to it regularly. There are only two points connected with it that I want to straighten out for you: (1) I do not recognize your right (given that you choose to have me for your spiritual adviser) to go without consulting me, and (2) never more than one such retreat, or any retreat, a year. The more swimming in your element you feel, the more will it be wise to use this moderation about it. But by all means stay the full time, or choose one of their longer retreats, not beyond a week however.
>
> (1) *Practices.* I do not doubt that your present mixed consciousness and action (in spite of the apparent loss of what seemed or even was prayer of simple quiet) is a gain in genuine spirituality.
>
> Make your *External Religion* consist for the part you never miss, of Weekly Holy Communion; at most twice a week. And persevere in this even if your present attraction goes (which it certainly may do). But do not make decisions, nor construct a theory, etc., against devotion to the Holy Eucharist *extra usum*.... This devotion has formed Saints and great Saints.
>
> (2) *Visiting the poor.* All this is in excellent working order. You have only to persevere, especially with your readiness to utilize unforced opportunities for spiritual help, and the cheerful acceptance of merely physical and natural humane helpfulness. And do not try to pick out the people specially repulsive to you; enough, better, if you end by

taking the repulsive and the attractive ones, just as they
come.

(3) *Direction work.* This, too, is all in order. I particularly
like "the collections of clergymen"!

(4) *Detachment and general behaviour.* Your *a, b, c,* show real
improvement, and you have got, I think, quite the right standard. Except that I do not like, "Unless I can leave all professional vanity at the foot of the Cross I may as well give up
altogether." This, of course, is excessive. For to the very end
of your life you will be more or less tempted to, and you will
fall into such faults; yet it will be abundantly worth while to
fight on and thus gradually to diminish such faults, and even
upon the whole the strength of the temptation to them.

Strains and conflicts: desires not to appear pious. I would not
fight these directly but would try gently to get thoroughly at
home with them, saturated by your joy. You will find, acting
thus, that people will (as to this matter) become more shad-
owy, more distant to you. And this will, of itself, correct this
failing. But I would certainly, now and always concentrate
my will upon not missing my Sunday Holy Communion,
wherever I was. God will help you on in proportion to your
generosity in this respect.

As to *Self Oblivion,* never try directly for this—a sure
means of strain, scruple, and much self-occupation. And if
while turning to God, other souls, your several objective
interests, etc., you still catch yourself in self-occupation;
thank God gently for the sight; to see this is a grace and a
mark that you are getting on.

(5) *Prayer.* By all means practise the mixed kind of prayer
you describe and no formal meditation; also let this prayer be
at least one hour long, or at most an hour and a half every
day; this to include morning and night prayers but not the
odd five minutes during the day. Also, when you cannot get
to the Carmelites in the afternoon, or can get to them only
at the price of over-fatigue, you will give that quarter of an
hour to some kind of prayer or spiritual reading, which

humbles yet braces you at home. As to your *Intercession,* you
are evidently not yet fully or steadily awake to its reality and
power. But pray do not strain after a comprehension of it. Be
very faithful in your service of the poor, in your Holy
Communion, and in your (very humble) mixed prayer and it
will come to you in the form and degree intended for you;
it will come, and perhaps soon. We must always thus, in our
own efforts, strive to reach what we have not got, by the
faithful practice of what we have, although God is in no wise
tied in His dealings with us, to this procedure.

As to what is meant by "keeping as continuously as possible in the spirit of prayer," it was partly the gently retaining
and feeding of the dim background; but also and specially the
doing of your studies, composition, speaking, etc., with a
sense that all you are doing is, in its perfection, always beyond
you. All that you are doing should always have a certain awe-
inspiring Over-againstness; something of the great *contrata,*
the infinite country of God. You will find that this will not
split up your attention, for it does not consist of any direct
consciousness of God Himself. I would only ask you, over
and above this, for a little aspiration to God or Christ, at the
breaks or the movings away from one occupation to another.

(6) *Christocentric devotion.* I am indeed delighted that you
are thus getting away from that more or less Unitarian frame
of mind, and I beg of you to feed this your new orientation
carefully and wisely—the ways you mention are excellent. As
to Nicene and Platonic language, I much want you quietly
to escape from your natural trend, from the alternative of
either forcing yourself to accept and proclaim, or definitely
rejecting these terms and thoughts. Do not throw overboard
anything here. Your and my chances of genuine growth
depend very largely on our persistent refusal to identify the
ultimate truth or even our own ultimate capacity with what
we actually see or even what we hope and now are capable
of. Simply feed your soul on the great positive facts and
truths you see already: pray for fidelity to your light, and for

as much more light as may be within God's plans for you.
And as for the rest, neither force adhesion nor allow rejec-
tion, but let it alone, as possible food for others and indeed
for yourself later on. It only does not concern *yourself at present.*

(7) *Historical values in religion.* I am delighted at your growth
here, and that you feel the factualness, the happenedness of
our Lord, of His Passion, and of the Holy Communion. I
certainly do not doubt that, as an Anglican you do and you
ought to feel so, also as regards the Holy Eucharist.

He repeats what he has said before as to the need for sense stimulation in all forms of life and especially in Religious Life, and
again, solemnly asking her to forgo all blocks to the doing of
God's Will, in regard to her allegiance to Anglicanism or to Rome
by saying: *I can never do this or that.*

"You must be ready," he ends his bulky affair, "to take this or
any other step if conscience calls."

It was the direction she followed and held to all her life, for her
questionings about Roman allegiance did not end suddenly, but
were always part of her testing. But, as she wrote to Dom John
Chapman years later, she would know "the push of God"; and till
then she would do the work to which God had called her in the
Anglican Communion, which she accepted whole heartedly, as
part of the Holy Catholic Church.

The Baron added a few weeks after a second thought on
another subject.

> *Activities not directly religious and behaviour in times of spiritual
> dryness.*
>
> I have been pursued by the sense of not having last time,
> insisted upon these closely related matters. They are, I am
> sure, your chief preparation for the grace of final persever-
> ance, grace great for us all, and a miracle for yourself.
>
> Your professional work is directly busy with religious
> matters, but this makes it all the more important you should
> keep up or revive activities and interests of a not directly reli-
> gious kind. It doesn't matter what these activities and inter-

ests are (I need never know what they are), provided they are wholesome, provided you have a relish for them, and provided they really are not directly religious.

Now what I advise you to do, when spiritual dryness comes markedly into your soul, is to drop all your continuous though mixed prayer—all, that is, except short morning and night prayers; little aspirations during the day, especially acceptances of this dryness; and on Sundays, your Holy Communion.

If at these times you really must write or speak on religion, God will help you; but I should be glad if you would adjourn such writing or speaking, whenever possible, to the season of light. As soon as without self-probing, you see that the dry bout is over, quietly resume your full rule—but not till then.

This advice, though contrary to many exhortations in spiritual books, is not really a contradiction of them. We live quite abnormal lives all of us, in these feverish times, and our nerves are on edge and require wise attention. Treat your soul as the captains in the old pre-steam days treated their crew. These men had always to be busy, but not always sailing. Weeks of no wind, or of wrong wind would keep them from sailing. What then? They would at once, *as part of their work and life,* drop the sailing and take to the mending and making of sails and nets, etc. So do you.

F. v. H.

So in obedience to this she took up a new pursuit, which I fancy gave her the same sort of pleasure that she had as a bookbinder. She learnt to do script writing, and used to please her friends, by transcribing for them, some of her favourite sentences from the Mystics or the Fathers.

She sent the Baron for Christmas a passage from St. Cyprian in half uncials which pleased him very much.

Five years later she wrote in a letter one of her deepest debts to the Baron in 1922.

Until about five years ago I never had *any* personal experience of our Lord. I didn't know what it meant. I was a convinced Theocentric, and thought Christocentric language
and practice sentimental and superstitious.... I had from time
to time what seemed to be vivid experience of God, from
the time of my conversion from agnosticism (about twenty
years ago now). This position I thought to be that of a broadminded intelligent Christian, but when I went to the Baron
he said I wasn't much better than a Unitarian. Somehow by
his prayers or something, he compelled me to experience
Christ. He never said anything more about it—but I know
humanly speaking he did it. It took about four months—it
was like watching the sun rise very slowly—and then suddenly one knew what it was.

Now for some months after that I remained predomi-
nantly Theocentric. But for the next two or three years, and
especially lately, more and more my whole religious life and
experience seem to centre with increasing vividness on our
Lord—that sort of quasi involuntary prayer which springs up
of itself at odd moments is always now directed to Him. I
seem to have to try as it were to live more and more towards
Him only—and it is this that makes it so utterly heartbreaking when one is horrid. The New Testament, which once I
couldn't make much of, or meditate on, now seems full of
things never noticed—all gets more and more alive and
compellingly beautiful.... Holy Communion which at first I
did simply under obedience, gets more and more wonderful
too. It is in that world and atmosphere one lives.

10

"In We Are, and On We Must"

The Evelyn Underhill of 1922–3 whom we have seen to be so humbly ready to be taught, so ready to confess the gaps in her own spiritual make-up, was, all the same, never ceasing in all the work that came to her, to help other people. She did not have to look for it and it was varied. The addresses of hers which are still available in this year are one to girls' club leaders, one to the Guild of Health, and one to an Interdenominational School of Social Service at Swanwick. Her speaking was always excellently prepared. It was refreshing both in its demand and in its form. It was often movingly lovely and often irresistibly witty and amusing. It was always salted with the wisdom that she had collected from her wide reading of the Saints and Mystics. It had a breadth that came from her study of philosophy. Fr. Curtis[3] notes that as you listened you asked yourself, Oxford or Cambridge? and then realized with a start that she was for the most part self-taught, and that though she owed a certain amount to the start and trend that King's College had given to her studies, she owed most to her unwearied zest for the truth, to her admiring love of sanctity, her diligent and enthusiastic study.

Her address to the Guild of Health can be seen to contain much of Baron von Hügel's often repeated advice not to strain after spiritual things. Its first paragraph is a summing up of her own religious history as we have read it:

> Here we are, little half-animal, half-spiritual creatures, mysteriously urged from within, and enticed from without to communion with spiritual Reality. If and when we surrender to this craving and this attraction, we enter thereby—though at first dimly—on a completely new life full of variety, of new joy, tension and pain, offering an infinite

opportunity of development to us. Such is the life of prayer as understood by the mystics, and as practised with greater or less completeness of surrender and reward by all real lovers of Christ.

Here is a sentence which became almost a refrain with her in her care for souls: "We take as our first principle the humble and diligent use of the degree of prayer natural to a soul at any particular stage of its course, and not the anxious straining towards some other degree yet beyond it."

Her writing work this year was the completion of a new edition of the *Cloud of Unknowing,* with an Introduction; and she must have been working about this time on a new edition of Walter Hilton's *Scale of Perfection,* also with a biographical and critical introduction. She loved these two mystics, the unknown one and the other whose Midland breeding was the same as her own, and she quotes from them in her Guild of Health address: from the *Cloud:* "God may well be loved, but not thought," and from Walter Hilton, among other passages, this which shows how from century to century the mystics have echoed each other: "When thou disposest thee to think of God, if thy heart be dull and dark, and feels neither wit nor savour nor devotion for to think of God, but only a bare desire and a weak will that thou would'st think of God then I hope it is good to thee that thou strive not much with thyself as if thou would'st by thine own might overcome thyself."

Another address which I have found among her papers is one for club leaders in girls' clubs. It must have been given in 1922 as it was printed in the *Girls' Club News* of 23 January 1923. It is full of the sort of bracing wisdom, and with a good deal of the refreshing and unconventional love of people which was characteristic:

> However ardent the spiritual or idealistic inclinations of the club leader or worker may be, these inclinations should not be too prominent in her behaviour and must *never* be taken as a standard to which others are to be deliberately tuned up. They make their best effect casually and without observation. Keep the home fires burning by all means; they are the

fires which raise the steam by which you do your work. But don't keep poking them in public and remarking on the quality of the coal. The gentle glow they spread is their best recommendation.

As well as—or even instead of—being what you think best, the club world and atmosphere must be all that the girls think homely and sympathetic if it is to feed them.... Begin where they are, not where you are.... Do not be afraid of Ella Wheeler Wilcox or *The Soul's Awakening* or fail to be thoroughly sympathetic about camisoles and jumpers. You may think this has little to do with spirituality, but it has, as a matter of fact, a good deal. The universal spirit is universal; it does not stop short at homely and common things.

Finally [she ends] be sure that religion is never offered to the young as primarily something which will be a comfort to them, or out of which they can get something for themselves. They are in the mass generous hearted creatures, and generosity of outlook is one of the qualities most needed for a healthy spiritual life.

In July 1922 she was at Swanwick, at a Conference which met to consider "A Christian Order of Society."

It says a good deal for her influence among Christians at this time that she who did not profess any special knowledge of social work, though it had always compelled her attention even at sixteen, should have been chosen as a speaker at this Conference.

But it was not organizing and schemes of social betterment that people were wanting from her, but that strange sense of God which she conveyed, even when her own vision was gained through so much journeying in the dark, and that feeling of oneness with the great human spirits who have received Him into their hearts. This sort of thing perhaps:

There is in William Blake's *Jerusalem* a marvellous drawing of the pitiful and energizing spirit of Christ brooding over Albion; stretching His wounded hands to the two limits

which Blake called Adam and Satan—all the possibilities of
our humanity (for Christ is, after all, the Son of Man) and all
the worst we have become. It seems to me we too are bound
to strive for such a spiritual gesture; the stretching out as it
were of one hand towards His perfection, the limit where
Divine and Human meet, and of the other, in complete
friendliness and generosity, towards the sins and imperfec-
tions of men. Neither action is particularly easy in a practical way; but unless we try to manage this we need not regard
ourselves as genuine friends of Christ. It is the double simul-
taneous outstretching that matters; this only can open the
heart wide enough to let in God, and so make each man
who achieves it a mediator of His Reality to other men. The
non-religious socialist seems to stretch out one hand, and the
non-social pietist the other. But one without the other is
useless. Both at once: that is where the difficulty comes in.

It sometimes seems a demand which we can hardly
meet.

That phrase "mediator of God's reality" is one that seems to suggest all that is most true about her own vocation. The year 1922,
as we see by her report to the Baron in 1923, was one of liberating spiritual experience for her. What George Fox used to call
"openings" came to her spirit and mind with compelling force.
"In we are, and on we must," Bishop Selwyn used to say. It was a
time of "on we must" for her, a time, as she admitted, of a great
deal of nervous tension, a costly year of progress.

Some time in 1923 she made the acquaintance which grew
into a close friendship with Elizabeth Rendel, whom she first met
at Mrs. Skrine's house in Oxford. Travelling home from Oxford to
London together, Mrs. Rendel was bold enough to say that she
didn't like Evelyn's *Mysticism* very much and preferred von Hügel.
To Evelyn it was much more important to find a friend who
shared her feeling for the Baron than to have her own work
approved, and they struck up a friendship over it which was very
much deepened by a chance visit to the Rendels' home one night
when Evelyn and Hubert needed a shore lodging during a cruise.

They came in late and tired and Mrs. Rendel put Evelyn to bed in an eastward-looking room which reminded her of that "chamber whose name was Peace and which opened towards the sunrising," where Bunyan's Pilgrim was laid in the Interpreter's house. Evelyn wrote the next day: "It was one of the very nicest sudden adventures we ever had, and we are so grateful to you both for your kindness. It was specially lovely for me to have the opportunity of making real friends with you. Christian friends do help one such a lot, and I have not very many of them. It is beautiful to think I can add you to the permanent list; as even without meeting, one can always keep in touch."

It was, I think, a relief to Evelyn to have a friend whom she was not directing; so many of her Christian friends came to her as souls to be directed, which meant that the friendship was carried on in an atmosphere rather too heavily weighted with responsibility.

She wrote again of this visit to Elizabeth Rendel: "It was a marvellous interlude of perfect peace for body and soul, and fairly saved my life! I felt a criminal arriving in that dead-beat condition—and went off as brisk and happy as Christian after his week-end at the Interpreter's house. We got on board just before the storm broke, and had a good old tempestuous night."

Another friend who came face to face with her in 1923 after six years of exchanging letters was Lucy Menzies. She wrote in her own notes for this book: "Having corresponded with Evelyn for some years, it was rather in fear and trembling that I first went to see her in her own house. But it was all right from the first. What impressed me about her that day was the great depth of her very grey eyes, which seemed to search deep down beneath all the shyness of a shy Scot, so that intimate talk was easy and I went away on wings knowing I had found a true and understanding friend."

Evelyn must have written more letters to Lucy Menzies than to any of her "family." In every year there are twenty or so, and they give the surest account of her doings and movements. They are full of loving concern for this friend and "child" who was so often in deep waters spiritually, but they also record much of her daily life, and there is a delicious vein in them which Lucy Menzies recorded: "Danny, my dog, and David, her cat, carried on a gay correspondence for some years. Evelyn never stood on her dignity and Danny would make pointed remarks about Evelyn, to which David replied with great gusto. We both entered into this with zest, and it somehow led to greater intimacy."

David was sometimes allowed to send an article to the papers, one of which, a review of a book on cats, ends: "It is pleasant to read of so many examples of the rightly ordered home, happy and cheerful under the control of its cat, keeping for him the best chair, arranging his food on the best rug, rising with alacrity in obedience to his lightest mew, and opening and shutting doors with promptitude and zeal."

SKYLIGHT PATHS PUBLISHING
SUNSET FARM OFFICES RTE 4
PO BOX 237
WOODSTOCK VT 05091-0237

We hope you will enjoy this book and that you will find it useful and use it to enrich your life.

Book title: _____

Your comments: _____

How you learned of this book: _____

Reasons why you bought this book: (check all that apply) ☐ SUBJECT ☐ AUTHOR ☐ ATTRACTIVE COVER
☐ ATTRACTIVE INSIDE ☐ RECOMMENDATION OF FRIEND ☐ RECOMMENDATION OF REVIEWER ☐ GIFT

If purchased: Bookseller _____ City _____ State _____

Please send me a SkyLight Paths Publishing catalog. I am particularly interested in: (check all that apply)

1. ☐ Spirituality
2. ☐ Mysticism/Meditation
3. ☐ Philosophy/Theology

4. ☐ Spiritual Texts
5. ☐ Religious Traditions (Which ones?)

6. ☐ Children's Books
7. ☐ Prayer/Worship
8. ☐ (Other)

Name (PRINT) _____

Street _____ Phone _____

City _____ State _____ Zip _____ E-mail _____

Please send a SkyLight Paths Publishing catalog to my friend:

Name (PRINT) _____

Street _____ Phone _____

City _____ State _____ Zip _____

SkyLight Paths Publishing

Sunset Farm Offices, Rte. 4 • P.O. Box 237 • Woodstock, VT 05091 • Tel: (802) 457-4000 Fax: (802) 457-4004
Available at better booksellers. Visit us online at www.skylightpaths.com

11

"CALLED OUT AND SETTLED"

In the June of 1923 Evelyn wrote her report, covering a year, for Baron von Hügel.

(1) *General.* I feel quite different from last year: but in ways rather difficult to define. Deeper in. More steady on my knees though not yet very steady on my *feet.* Not so rushing up and down between blankness and vehement consolations. Still much oscillation, but a kind of steady line persists instead of zigzags.

I have been trying all the time to shift the focus from feeling to will, but have not yet fully done it, and shall not feel safe till I have. The Christocentric side has become so much deeper and stronger—it nearly predominates. I never dreamed it was like this. It is just beginning to dawn on me what the Sacramental life really does involve: but it is only in flashes of miraculous penetration I can realize this. On the whole, in spite of blanks, times of wretched incapacity, and worse (see below) I have never known such deep and real happiness, such a sense of at last having got my real permanent life, and being able to love without stint, where I am meant to love. It is as if one were suddenly liberated and able to expand all round. Such joy that it sometimes almost hurts. All this, humanly speaking, I owe entirely to you. Gratitude is a poor dry word for what I feel about it. I can't say anything.

The moral struggle is incessant, but there is a queer joy in it. I don't think I need bother you much about that. Small renunciations are easier, but real ones still mean a fight. Nervous tension or exhaustion means a renewed attack of all my old temptations at full strength and I feel invaded by

109

hard, exasperated, critical, hostile, gloomy, and unloving inclinations.

Of course my will does not consent to these horrors: I do struggle with them: all the same they creep into my mind, and stick for days. Another proof at bottom I am un-Christian still (for surely mere nervous tension should not mean these odious feelings?). And that lovely gentle suppleness and radiance I see in all my real Christian friends, and long for, I can't get. I don't think I have ever seen the deepest roots in myself of pride and self-love.

Many religious practices I still can't do, e.g. self-examination. I did make myself do a long written one at my retreat, which perhaps I ought to send you. It looked horrid—but somehow I can't feel much interest in it, or that these curry combings matter much. So much more worth while and far more humbling, just to keep on trying to look at Christ. I know instantly by that when I do anything odious. Even before Holy Communion I don't do much else but, as it were, let that love flow over and obliterate everything. There is so little difference between one's best and worst.

Probably I ought to tell you this. Last October, one day when I was praying, quite suddenly a Voice seemed to speak to me—with tremendous staccato sharpness and clearness. It only said one short thing, first in Latin and then in English! Please don't think I am going in for psychic automatisms or horrors of that sort. It has never happened again, and I don't want it to. Of course I know all about the psychological aspect and am not *hallucinated.* All the same, I simply cannot believe that there was not something deeper, more real, not me at all, behind. The effect was terrific. Sort of nailed me to the floor for half an hour, which went as a flash. I felt definitely called out and settled, once for all—that any falling back or leaving off, after that, will be an unpardonable treason. That sense has persisted—it marked a sort of turning point and the end of all the remorse and worry, and banging about. I feel now if all consolations went it ought not to matter very much; though as a matter of fact derelictions are more painful and trying than they used to be, but have their purifying side. I feel a total, unconditioned dedication is what is asked and it is so difficult. I shall never do it—one fails at every corner.

There have been other things since from time to time, but quite formless, and unspeakably sacred, penetrating, intimate, abasing. Now and then new lights, too, sort of intellectual intuitions, and quite clear of "sensible devotion"; but they are so quick and vast one can only retain about half. I would like to get away from the more vividly emotional feelings: I don't altogether trust them—but how can one help feeling pretty intensely. One has only one soul and body to do one's feelings with after all.

Prayer, at good times though still mixed, is more passive: a sort of inarticulate communion, or aspirations, often merely one word, over and over. Sometimes I wonder whether this is not too much taking the line of least resistance; but it is so wonderful, sweeps one along into a kind of warm inhibited darkness and blind joy—one lives in Eternity in that—can't keep at this pitch long, twenty minutes or so.

I do try to say a few psalms each day and do Intercessions, but one forgets everything then. Of course it's not always like this, often all distraction and difficulty.

As to Intercession, if I ask myself whether I would face complete Spiritual deprivation for the good of another: e.g. to effect a conversion, I can't do that yet. So I have not got real Christian love: and the question is, can one intercede genuinely for anyone, unless ready to pay, if necessary, this price.

Special points (*a*) A terrible, overwhelming suspicion that after all, my whole "invisible experience" may be only subjective. There are times (of course when one has got it) when it seems incredible that these things could happen to me, considering what I have been. All the books say in unmortified beginners they are very suspicious, so what is one to think?

And further, there is the obvious fact that consolation and deprivation are somehow closely connected with the ups and downs of one's nervous and even bodily life. There is no real test: I may have deceived myself right through, and always studying these things, self-suggestion would be horribly easy. These doubts are absolute torture after what has happened. They paralyse one's life at the roots, once they lodge in the mind. I do not want to shirk *any* pain, but this does not seem a purifying kind. I have read over and over all you say in the Mystical Element—one must have suffering and in a way I wish for it, but I don't get any certitude for myself. The one hopeful side is, what happens, though recognizable, does not really match the books; it does seem my own, yet *infinitely* transcending anything I could ever have imagined for myself—and grows in depth, mystery, and sweetness.

You said the first time of all, it was all right, I need have no doubts. You know me better now—if you could and would say you still feel absolutely sure, I think I could accept that once for all, and turn my back on all these horrors whenever they come. So far I have struggled through all right, generally by deliberate forced prayer—but this only shelves the problem, does not solve it—and it makes one feel horribly unsafe. The return to peace and certitude is wonderful; but how am I to know for certain this is not just some psychic mechanism? There are times when I wish I had never heard of psychology.

(*b*) Sometimes an even more terrifying visitation, when not *only* my own inner experience, but the whole spiritual scheme seems in question. The universe seems cast iron and the deterministic view the obvious one. All the old difficulties come back: and especially that chasm between the universal and the historic experience of Christ. I see clearly that for me religious realism is the only thing that is any use. Generally I seem to have it with an increasingly vivid sense of real approach to, or communion with God and Christ as objective facts, completely other than myself. I can't love on any other basis than this: even human love can't be spun from one's dreams, and this is far, far beyond that. But in these black times of doubt, it seems possible that one's hours of prayer and adoration simply react on oneself and produce the accompanying experiences. I have no guarantee of genuineness. It is not the awful moral struggle I knew I should have once I gave in; that has a sort of joy in it; those mental conflicts are just pure horror.

Mortification. I still feel I ought to do something about this, partly for love, partly as a training for suffering: years of softness to make up for. But I don't know the right principle: the books seem to conflict. Fr. Doyle's *agere contra* in everything, even trifles, seems fussy and self-occupied, e.g. always looking out for an opportunity of doing or even eating something you don't like! I simply couldn't be bothered! The other idea, doing and accepting what comes and never deflecting for one's own likes and dislikes, seems better and far from easy, but perhaps not quite enough? But so far you have almost encouraged me to do the things I liked? Non-religious interests, etc. Like the comfortable camel in Ferishtah—bit of chervil and all? but I have a sneaking sympathy for the other camel! Please would you give me some direction about this?

Psycho-physical tangles. The parallels between nervous states and spiritual sensitiveness worry me: nerves and soul seem hopelessly mixed up; one thinks one is out of grace and finds it was only mental fatigue and impotence. Don't know how best to run my devotional life in nervous exhaustion. Often too stupefied to think, will, or love at all. I do keep my whole rule somehow—merely kneeling on a hard floor the proper time seems better than nothing—but the struggle to pray is fruitless then. This rule keeping tends to a sort of rigidity. I am restless and starved when my particular routine is upset. And during holidays, or when travelling, lecturing, etc., approximately a quarter of the year—I can't rely on keeping it. Often no privacy, no certain free time, safe from interruption: and the desperate struggle to get it at all costs induces a strain which is hostile to prayer. Lately, in fact, "holidays" have been periods of misery on this account. Of course, I never sacrifice Communions unless they are quite impossible—even these I cannot be sure of when we are yachting. What I want here is permission to be more flexible about the external rule and make up by taking every opportunity of quietude or of short aspirations, for any irregularity in long recollections. I believe I should do better like this and am sure it would not mean slackness. And there must be some way of super-naturalizing one's active life when one can't have one's usual solitude and fixed adoration. After all it's not my choice that I have to be at other people's disposal the whole time. Could not one turn these conditions into something worth offering?

Retreat. May I go to two three-day retreats in the year instead of the one whole week retreat which you allowed but which is so difficult to manage? *Please* say yes to this! It is such a help and refreshment in one's driving incessantly active life! I come back completely renovated. But a year between is a long time to wait.

Vocation. I feel great uncertainty as to what God chiefly wants of me. Selection has become inevitable. I can't meet more than half the demands made. I asked for more opportunity of personal service and have thoroughly been taken at my word! But there is almost no time or strength left now for study for its own sake; always giving or preparing addresses, advice, writing articles, trying to keep pace with work, going on committees and conferences—and with so little mental food I risk turning into a sort of fluid clergyman! More serious the conflict between family claims and duties and work is getting acute. My parents are getting old: they don't understand, and are a bit jealous of the claims on my life (especially as it's all unpaid work). I feel perhaps I ought to have more leisure for them, though I do see them nearly every day. But this could only be done by reducing

what seems like direct work for God, or my poor people or
something. I confess the work and the poor people are congenial: and idling about chatting and being amiable, when
there is so much to be done, a most difficult discipline—so I
can't judge the situation fairly. It is not a case of being needed
in any practical sense: just of one's presence being liked, and
one's duties slightly resented!

Disobedience. When I have been alone and have had the
opportunity, I have sometimes gone to Holy Communion
oftener than you said. Otherwise I believe I have kept on my
collar and chain.

Guilds of Prayer. Constantly being urged to join Guilds of
Prayer, Intercession, etc., and reproached for refusal. Ought I
to? I do so want to keep free and hidden in prayer: feel very
reluctant to take on these extra rules—but don't wish to be
unsocial.

The Baron did not leave this report for long without an answer.
He must have seen the signs of strain from which he always tried
to save Evelyn. To the end of her life she bore the strain of that
longing to be sure. It was her Way.

On 12 July the Baron wrote to her:

I have had to wait for a break in my present work and a
leisure of mind sufficient for ruminating your report and
making suggestions thereon. I have had a free day today: and
the best of the morning and afternoon have been given to
the little work. May God bless it abundantly.

I do not doubt you have got on substantially during this
last year, especially your General Notes make me think so.
This means that we must not make any radical or very tan-
gible changes. The following points, however, have all got
their importance, especially two, which I shall treat as fundamental. I think that a gentle, genial approximate practice of
the habits proposed will considerably simplify, expand, pacify,
and feed your soul.

As to self-examination. No long written out affairs! Be
satisfied with a short examen, only of the day just passed, in

your night prayers. Say three, at the most five, minutes will be ample: no straining, no scraping, as it were, the very bottom of your soul; no assuming, even if you find nothing, there *is* something; no contrition for possible sins. Develop a general, gradually increasing habit of dropping all voluntary self-occupation during the day and gently turn instead to God in Christ. This double practice will be your substitute for much self-examination; for you will thus grow into a general but most real self-contempt; and God will then, off and on give you glimpses also of particular wrong and imperfect dispositions of yours. Such glimpses you will gratefully receive but you must not then break up your recollection by any prodding at yourself, any active and detailed self-examination. A gentle general horror of self and a simple flight away from self to God and Christ—to Christ-God—this will brace you finely.

The Divine Office. The praying of a few psalms, or even only snatches of psalms is good. But I would not take to the recital of an entire Office, however short. Not your *attrait*.

Your test of *purity of intention* is incorrect because excessive. Such purity requires only two things: a general readiness to accept and to will when God shows it to us, whatsoever He may wish us to do, to renounce, suffer, or to be; and a particular acceptance by our will of whatsoever He has already shown us or is now showing us. We only weaken ourselves if we attempt a third thing—if we anticipate possible demands of God; for such demands, so long as they are merely possible, lack all the corresponding support which they bring with them the minute they become actual. So please drop all such mere possibilities which can only depress you, without any spiritual profit.

Special points. Here is the first fundamentally important point. I do not at all like this craving for absolute certainty that this or that experience of yours is what it seems to yourself. And I am assuredly not going to declare that I am absolutely certain of the final and evidential worth of any of those experiences. They are not articles of faith, are they?

God and Christ, and the need for our constant death to self, remain simply certain do they not, even if your experiences are mistaken ones? And for what are even the most genuine of such things given to us than to help us still further away from self and self-occupation? You are at times tempted to scepticism (who is not?) and so you long to have some, if only one direct personal experience which shall be beyond the reach of all reasonable doubt. But such an escape from scepticism would even if it were possible (which it is not) be a most dangerous one, and would only weaken you, or shrivel you, or puff you up. By all means use such lights; by all means believe them, if and when they humble and yet brace you, to be probably from God. But do not build your faith upon them; do not make them an end when they exist only to be a means. So practising you will escape one more entanglement, to which kind of *emberlificotage* you are distinctly prone.

Other problems. Here is the second fundamentally important point as to mortification. You quote Fr. Doyle's rule of always going against what we may like—a ceaseless *agere contra,* and you most justly find in such a scheme no room whatever for what I mean by non-religious interests. I do not doubt that Fr. Doyle's rule contains very precious truth, and even that perhaps it would have been God's call for him if he had lived say, to seventy. Yet it is certain that the call, even of the same soul, often changes as the soul reaches maturity and then old age. And again it is certain that the grand truth enshrined in this position is capable of, indeed for souls at large requires, further discriminations. The great founder of the Trappists, de Rancé, doubtless clung to this *simpliste attrait* up to old age. But then Dom Mabillon, his saintly Benedictine contemporary, as faithfully followed a much more *nuancé* attraction, and indeed also exemplified what I mean by the practice of the non-religious interests.

Now the latter ascetical type, I submit, is yours and not the former. You would only further accentuate what is excessive in you, and would lose your peace instead of deepening it.

Vocation. I am not sure that God *does* want a marked preponderance of this or that work or virtue in your life—that would feed still further your natural temperament, already too vehement.

As to *helping others,* I find a great relief in what I have now practised only these last two years. I now know, roughly, how much I can try to help others without getting markedly empty myself. So now, when I have got to this point, I politely refuse to answer any fresh correspondents: I tell them frankly how matters stand and that God will find them, if really necessary, some helper with sufficient leisure for the purpose. As to your attending to your parents, that is assuredly an excellent thing for you, not to try to lengthen your visits, but to try gently and humbly to increase their quality—from your parents' standpoint I mean. How great if you could end by a certain real interest in those nothings, an interest springing from the purest love of those souls!

Rule. You ought already to know well that I do not want you to keep your entire rule "when too stupefied to will or think or love at all." "Kneeling on a hard floor making fruitless struggles." This cannot certainly be good for it is clearly not wise. I have wanted you all along to have two rules: a maximum rule for fair weather and a minimum rule for foul. For foul weather, morning and night prayers (with examen) all quite short, and two Holy Communions a week. For the rest, some extra needlework or gardening or what not. The fervour will then return much sooner and you will not have worn down your nerves to no purpose. When you have lectures, etc., to do, at such times also the minimum rule with such bits of recollection as you can manage. (You will get such bits if you do not attempt to give out beyond your interior resources.)

Retreats. By all means have two a year of three days each. But do not utilize them for elaborate examinations of conscience or for confession when you have not some definite fairly grave matter, not hitherto confessed. Evade all Guilds, etc., for yourself, but encourage them in others who find them helpful. There are many such ways to God.

Of course, all my advice should be taken *bonnement, cum grano* on the whole. Thus as to Communions, you would go occasionally three or four times a week: but your rule would still be twice a week.

Yours most sincerely,
F. von Hügel.

No report till June 1924, supposing I am still alive then.

It must have been a little bit difficult for Evelyn to reverse her policy and to write to the Baron asking if she might join the Order of the Holy Dove. This was a Lay Order of contemplatives, living not in community but in the world. It was to be an Order for those to whom "the search for Union with God is the chief quest of their lives." It was in the hands of two anchoresses living in the Isle of Wight; it did not ask more than Evelyn was already prepared to do. The members who knew each other prayed for each other and the Order, saying the *Veni Creator* on Thursday mornings at a set time.

The Baron suggested some questions for her to answer. I think he must have smiled as he wrote: "You had just been asking me to fortify you against joining any guild.... Do you feel quite quietly and clearly that this is substantially different? that it will in no wise complicate and trap you but will only gently support and steady you? And do you know the personnel? Solid, simple, sober souls? It seems to me that if *Yes* comes fully to these questions you can join with security. May God bless and help you to moderate yourself even in good things."

Evelyn belonged to the Order for some years till the chief anchoress died and the Order ceased. She brought Lucy Menzies and one or two others into the Order.

She was working hard at reviewing all this year. The sort of books that came her way were McDougall's *Outline of Psychology* for the *Westminster Gazette* and a multiple review concerned with Gore's *Belief in Christ,* Garvie and Anderson on the Fourth Gospel and the Epistle to the Hebrews and Principal Galloway's *Religion and Modern Thought,* for the *Daily News.*

Of McDougall's work she writes rather wickedly: "A work of 450 pages which contains, according to the index, only two references to Freud as against eight to apes, and none at all to auto-suggestion or the subconscious mind, must instantly attract us."

12

A TREMENDOUS YEAR

In 1924 Evelyn was ready to explore all sides of her varied vocation. It was the year of the Conference on Politics, Economics, and Christianity, called COPEC, and she was a member of the commission which drew up the Report on the Nature and Purpose of God; and was, I think, responsible with one other member of the commission for its final form. "I have been having a lurid weekend," she wrote in February to Lucy Menzies, "going through proof sheets of galley mostly by my co-editor, who has a talent for pouring forth floods of heliotrope prose.... My own contributions stand out with the stark austerity of quotations from the Stores list."

On this commission she worked with men of the quality of Fr. Edward Talbot, C.R., Principal Cairns, W. R. Maltby, W. H. Moberly, Oliver Quick and Charles Raven. The only other women were Miss Lucy Gardner, a member of the Society of Friends, and Miss Lily Dougall, who died before the conference met. Evelyn was described in the list of the Commission as "Lecturer on Christian Mysticism and Religious Psychology." But though this was an important bit of work, and the report turned out to be the most valuable part of the conference, something more vital happened to her in the early months of 1924. She was asked to conduct her first retreat at Pleshey. She had been to Pleshey quite often by now, and had come to love its peace and its long tradition of a place of prayer. She knew the Chaplain, Henry Monks, and Mrs. Harvey, the Warden, was a great friend. Even before the new chapel was built Pleshey had a beauty and simplicity of its own, the little rambling garden with the moat beside it, deep in the Essex countryside. It became more dear to her than any other holy place, and her first and her last retreats were given there.

It was Dorothy Swayne who asked Evelyn to conduct her first retreat, after meeting her at a small conference in 1924, where: "she at once impressed me with her vitality, her deep spirituality and quick wit."

> At that time [she wrote] I was warden of Time and Talents Settlement (Interdenominational) and had started having an annual retreat for an Interdenominational group. It was not easy to find people who could conduct a retreat for such a group and I at once felt that E. U. could do this. I therefore invited her to conduct our retreat at Pleshey. Her whole face lit up, and she said that to conduct a retreat was something she had longed to do, but that so far she had not been given the opportunity; and so in March 1924 she conducted a retreat for the T. and T. Settlement at Pleshey.

To Laura Rose, Evelyn wrote: "I have just been asked to conduct a three-day retreat at my dear Pleshey in Lent. I forget if I told you I might do it. It seems a great responsibility, but I think I have to do it. Of course, the Chaplain will say Mass, but I shall take the addresses, meditations, and interviews, so you must pray for this."

There were at least five solid bits of work to get through in the early spring of that year, as well as the work on the Mystics of the Church which she must have been beginning. She had two addresses to clergy and adolescent leaders, and an address to the Sunday School Council in January; there were two lectures for the University of St. Andrews, and the Pleshey addresses, all before the middle of March, and talks on Mysticism at York, Leeds, and Darlington shortly afterwards. It was a heavy programme to undertake, and although she was a lightning quick worker, it seems as if she must have been rather overspending her forces of mind and spirit.

She was looking forward enormously to the St. Andrews visit, to the prospect of staying with Lucy Menzies, and having plenty of time to talk to her. They had written to each other constantly after the meeting in 1923, and had become really intimate. Here is a letter of Evelyn's fixing up the St. Andrews visit:

> Lucy, my dear, Yes, it really is fixed, and the first lecture is written which I began to think would never be. Owing to an agitated letter from Mr. Russell saying that the words Spiritual Life would cause the students to suspect piety and keep them away (!) the tide is now: Man's Relation with Reality. My feeling is in favour of coming up on Sunday, and departing to Edinburgh on Saturday. That will surely, in spite of your giddy proposals, give us some evenings to ourselves. Indeed it must for I am coming to see you aren't I? and Danny? [Lucy's dog].... For heaven's sake don't "abandon your light manner" or I shan't be able to bear it. When treated with gravity and respect I sort of shrivel. And the Adolescent Leaders like rows and rows of grim bunny rabbits, and not understanding *one word* have much reduced me. So do let's be a little frivolous.
>
> It was such a perfectly happy week [she wrote later to Lucy Menzies] and I loved every moment of it, both the sacred and profane. Hubert was amazed and almost alarmed by the condition of rude health in which I have returned, so you see what all your sedulous spoiling and cockering up did for me.

Lucy was passing through a time of great spiritual stress, but the two friends seem to have managed to lay that aside and be happy together, though Evelyn was quite aware of the suffering of this very sensitive spirit. "It is horrid to have to stand by and see you suffer, but it is the sort of pain which is one of the soul's privileges and makes 'affirmative religion' look pretty thin. How can we expect God's action to be other than torture to us, weak and unpurified, and yet sensitive things as we are."

But she has some practical advice, too, to give to her spiritual child: "I do hope, dear Lucy, you are going to be really good, rest and consider your nerves, and generally look after yourself. I am absolutely sure it's your immediate duty to do this as well as the quickest way to recover your spiritual balance. Ovaltine, gentle aspirations, no strain and no fixed rule, preference given to secular interests. Be 1/10th as kind to yourself as you were to me and you will do nicely. I hope at Pleshey to see you with steadier nerves and a less careworn face."

Some advice was administered to Lucy through Danny (the dog):

> Thank you for your charming letter. I see you will be a most useful correspondent, so observing and unprejudiced, and telling one just what one wants to know. I hope Pleshey will be a success. Tell her to keep calm and not overdo it, and tell her that the nicest place in the house is the tiny oratory at the end of the corridor. Advise her to let herself alone.

The Pleshey retreat came less than three weeks after her Scottish visit. On 2 March she is writing: "Been working hard all the week at my Pleshey stuff. Got four of the eight addresses ready. They are coming out a bit on the cheerful side, but perhaps that is better than the opposite."

We come at this point to another vital black notebook: the notebook in which she wrote the very full notes for her first retreats. At retreats and conferences Evelyn never spoke extempore. Although she had perfected her technique in speaking in the intimate circle of retreatants, as though she were speaking without notes, it was all there in the book that lay on her knee, and so were the prayers and hymns, chosen long before. All her books in the last fifteen years of her life, except *Worship,* were based on these retreat notes.

She had two preparatory addresses, for there were a number there making their first retreat. She told them about her own first retreat, the one about which she had written so enthusiastically to von Hügel. "I remember my own first retreat, the apprehension and vagueness with which I entered it and the wonderful revelation that it was; my alarm at the idea of silence, and the mysterious peace and light distilled by it; my absolute distress when it ended, and clatter began."

Her main thought in the preparatory addresses was that they should be more concerned with God than with themselves: "Don't let us waste too much time gazing at ourselves. A deepened and enriched sense of God is far more important than increased and detailed knowledge of self."

Then for her five main addresses she chose Love, Joy, Peace, Prayer, and the Communion of Saints. Love the complete answer to and cure of sin. St. Teresa's love, work, and suffering. And joy that comes from humble self-oblivion, and Peace which is the quality that springs from abandoned obedience, and so is able to face everything.

It is nice to find the cats straying into the retreat addresses: "It won't make you grow to get inside a comfortable religious system that suits you, and look over the edge like a cat in a basket.... Love and do as you like.... St. Augustine did not say love and do nothing if you prefer it; sit on your devotional cushion purring."

I wonder when she chose this very severe black notebook if she thought of the other. Her later retreat notes were put into the loveliest books bound in Italian handmade paper; but the black notebooks are landmarks.

She slipped quietly into what was certainly her most distinctive work. It was a new step in the Church of England for a woman to conduct retreats, and no one can have brought this particular work for God to greater perfection. As the years went on she conducted seven or eight retreats during the year in different retreat houses; two of these were always at Pleshey, and her memorial in the chapel there is a witness to the love she had for that place.

Just before she went to Pleshey for this first retreat she was asked to be one of the speakers on the first day of the COPEC Conference. "A horrifying responsibility"—she writes to Lucy Menzies. "Dr. Raven for Anglican, Mr. Maltby for Free Church, and I, I suppose, for 'any other colours' as they say at the cat shows." "Meanwhile," her letter goes on, "I am going every night *Back to Methuselah,* and finding it most stimulating. Somehow the spiritual plot in it comes out more vividly when acted.... He is a marvellous creature, with a rare visionary touch, though so often exasperating."

Evelyn went north again before the end of March to speak about Mysticism, and writing again to Lucy, then on holiday in Italy, she says:

> The Yorkshire trip was good fun, and York itself specially lovely....The High Celebration on Lady Day, in the Minster, was the most perfect thing of its kind I have ever lived through, with the right blend of beauty and austerity. In Darlington I stayed with a nest of Quakers, and in Leeds with the Professor of Literature who is also an emancipated poet, so if one's mind is not supple it is not the fault of environment. Say a prayer for me at the Portiuncula, won't you? and please dear child take care of yourself, and stay quiet, and let peace soak into you.

Her mother fell ill during the Yorkshire visit, and so did Baron von Hügel; he recovered partially after receiving Extreme Unction, but Evelyn's mother died after a short illness. She wrote to Lucy: "We have had a great sorrow since I last wrote. My mother, who had been ailing for some days, became very ill on Thursday night and died early this morning. We can only be glad she went from us so quickly and peacefully, for had she lived it would have meant great pain and distress. I am staying with my father for the present. He is much broken, poor old man, for she had been his one thought."

So on the top of all the work that spring came a loss which is always fundamental. It is difficult to know how much sympathy there was between Evelyn and her mother. Barbara Gnospelius told me that they seemed to be made of different material, but Evelyn had always loyally helped her mother in her philanthropic efforts, they had enjoyed travelling together, and if they never understood each other very well, they had devised a companionable relationship, which she must have missed.

It must have comforted her to get this very understanding letter from von Hügel: "—Your mother's going—the very difference of outlook between you must be adding to the trial, must indeed be giving a special discomfort to it. I can but pray that God who knows so well how to bring—in the long run—special lights and aids to those who seek him much, will somehow do this for you, instead of us, your clumsy fingered friends!"

So she didn't go to the COPEC conference which was just at that time. She felt that her father was not fit to be left, and she sent her paper to be read by Professor Moberly.

It fell with a strange sense of refreshment into the atmosphere of the conference hall. She must have been making it during those evenings when she was seeing the great Shaw play, for it began with a quotation from *Back to Methuselah*.

> "Enoch…has given up his will to do the will of the Voice": We are here [she said] because the Churches and Christian bodies that we represent are all committed like Enoch to the walk with God and want to learn to interpret the will of the Voice. We have been not so much wicked, as stupid, muddled, vague. This very Conference has come into being as a result of the pressure of God upon history. It is a part—we don't know what part—of His great, mysterious and unceasing action on human thought and human life. All limitations to that action are ours, and are the essence of our sin. It is our frightened selfish resistance, or worse than our resistance, our disgusting pious apathy, our dull certainty that social regeneration won't happen, which stops it from happening; our frightful lack of the dynamic virtues, Faith, Hope, and Charity.
>
> Christianity was given to us as a complete revelation in human terms of God and His purpose, demanding from us a completeness of surrender and response. But we have snipped it at both edges, limited both its supernatural and natural outlook and made it ineffective and incomplete. We have reduced its supernatural vividness and splendour, its holy beauty, its hardness and romance.

The paper ended with a fairy story. It was such a delightful surprise that perhaps we didn't realize till afterwards how sharp a dart had been aimed at our complacency.

I read the other day the story of a Brownie who lived in a

wood. He had a little wheelbarrow and passed his time in a very moral and useful manner picking up slugs and snails. Yet there was something lacking in his life. The King of the World passed through that wood very early every morning, and made all things beautiful and new, but the Brownie had never seen him. He longed to, but something prevented it. He had one cherished possession, a lovely little green blanket which had once fallen out of the fairy queen's chariot and which he had not been able to help keeping for himself. It was very cold in the wood at night but the blanket kept him so warm and cosy that he never woke up to see the King of the World. And one day there came to him a Shepherd, who looked deep into the soul of the Brownie and said to him: "Haven't you seen the King of the World?" And the Brownie said, "No, I do so want to, but somehow I can't manage it." Then the Shepherd replied: "But I seem to see something in your soul that keeps you from the vision; something that looks rather like a blanket." And at that a terrible fight began in the heart of the Brownie, a battle between wanting to go on being warm and comfortable in his blanket and longing to see the King of the World.

Perhaps [she ended] the ultimate choice which lies before us may turn out to be the Brownie's choice between the Heavenly Vision and the blanket.

She had quoted Shaw and Ruysbroeck and Bertrand Russell, but the thing that we couldn't quite evade was the little green blanket. How valuable it was to that conference.

The Baron wrote to her about it: "How attractively and helpfully touching is the enclosed paper which I wish you could have read yourself to the Copecs, but which anyhow so well deserves printing."

Into this turmoil of composition and speaking and lecturing came now all the weariness of clearing up which follows a death. "I am living distractedly in two houses at once, and have a mass of things looming up to see to. Papers and possessions to sort up and deal with and all that. At this moment Holy Poverty seems to me more a luxury than a virtue."

She had to decide with Hubert that summer whether they should leave their own house and go to keep house for her father, but fortunately this was one of the occasions when Hubert's feeling, which she wormed out of him, was for the sensible plan of staying in their own house, and Miss Corisande Thorne, a cousin, came to look after Sir Arthur till his death, and made him very contented. So again, Hubert saved her for her vocation.

Lucy (in Italy) had been making friends with Sorella Maria, and Evelyn writes to her: "I felt sure she was wonderful, but you have made me see her quite vividly and now I feel I know her much better than before. I wish she would undertake your direction. She is much better fitted for it than I am." She had a chance when Lucy passed through London on her way home to introduce her to Laura Rose. Her friends very often became dear to each other, and Lucy, Laura Rose and Sorella Maria all grew together in the warmth of her friendship.

She had to take her mother's place with her father at some legal occasions in the summer: "I've had a worldly week with all the parties to these 'ere American lawyers, and last night with a really splendid show, the Lord Chancellor's reception in Westminster Hall. It was a sight, that glorious architecture and roof brilliantly lit up as one never sees it, and everyone in their best, swords, orders and all. I went with my dear old papa, who looked very sweet in his black velvet and buckled shoes."

The Baron had written that he would expect another report from her in 1924 "if I am still alive." It had been a difficult summer for him after his desperate illness. With affectionate understanding Evelyn had kept him supplied with jig-saw puzzles, just the distraction he could attempt. But she did send him a report, which unfortunately does not exist, and he replied in August.

Now here I come, with my little answer, first to yourself, from amongst quite a number of important long unanswered letters. Yet I must make my observations short, even though I have carefully considered and prayed over your report in its several points.

As you know well there is never anything quite new to advise, provided one has already advised a soul at all truly and wisely. But the following two suggestions will, I believe, be worth your praying over quietly, without strain or rush of any kind.

(1) I notice how well you are aware that self-satisfaction, or even simply the appearance to our eyes of our state of soul as satisfactory, are no genuine tests and measures of solid spiritual advancement. And yet, I think, you allow yourself to attend to, or at least to notice vivaciously, this sight of yourself in your real condition of spiritual misery. I should like you *gently* to try to alter this, still less (in any direct way) the substance of this your soul, or your estimate of such substance: but simply the vivacious, irritated, or confusing attention to these things or impressions. Drop, gently drop by a quiet turning to God and Christ and the Poor, and you will grow in peace and power.

(2) Perhaps you have now inherited a little money from your mother so that you can more easily somewhat restrict your literary religious labours. My ideal for you continues, say two-thirds of your output during the average of the last ten years. This, too, would much help towards advance, hidden under apparent retrogression. God bless you: pray for me.

Yours very sincerely,
F. von Hügel

Evelyn and Hubert got away on the yacht in August after the Anglican Fellowship Conference for Evelyn at Oxford. "Mostly clergy and ladies, some intelligent, and all deeply anxious to be. But I met one real golden soul, humble and simple, and contemplative without knowing it, and shyly astonished at his own happiness."

It felt strange to her on the yacht to be the mistress after so many years, but she was glad to find that her father was really enjoying it and not possessed by sad memories. That month's cruise, and a holiday in Italy in the autumn, set her up for her second retreat, which proved to be a really satisfying experience.

> I loved Pleshey this time [she wrote to Lucy] and indeed it was more like having a retreat than giving one. They were a splendid set, and the full flavour seemed turned on all the while. I had nothing to do but swim along. On Sunday morning before the ten address it was very wonderful somehow—a kind of living stillness filled the chapel. I daren't go on for a bit. All the country was wrapped in a lovely golden russet too. I thought of you listening for the little threefold bell, and could feel you and the Baron, and Gwen,[4] and Mrs. Rose with your dynamos turned on and helping.

The year's work was not quite over.

> My next job is speaking at the West London Copec Conference on the 20th at 2.30 with Bishop Gore as partner, who greatly oppresses me, and the following Monday at Woodbrook, and on December 2nd at Bath, and after that Peace.
>
> Copec and Bishop Gore went off all right [she wrote later to Lucy]. I thought he looked at me a bit as a gamekeeper looks at a poacher, but he didn't say nothing. In the evening we had Studdert Kennedy whom I'd never heard before—a really great experience...he speaks like a white hot prophet. He said quite simply that the whole social gospel was summed up in the Blessed Sacrament and spoke from that central point for half an hour.

The pressure of work was still pretty fierce even after the address at Bath. She was contemplating addresses for the spring, one part of a set at King's College on the Philosophy of Religion, "and I've not yet thought of preparing it."

And then there was this sort of thing: "I've got such a dreadful new 'case'—an awful jumble of sin and perverted instincts, and religious cravings and shifting. Real mud, and yet a good gleam here and there. It makes the troubles of your type seem like difficulties of white violets."

She and Hubert had meant to get out of London at Christmas time, but both had such bad colds that they stayed in town having an "agreeably lazy time."

One charming reminder from their Italian holidays gave her great pleasure in Christmas week, and she recounts it to Lucy with delight:

> Yesterday was much enlightened by a letter and Christmas parcel from my darling Fra Raffaele at the Carceri. I'd sent him a tiny offering from notes left over from our Italian trip. "Most illustrious and beloved benefactress" seems a bit strong for what works out at about 15s. 2d. at the present exchange. I get also his prayers that I may receive "all the riches of Paradise" and his "paternal and affectionate blessing" as a wind up. Accompanying this was a nightlight box! containing a *very* nice silver medallion in a case of the Crucifix, and St. Francis embracing our Lord; a silver cross with the Benediction of St. Francis, various other medals and crosses, a wee rosary, a rich selection of cards, *and* the dear man's own photograph! You can imagine the excitement of unpacking them. They seem to bring a breath of Umbria right into the room.

It had been a tremendous year: her first retreats, all the work for COPEC, which included speaking at quite half a dozen big meetings; her mother's death and the new responsibility for her father, the work on the *Mystics of the Church,* which included short biographies of all the notable Mystics of the Church from St. Paul to Sundar Singh with an appraisement of their contribution to the Way; and quite a lot of reviewing and articles like a ten-page one on Christian Fellowship for the *Interpreter,* and a shorter rather delightful one on Mother Janet Stuart, and Mother Mary Aikenhead. This saint declared: "If I could, no one should join our Order who has not a real spirit of labour.... All piety which does not assist us to fulfil these duties which belong to our vocation is questionable."

We might leave the Evelyn of 1924 in the company of these heroic women and yet hope that she will take the Baron's advice and reduce the volume of her writing. For looking at her life it is impossible not to feel that she wrote too much in the early years. She had published fourteen books in the fourteen years since she wrote *Mysticism,* besides a vast amount of lectures, addresses, and reviews. It is possible, as the Baron's letter suggests, that she was writing some of the review work because she needed the money for her holidays and her very lavish gifts, or even to meet the expenses of a London establishment. But it was also her gift, and she delighted to use it, and to set her first-class brains to tackle a worth while bit of work. None of her work was scamped and it was always notably well documented, for behind it lay her wide reading. She did not shut herself up in her work, and one must think of her as a person with a varied set of friends, who liked to see them, and go to parties and concerts with them. She belonged to one or two London musical societies.

Hubert was one of the early "wireless" fans. There is a picture somewhere in her *Letters* of his fixing up a set on the yacht so that Evelyn can listen to a broadcast about cats! He had acquired a motor-bicycle and sidecar and this meant that they could get into the country more easily to her flowers and birds and trees which she loved, as poets love things, with an eager delight. The pattern of their London Sundays was that Evelyn would go out early to Church, and then after breakfast she and Hubert would go off together, first using the motor-bicycle and sidecar, and later the car, to some favourite place near by. Sometimes they got as far as Windsor, but more often to Richmond or Kew. Luncheon with Sir Arthur followed, and then a regular Sunday tea party with guests varying from Evelyn's latest "case" to old Sir Frederick Pollock with whom she exchanged postcards in Latin. These were most happy parties, with sparkling talk and plenty of amusing gossip.

13

"In Torment and Effort to Serve the Brethren"

Evelyn had produced for the January number of the *Hibbert Journal* in 1925, a ten-page article on "Our Twofold Relation to Reality." It may have been rather a *réchauffé* of her St. Andrews lectures; for it contains a good deal that she had been thinking about in 1924.

> The devotee and the practical man alike represent subtractions from the richness of human life. For the devotee, if he turns away from the visible and contingent, is failing to accept those humbling lessons and homely opportunities, those strains and tests in which it abounds: whilst the practical man is still more hopelessly divorced from full experience, for he fails to look beyond the contingent to that assigned end which alone gives it meaning and puts us in a position to deal with it properly. He flagrantly disobeys the first and great commandment of the Gospel—the Charter of spiritual life. Thou shalt love the Lord thy God with all thy Heart and with all thy Soul and with all thy Mind and with all thy Strength.... For the individual, this means making a place in our flowing life for a deliberate self-orientation to the Eternal Order. For the community it means providing an environment in which these interests can be cherished and taught. Religion in its special language calls these two essentials of full life Prayer and Church. But the values and needs which they represent are deeply rooted in the facts of human nature, and stretch far beyond the narrow meaning commonly attached to them, and the crystallized form they have been allowed to assume.

Lucy's Confirmation was to happen in London early in the

year, and Evelyn's first letters to her are full of dates and plans for this. But she writes with a sad sense that the Baron's death is near, and she must be prepared to throw up plans so as to be at his Requiem. "We really long for him to be at peace, for lately his control of speech has been failing, and he knows it and struggles in vain to say what he wants."

Baron von Hügel died before the end of January. He recovered some power of speech at the end, and Mrs. Plunket Greene (his niece) sent Evelyn notes of his last talk to her: "How delighted he was to give himself to God, and grateful for being clear in mind and without pain. How God was so generous to us, and we oughtn't to be niggardly in self-offering." It was the last word she had from him and matched well with her own generous giving of her powers. She felt that she must write a little of what it had been like to be helped by him, and put together the short article in the *Guardian* which was reprinted in *Mixed Pasture*. His going was a serious grief to her, though not an unexpected one. "It has been a bit hard now it has come, in spite of one's rejoicing for him [she wrote]. There were lots at his Requiem, of course, including many who obviously loved him."

But Lucy's Confirmation brought great joy, especially as it meant great peace of spirit for Lucy. They had two happy days in the country together before it. One of her real joys this spring was that Lucy, who had been so troubled, came into a time of real peace after her Confirmation.

It was one of those springs when influenza was rampant, and Evelyn, of course, got it, and in the course of it some rather more deep-seated trouble was revealed, probably all part of her future attacks of asthma. She had some weeks of bed and indoor life in compensation for the strenuous months behind her, but after a spell in the country at Beaulieu, which she loved, she came back restored: "No patch, no asphyxiation, sleeps and eats well." In June she got another little spell in the country, loving birds on Chesil Beach: "Terns, and other lovely things. Also the Swannery was very lovely to the eye; 800 adults and I know not how many cygnets, numerous lady swans majestically sitting on nests, and the others swimming on the mere. I am now struggling with a welter of minor engagements before going back to Appledore next week, when I am going to give a simple and not pious address to the villagers on St. Francis! a bit of a job! It will have to be mainly the Dumb Friends League view of the saint." She writes a little later of this talk: "Appalling!... I think they probably thought he was an amiable lunatic, and fortunately a foreigner."

It was some time in this year when she went to interview the secretary of a large church society, and describes her wickedly to Lucy: "The general secretary is like a compound widow of several generations of clergymen, and talked about good churchmanship in a way that made me quite uncomfy; in fact I had to spend half an hour in Westminster Cathedral to get rid of the taste."

A rather different engagement was her taking Maude Royden's[5] place at the Guildhouse one Sunday evening. "They call it preaching the sermon, though I insist on calling it giving the address."

She was also acting as hostess for her father at a large party in Lincoln's Inn. She did really like parties, but perhaps not formal legal parties.

Somehow the spring and early summer seem to have been a succession of not very congenial things, and the summer brought a crush of conferences. The Church emerged from the First World War very much shaken, and convicted of dire negligence and ignorances, longing for something new, for a better standard. And Evelyn had something new to say, or possibly something very old to say again in a new voice. One priest who knew her well was to write: "The tinge of intellectual austerity in her was one which had a special appeal for the age in which she lived." Like all true mystics she spoke with authority, the authority of the search for Reality which dominated her own life. So it was no wonder that groups of Church people turned to her hungrily for something they sensed in her which gave her words both beauty and integrity; something which reminded the Church of England that it was part of the Holy Catholic Church and heir to great renunciations and consecrated achievements; and to the strange unguessed-at beauty of holiness.

Many Church people had turned eagerly to von Hügel for this new outlook, but he had never been easy to understand for English people; one suspects that he always thought in German. Now here was his disciple speaking with an exquisite clarity.

Evelyn went to three conferences in the summer of 1925. The first was one which must have taught her a good deal about the Church of England. It was a conference concerned with deepening the spiritual life of the Church, and she calls it in a letter to Lucy "an interesting and illuminating affair."

> A mixture of eminent and progressive ecclesiastics of all parties, four bishops, and quite a bunch of canons, with boys and girls from the universities (who told the bishops without any tact or reserve just what they thought of the Church), representatives from missionary societies, Studdert Kennedy, Oldham, the Head of Cowley, and so forth. Most of the mature persons freely confessed to being spiritually impotent and tired, but when we were asked to give quarter of an hour a day to prayer for the object of this conference a surprising number were alarmed by this dreadful demand.... We now form a more or less permanent body, and meet again in October. We are to meet in the Jerusalem Chamber, and have silent prayer before the high altar of Westminster Abbey, at 10 p.m., which is rather wonderful.

There was another conference at High Leigh on Prayer, and at this one she met B. K. Cunningham,[6] "who gave a beautiful address on Prayer and life in which he revealed himself as being the Real Thing." Evelyn herself was speaking at this one, and planning to repeat her paper to the Student Christian Movement Auxiliaries in October. And still she had one more conference, the Anglo-Catholic one at Oxford, whose members she describes as "nice, keen, and some even broadminded." Looking ahead she envisages a Liverpool Cathedral job, and two retreats at Pleshey in the autumn; so that it is quite a relief to find her on her father's yacht, *Wulfruna*, at the end of July, and to hear that "I am lounging comfortably in my own roomy cabin, and

Hubert is busy tuning up a new and gorgeous set of wireless, ready for a talk on cats."

Amongst all the lecturing, the addresses and retreats, the steady stream of people whom she called her Family kept coming to her one by one, taking long hours of her time, and a constant share of her prayers.

Here are some typical ones whom she mentions in her letters to Lucy:

> Yes, the family does seem to take a lot of time lately. The last addition, who is very interesting, is a man of fifty-six, once a doctor, now a diplomatist and political expert—to all appearance a finished man of the world, but driven and possessed by a feeling that he has got to give himself to God.
>
> I've rather a special young person coming to Pleshey, a secondary school teacher who has been writing to me for a while—a true wanderer in the jungle, hungry, intelligent, was never taught any religion, isn't even baptized, and has had a very hard and friendless life. One of my dearest and naughtiest ones has given me a rare time of it, having tried to break away and be very bad, and had to be pulled back by invisible means to penitence and peace, so there was a good deal doing. I acquired a new child...a dear thing, answering to the name of Faith, tho' not yet overburdened with that commodity.
>
> I must stop and address myself to a new case sent to me...a nice child who has been encouraged by silly clergymen to take her inner experiences much too seriously, and who informed me that she had just been reading a perfectly sweet little book by St. John of the Cross!
>
> The Family has now added to its number a young doctor, first Quaker, then agnostic, and now I trust safely Christian. I escorted her today to be confirmed by Bishop Gore at the Grosvenor Chapel and she will, I hope, make her first Communion next Sunday.

All this time she did not forget her back-street friends. So many of the letters end, "I must stop and go round to see Mrs. Rose."

Lucy Menzies was very faithful about sending little garments for the children in the streets. Evelyn found a good deal of very solid comfort in Mrs. Rose, to whom she used to recount many of the tiresome and ridiculous encounters with people. She also counted a great deal on Mrs. Rose's prayers. In the end she managed to get her down to Pleshey, which was a great joy to her. The whole relationship with her poor people was very natural and loving and humble.

One of the happiest things for Evelyn in 1925 was that in the autumn she actually got to the Rifugio and saw Sorella Maria, stayed a night there and had a long talk to her. It was their one meeting in a lifetime, but like the single meeting between George Herbert and Nicholas Ferrar it led to a spiritual intimacy. Years afterwards I remember Evelyn telling me how she could write about her spiritual troubles to Maria, and how the short and telling replies comforted and sustained her. Of this one visit she wrote to Lucy Menzies:

> I found your letter here all right when I got to the Rifugio. It was so nice to get it and made me feel that a lot of you was there. It was a lovely time. I got there about 5 together with a talkative tho' excellent Roman priest [she notes in her letter to Laura Rose that this priest came to meet her because he had known the Baron and wanted to hear about him] who was the one unnecessary feature—though perhaps not quite unnecessary, as he said Mass on Tuesday morning, at which Maria served and the Sorellini made their communions, and that was lovely beyond words. She is wonderful, and when it comes down to hard tacks extraordinarily like the Baron in her outlook. We had a good bit of talk, and she said perfectly lovely things. She really is *it*. I think it is a very great privilege to have been with her. She is concerned about you and asked me to say that your soul was very present with her.... It turned out that she fears intensity for you, just as much as I do, and said "I should like to recommend to Lucia, above all the ways of simplicity."

> Hubert stayed at Assisi while I was at the Rifugio, and

picked me up by motor…a bit astonished, I think, to come in for saying the Angelus on the stairs, and to see me passionately kissed by all the Sorellini on departure. Maria gave me at my request a "Word" to take away with me, and a very ferocious one it was.

To Laura Rose she wrote of this meeting:

> Maria is all that we felt. I got to the little station at 5 yesterday evening. It was just getting lovely after the heat; and then drove in the little village cab through the most beautiful country, olive woods and vineyards to the hill beyond—and just as we neared the Rifugio Miss Turton and Maria met me and I walked up with them. Maria and the sisters wore white cotton frocks and grey linen aprons, the cord of St. Francis and sandals on their bare feet…. Maria has the most beautiful expression, strong and humble, and a low, gentle voice. I got quite a long talk with her, and it was wonderful to find how exactly she and my old man [v. H.] agree in spite of great differences in mind and language in all the deep things of the spiritual life. I asked her for something for myself and she said, "In torment and effort to serve the brethren." Maria loves Ruysbroeck too and was so delighted to hear how much you cared for him and for Dante—both of them her dearest friends.

The Rifugio was linked up with her next retreat at Pleshey: "I've translated that little prayer of St. Augustine which Maria puts in all the guest rooms at the Rifugio, and am putting a copy in all the cells, also at starting points of meditation the Baron's 'The soul is primarily a force or energy, and holiness is a growth of that energy in love, in full being, and in the true spiritual personality.'"

Her Student Christian Auxiliary Sunday at Guildford seems to have been settled over her head. "Next Saturday afternoon I go with a lot of Student Christians to Guildford, and talk to them on Sunday morning about prayer. I conduct a little undenominational service which I'm told must not last more than 20 minutes—rather a thin way of celebrating All Saints, but as Mrs. Rose observes: 'You won't like it but the Saints will!' Let us hope so! I feel that it is the Baron's feast now."

But that November Pleshey retreat brought her an enheartening experience that was almost startling. "I had the nearest possible shave of not getting there, as I was suddenly laid low with flu the previous week-end. I was in bed till Thursday, but by firm steady prayer and determination got up on Friday *perfectly* well, and remained and still remain so—shouldn't have known I'd had an illness! It's really rather startling. I feel like a Lourdes Miraculée. No cough, no asthma, no wobbly sensations."

There was another retreat before the year's end at Pleshey, a snowy one, with a rather mixed company, but four really grand people who "kept things going."

Her book, *Mystics of the Church,* was out and she notes: "It was reviewed with great respect by *The Times;* enthusiasm by the *Church Times*—which was sorry, however, that I went to the length of supposing that non-Catholics ever found God—great reserve by the *Record*—and pure spite by *Blackfriars.*"

She had one other special joy before Christmas, and writes to Lucy Menzies:

> I have been having a wonderful time with the Baron's letters. His niece, Gwen Greene, who was his pupil, has entrusted a lot of wonderful ones to me…to arrange and study, with a view to many of them being included in the book of letters Bernard Holland is getting up. They are extraordinarily deep and beautiful, full of his peculiar wisdom and supernaturalness, and I feel I now know far more both of them and of his doctrine than before. Here is one bit for you:
>
> "At one moment…silent adoration in church: at another dreariness and unwilling drift; at another the joys of human affections given and received; at another keen suffering of soul, of mind, in an apparent utter loneliness; at another external acts of religion; at another death itself. All these occupations, every one can, ought and will be: each when and where duty, reason, conscience, necessity, God, calls for it—it will *all* become the means and instrument of loving, of

transfiguration, of growth for your soul, and of its beatitude. But it is for God to choose these things, their degree, combinations, successions; and it is for you, just simply, very humbly, very gently and peacefully to follow their leading."

Isn't that lovely?

He has one lovely bit about "Gentle attempts gently to will whatever suffering God may kindly send us; the grand practice of at once meeting suffering with joy. God alone can help us to succeed in this: but what is Christianity if it be not something like that."

14

Speaking to the Clergy

The year 1926 which was to be such a turbulent one to many people in England was another year of growing for Evelyn. I do not feel as if the crux of the General Strike touched her very deeply. Politics never possessed her. I do not ever remember her talking about them. When the Strike came it meant a hold-up to work and plans, but nothing fundamental. She did become involved in this very year in the early stages of the Prayer Book Bill. That was her country and she was prepared to take steps there and to suffer there.

She began the year in bed, with a pneumococcus germ which she did not shake off completely till Easter. It was rather worrying because there was much work ahead, three retreats, and the Water Millock clergy school, a quiet day at Ramsgate, and the Anglo-Catholic Conference; and, more important still, a book, *Man and the Supernatural,* in which she was trying to express and bring together the things that she had learnt under von Hügel's guidance. She was using as a basis some of her articles and lectures and addresses, but "all this material" she writes in the Preface, "has been recast for the purposes of the present book." She was very conscious of the Baron's influence on this bit of work, the first book she had written of this kind since he had directed her. "I felt almost," she wrote to a friend, "as if he were leaning over my shoulder." She was irked by the quite inevitable interruptions of so much speaking: "It is going to be difficult enough to get the continuous concentration without which this kind of work simply can't be done."

Hubert and she were wondering about buying a little car. "I can't get Hubert to feel he needs it," she writes, and it was in fact not bought until the following year.

A retreat for the Guildhouse congregation had to be given up, but one at Pleshey in Lent was carried out, and by Lady Day she was feeling set up in health, giving a lecture to the Royal Society of Literature "and enjoying it."

The most notable thing in this year was her talks to the Conference of Clergy from the Liverpool diocese at Water Millock, which were published the same year by Methuen, and called *Concerning the Inner Life*. It was a new thing for a clerical conference to be addressed by a lay woman, one of Evelyn's pioneer bits of work.

> The Liverpool Clergy [she wrote to Lucy Menzies] were a most mixed and touching lot, twenty of them, and me the only woman present. I felt funny, but *they* at the beginning more so, and clearly very frightened of me. However, most of them got quite tame by the end, and some extremely friendly.... They looked awfully startled when I told them what a huge difference it made to us if they did their services in a recollected way.

She had two fellow lecturers, Charles Raven and Canon Cooper. She began her talks with disarming humbleness:

> I feel a great diffidence in coming before you, as an ordinary laywoman, to speak of such matters; since they are, after all, your peculiar and professional concern. Indeed I only presume to do so because I care about these things very much, and have some leisure to think about them; and so venture to put at your service certain conclusions to which I have come. The primary thing, I believe, that will be of use is a conception as clear and rich and deep as you are able to get it, first of the Splendour of God; and next of your own souls over against that Splendour of God; and last of the sort of interior life which your election of His service demands.

She was giving them a picture of her own experience when she said:

> The soul of a priest, in fact, the soul of every religious

worker—stands in a special relation towards God and other souls…. He is one of the assistant shepherds, not one of the sheep. He has got to stick it out in all weathers; to be always ready, always serving, always eager to feed and save. An unremitting patient-fostering care, the willing endurance of exhaustion, hardship and risk: all these things may be asked of him.

Here is the part which she felt had startled them:

You do far more for your congregation, for helping them to understand what prayer really is, and to practise it; for quickening their religious sensitiveness, by your unselfconscious absorption in God during services, than you can hope to do by any amount of sermons…. These congregations are probably far too shy to come and tell you what it is that helps them most in the things you do; but there is no doubt at all that your recollectedness, your devotional temper will be one of the things that do help them most.

She spoke to them a great deal about their individual work for souls, about spiritual direction, for which she herself had such a particular aptitude, about the height and depth of intercession for souls. One very simple thing she asked of them was that they should pray in their own churches, not only saying matins and evensong there, but their other prayers. "That is the first move towards making these churches real houses, schools, and homes of prayer."

The clergy who were at Water Millock must have felt her special power of making the things of the Spirit seem both tremendous and homely, and curiously attractive, for they very soon asked her to come again and to do the same work another year.

It was not only the Church of England that was benefiting by her power to vivify the Way of the Spirit. In the records of these years one finds how much time Evelyn was giving to the Free Churches, speaking to Ministers, and congregations. This year she was at Birmingham speaking to a Wesleyan congregation, and a little abashed at being conducted to the pulpit.

One engagement this year gave her great pleasure. This was the expedition to Thurgarton to speak in the vicarage garden which was on the site of the Priory where Walter Hilton, one of her favourite mediaeval English Mystics, had lived and written his books. She felt that the whole afternoon was tinged with the proper monastic flavour by the arrival of Fr. Tribe and a company of novices and students from Kelham. Of Hilton she said:

> His sanctity is assured to us not by his exhibition of startling and difficult virtues, or by outwardly heroic acts, still less by any of the extraordinary phenomena, ecstasies, and visions which are too often regarded as the marks of the mystical saint—but for a far more Christian, more truly supernatural reason—by the continuously life-giving power of his works. He is one of those hidden figures, those quiet and secret friends of God who have never failed the Church; and through whom Christ's gift of more abundant love reaches the world, and enters those souls that are ready to receive it.

Another expedition that pleased her immensely was an afternoon at Thaxted: "Quite the most beautiful and rightly ordered church I've ever seen. Conrad Noel who is an artist, as well as an enthusiast, has made everything as perfect as it can be made," she writes to Lucy Menzies.

They went as far as Blakeney in September, after a cruise with her father in August. She found Blakeney entirely fascinating, and describes its little cobble houses, the saltmarsh, and the superb old church at the top of the hill.

She had enjoyed reviewing A. E. Taylor's books about Plato, and one gets a glimpse of her scholarliness when she says that he had made her read the Symposium, and Protagoras, and most of the Phaedo over again.

The little paper-covered book of her Liverpool addresses, *Concerning the Inner Life,* was having what she called "appallingly reverential reviews"; perhaps its very simplicity and the informal style made it seem more approachable than some of her longer books. Such diverse newspapers as the *Spectator, The Times,* the *Star,* the *Cape Times,* and *Cape Argus,* the *Daily Herald,* the *Southern*

Cross, all wrote with enthusiasm about the little book, and about her own work. The *Spectator* (soon to ask her to come on to its staff) wrote:

> There may be more learned Christians...but there is no one writing in English better qualified to express in everyday life the high and secret conversations that the mind may hold with its Maker. There is something infectious about Miss Underhill's style with its deep rooted common sense, its virile idiom, and its creaturely appreciation of the beauty of the world. These addresses will bear reading and rereading, for they are the fruits of a life that is all too rare in this day and age.

The *Daily Herald* wrote: "A little book which Mystics will treasure, and in which all can find finger posts to some of the best things in life."

And her Free Church friends in the *Methodist Leader* say: "We can hardly render greater service to thousands of our readers than by calling attention to a small book by Evelyn Underhill, *Concerning the Inner Life.*"

All this made Evelyn write: "It makes me feel inclined to dive into the nearest burrow, but I think I am going to have my hair cut off instead."

October brought her time for some peaceful work. "My winter outdoor jobs are now done, and I have luxurious mornings by the study fire brooding over my book, and the Baron's last Essays which have just appeared," she writes to Lucy. "They are grand I think, especially the one of *Suffering in God,* but oh! how thin and arid he makes everyone else seem."

She was missing him very much all through this year. "Glad you like my *Spectator* review of the Baron," she wrote. "The more I read that book the more I feel—what else is there left to say; but it's awful to come from that atmosphere to niggling committees... full of timid notions about going slowly and not expecting too much."

And at Christmas she wrote: "Gwen [Greene] was here yesterday, and we talked about the Baron for an hour—a great refreshment."

15

THE REVISION OF THE PRAYER BOOK AND MATTERS OF REUNION

One could not be a member of the Anglican Communion in 1927 without having some concern for the Prayer Book Bill, and Evelyn was among those who were planning and praying for a peaceful passage of the Bill, rallying the central body of the Church of England, and setting it free from either extreme.

> Life has been complicated by a sudden access of publicity [she writes to Lucy]. I unwarily wrote a little letter to *The Times* about the Prayer Book to support Dr. Relton who talks sense, and they put it on the central page where everyone sees things, and I have lived ever since under showers of letters, some vitriolic but most grateful, and got up to my neck in plans and discussions for outwitting the fanatics and getting it passed on a basis of mutual tolerance.... All a very funny job for me....

She was evidently trusted with inside information, for she writes to Lucy in March about two crucial days at Lambeth about which she cannot divulge details.

"Aren't the scuffles about the Prayer Book silly as well as dreadful? I much fear it is going to be wrecked between the two sorts of extremists," she writes to Lucy.

Evelyn's individual cases flocked in on her and in March she is writing: "The ground is simply littered with cases from now till Easter, and I hardly know how to get through things, especially as one does like a little peace in Holy Week."

She and Hubert got away to the New Forest for an Easter holiday, but by the end of April she is writing in the train going to Chester to a meeting of bishops and clergy at which again she is

148

to be the only woman. The subject was the revival of prayer among the clergy; but the people she felt could have helped most, Fr. Talbot and Bishop Frere, were not able to come to it. She must have been getting used now to speaking to clergy and ministers, but it was a lonely experience, and one wishes that she could have had other women with her. The spiritual strain in avoiding any sense of superiority must have been rather fierce, but this attack on her humility she weathered amazingly well, and I remember the first thing that struck me two years later was her humble assumption that I should know all the things she knew herself. "Of course, you know all about this," she would say as I floundered after her through the rapids.

A rather comforting postscript asserts that she is "quite well." That was a good thing, as she had two lectures at St. Albans, a Quiet Day, and a lecture on the Prayer Book at King's College before 11 May.

It is a little difficult and perhaps unnecessary to distinguish between her various retreats. So far they were being held at Pleshey, but this year there was one at Water Millock in July for women, some of them the wives of the clergy who had heard her speak there, and she found these women really responsive. Later she was to go as far north as Cumbrae, and Leiston Abbey, Moreton, and Glastonbury were also open to her. She nearly always knew of some staunch and experienced souls coming to a retreat who would help her by their loving attention. But always, also, there were some people making a first retreat whom she carried in her spirit during the days. Some of them had come at a time of great stress. She had Laura Rose at this spring retreat at Pleshey. She always made sure that her retreats would be backed up by intercessors, whose names she revealed when they were prayed for on her last evening.

She was up at Water Millock at a second meeting of her Liverpool clergy when the total eclipse of the sun which made the summer of 1927 memorable, happened. "I saw the eclipse in the zone of totality, and though cloudy it was impressive," she wrote to Lucy. She had the most tremendous day of it. "Rose at 4.45, came back from the eclipse to Mass; lectured in the morning, afternoon shown over a large cotton mill, and attended lectures and discussions all evening."

Throughout this year she was serving on a commission, chaired by the Bishop of Liverpool, Dr. David, for the deepening of the spiritual life of clergy and laity. Evelyn's special concern was with the laity, and perhaps no one in those years did more to encourage ordinary lay people to be aware of a call to commit themselves to God for His purposes. She believed in us, saw in us capacities beyond what we had guessed, called us into the company of saints and made us free of their wisdom. Best of all she gave us her sense of God. She was experiencing all the time what it meant to bring people into communion with God, and so she had something very real to give to the work of this Commission. It was no guesswork with her.

Back in London there was the Anglo-Catholic Conference, at which somehow she did not find herself quite at home... "most odd, sitting in a row with three ecclesiastics in cassock and biretta." It was a little narrow for the one who had prayed, "I hope my mind will not grow tall to look down on things, but wide to embrace all sorts of things."

It is always good to hear of her getting even a short piece of real solitude, and she found it this year at the retreat house at Moreton. It convinced her of the superiority of private retreats. She had a lovely sitting-room, a private veranda next to the chapel, and a huge garden to roam in. She found the Lady Warden sympathetic, and a lover of von Hügel's books. The house was quiet and the atmosphere free. It was one of the retreat houses that she went to regularly to take retreats later.

This year she began a delightful connection with Canterbury. She went down in the summer to meet the Dean, and to plan a two days' meeting for women in the crypt of the cathedral. "We shall have Mass there, and the addresses, and use it for prayer and silence in between. I think it will be a lovely job to do," she writes to Lucy. It proved to be so when it happened in the autumn. "The place and atmosphere were perfect," and the forty to fifty people who came just the size of company that she felt able to hold.

In the summer of this year it became clear that Mrs. Harvey, the Warden of Pleshey, would not be able to go on with her work there because of a breakdown in health. Evelyn was very sorry about this. Mrs. Harvey was bound up with her own first retreat, and also with all the others that she had conducted at Pleshey. It was a matter of great concern to Evelyn who should be her successor. Pleshey must not lose its special quality of beauty and peace and holiness. She wondered if it were possible that Lucy's health would stand the racket of being Warden of a retreat house. "I feel it might be worth your while to make tentative enquiries into the possibility of trying it for a month or two…the need of securing someone who docs it for pure love and is a person of prayer overrides everything else." Mrs. Harvey also wanted Lucy, and in the end she was appointed, but did not go to Pleshey till the very end of 1928; and then began their eight years' partnership of Warden and Conductor, which meant so much to Evelyn in her work at Pleshey. The retreat house owed so much to them both, in beauty and in love and peace. It was during Lucy's wardenship that the new chapel was built, which now contains memorials to both of them. Lucy was bringing out her book on women saints this year. Interest in books by her friends was one of Evelyn's specially endearing characteristics. She found an attractive title for Lucy's book, *Mirrors of the Holy,* and mothered it with far more zest than if it had been one of her own.

She and Hubert took the little car up to Middleton in Teesdale, and loved their moorland holiday, and found the rare gentian that has grown there since Roman times, which pleased them both immensely.

There was a new edition of *Mysticism* looming. She did not alter its format though she said in the 1928 Preface that she would have written it differently with the emphasis on different points if she had been writing it afresh.

At the end of the year came the defeat of the Prayer Book Measure, an unexpected defeat as far as Evelyn was concerned, for she had taken Dean Inge's view that there would be quite a substantial majority for it. She once confessed to me, years later, that the bands of people praying in Palace Yard that the Measure might not pass seemed to her an example of a wrong use, a self-willed use, of prayer.

> Do you remember [she wrote] in 1927 when the Prayer Book was thrown out by Parliament and old Bishop ———— had a group of people praying with almost vicious vigour and bending their whole minds upon it? ———— told me that it felt in the House as if a spell had been cast on every-one who supported the book so that they did their very worst and feeblest. He said "It felt to me like an answer to prayer gone wrong."

It was a great blow to all who had been working for a reconcilia-tion between Anglicans, and Evelyn had played her part in it as a mediator and not as a partisan. But it never shook her loyalty to the Church; that was firmly established now on the experience of her years of teaching and direction, on her own growth in spiri-tual life, and on the sense that she was in the Church of England because God needed her to be there, as part of His purpose.

Before Christmas she had a day which was something of an ordeal, when she was formally received as a Fellow of King's College. The rather modest student who had made no splash in college life was now to be honoured as one of their most distin-guished scholars.

> The show at the college came off yesterday, [she wrote to Lucy] and was even more alarming than I had thought, as I was the first Fellow to be admitted, and after running the gauntlet of the Great Hall, and the intense curiosity of the students, had to walk up alone to the platform and stand in the open, while the Dean who presented me expatiated on my career and qualifications, ending to the joy of all present by saying that I enlivened my leisure by talking to cats.

She was pleased to be acclaimed as a poet as well as an exponent of mysticism.

> The college dinner was great fun, nearly two hundred there.

I sat at a table between X and Y and managed to be quite polite when they talked about "superstition." But Oh! how completely these intellectuals miss the bus.

The Prayer Book Measure was defeated, but the amended book was in being and one of Evelyn's early bits of work in 1928 was to attend a meeting at King's College "to see if some plan could be reached about the amended book. It was most interesting [she wrote to Lucy] but seemed pretty hopeless. We had Lord Hugh Cecil, Sir Henry Slesser, Lord Phillimore, the Dean of Canterbury, the editors of all the Church papers, and heads of societies, and a selection of prominent padres. Both sets of extremists are alike adamant, and quite unable apparently to understand each other. It's a desperate business."

Something of what she was thinking herself appears in an article she had written the autumn before for the *Spectator,* called "The Hill of the Lord."

It seems to be implicit in the very nature of religious controversy, that it so easily persuades those engaging in it to adopt an even lower and more limited standpoint. Like persons sliding down the opposite sides of a mountain they steadily recede from those summits where they might be at one; and each new shower of stones announces a constantly accelerated retreat, which inevitably drives them further and further apart....

In the discussions raging round the Prayer Book, and the secondary disturbances which these have provoked, dispassionate observers have seen—some with cynical amusement but others with bitter regret—this unfortunate process taking place. They have watched some of those specially entrusted with the spiritual guidance of man slipping down into positions from which the other tracks upon the mountain, and the end to which all must converge, are seen—if at all—in false perspective; and the large boulder in the foreground is identified with the rock on which the true Church is built. And it seems to some of these onlookers that a recovery of that sense of the mountain which makes the true mountaineer, and reduces to their true proportion the alpine adventures of men—in religious terms, a fresh perception of the overwhelming majesty yet actualness of God, over against these small achievements—can alone bring the contending climbers peace.

It is strange that modern men slowly opening their eyes upon the vastness of the universe, do not obtain from this revelation a more vivid sense of their own limitations and of the symbolic character of all their knowledge. We may well say of all realities, as St. Thomas does of divine things, that "they are not named by our intellect as they really are in themselves, for in that way it knows them not." Meditation on this liberating truth—and it comes from one of the most orthodox of the saints—might even teach us to look mercifully at the religious language our neighbours prefer to employ.

She was writing regularly for the *Spectator* all this year, reviews and articles. One on the Malines Conversations has the same message as the article just quoted.

A certain profound union of Christendom already exists. It is probable that the most spiritual minds of all Communions will come more and more to find their common centre in this truth; and that visible reunion, when achieved, will be the flower of a seed sown long before in the fields of the Spirit, and cherished in secret by a few.

She was one of those few, and was always alert to see any growing of that seed.

The establishment and work of the Moines d'Union, the growing *rapprochement* between the Anglican and Orthodox Churches, the Lambeth Appeal, the Lutheran High Church Movement, the swift success of such journals as Irenikon and Una Sancta, all these things witness to the kindling of a new fire.

We have seen how much she welcomed the Entente which Maria

and her sisters in Umbria had so much at heart.

One of her *Spectator* articles gives an account of Maria's little community, and a lovely picture of Maria herself.

> When I visited the group they were living in an old country house not far from the Fountain of Clitumnus. In the stable they had made a tiny chapel as poor and naked as the Poverello could desire. The head of the household and foundress, who is known as the Least Sister, came down the lane to welcome me. She was dressed like the rest of the family in a peasant's grey linen frock, an apron, and a little shawl. I shall not presume to describe her remarkable personality, or the simple beauty of the life she has inspired. That life, with its gracious suppleness and entire avoidance of rigorism, its spiritual deeps, its deceptive appearance of ease—even of gaiety—cannot fully be understood by a passing guest; nor does the Least Sister, whose friendship I count as one of my greatest privileges, easily disclose the secret of her unassuming power. Those who recognize her type will discover without surprise that her delicate courtesy, her serene and widespreading love, conceal a Teresian inflexibility of purpose; a profound sense of the pain and need of the world, and a passionate desire to help it. As we sat in the woods, I asked her to tell me something of her conception of the spiritual life. She replied in words startlingly at variance with her peaceful surroundings, *In tormento e travaglia servire i fratelli.*

Her articles were mainly reviews of books concerning Franciscan and other saints, but there was a notable one on Bishop Gore's *Jesus of Nazareth* and another on Middleton Murry's *Things to Come.*

Meanwhile she continued to serve the cause of Christian unity by speaking at Nottingham to a group of Nonconformist ministers. "Fifty in all," she writes to Lucy, "including six parsons and four Quaker women. We got on together quite nicely, though they were too shy to come into the vestry, which was my private lair."

Later on in the year she took her northernmost retreat—at Cumbrae, the island on the Clyde estuary. "I feel like an anchoress," she wrote from there to Lucy, "with my own little window opening into the Cathedral right opposite the Blessed Sacrament."

Evelyn was an enthusiastic pilgrim. She loved going to places where the saints had lived. She liked to take a rosary or a crucifix, and have them blessed in the holy places. In this year, she and Hubert and Clara Smith started off for Spain, a pilgrimage for her to the country of St. Teresa, and St. John of the Cross. They stayed at Gavarnie, and had the unexpected joy of finding lovely mountain flowers there, on the French side of the Pyrenees.

> I long to come here in spring [she wrote to Lucy] as it is an absolute paradise for alpine plants. Raimondia grows in thick mats in the crevices of the rocks, and a great purple iris, and asphodel, and beds of blue and yellow monkshood. And we've got the Pyrenean cranesbill, and alpine gypsophila, and a lovely mountain aquilegia, in flower even now, and see the remains of tiger-lilies and other exciting things. I never was in a more wonderful place for botanizing.

She never did go back there, as far as I can tell, but the letter gives one a picture of her intense love of flowers.

They moved on to Avila, a place that she must have visited so often in her mind. There was the Encarnacion, where Teresa began her convent life, and fought so long against the final surrender to her vocation; and where she returned in later life to be prioress, when she had established her reformed Carmelite Order; and also St. Joseph "a small and poorhouse where the primitive Rule of Mount Carmel was strictly observed," writes Evelyn in her *Mystics of the Church,* where Teresa established her first convent under the primitive rule. Evelyn wrote to Lucy from Avila.

> We went down to the Encarnacion and luckily fell in with a young American Jesuit, speaking perfect Spanish, who helped us a lot....You go into a little court with a splendid vine which must have been there in Teresa's day, and then into the actual parlours she used, with the original grilles

from behind which she talked to St. Peter of Alcantara and St. John of the Cross.... I think perhaps the most affecting thing is the little grille at which St. John of the Cross sat to hear her confessions, she being of course within the enclosure. The door into the choir through which the nuns receive communion is the one she used and where she had the vision of the Spiritual Betrothal. A very bad picture commemorates this—in fact a good deal has to be passed over lightly!

Later:

I went to Mass at the Encarnacion this morning; such a divine walk down from the walls, with early morning light on the mountains. There were two other women in the big bare church and, of course, the nuns behind the grille. They sang the *O Salutaris* and then the priest walked down to the west end and gave each communion through the little gold door Teresa used.... It was really lovely.

After breakfast we went to St. Joseph and were then shown the original Chapel of St. Joseph where the first Mass was said, and the first nuns took their vows, and then the relics, including Teresa's little drums and pipes in perfect preservation, her leather belt, one of her letters, *and* one of her bones! At the *Casa Santa* where the room she was born in is turned into a chapel, the sister who showed us round let me hold her rosary in my hand.

The whole town seems almost what it must have been in her day. You see the covered mule carts in which she travelled at every turn.... Altogether it is a dream of a place and ranks next after Assisi.

Hubert and Evelyn and Clara Smith went on to Toledo: "Nothing Teresian here but her convent and one tooth which I refused to see! Also the great fortress-like house of the Carmelite friars, grim enough to make prisons for a dozen inconvenient saints." But she describes it as marvellous, and full of Moorish and Mozarabic treasures.

We went to the Mozarabic Mass. I had not been able to get
a description of it so could not follow all the eleven points of
difference, though some were obvious, e.g. the Epiklesis
loudly and distinctly repeated *after* the words of Consecration,
the offering up of the elements at the very beginning of the
service, the Pax given all round, a quite different arrangement
of the Canon in short bits, a highly ceremonial washing of
hands with a big jug and basin, and above all a startling savage howl uttered by the choir at the end! They did it again at
Vespers! most peculiar!

She came back to the usual round of addresses, one of which
was to the "big meeting of S.S. teachers," at which, she writes in a
letter to W. Y., "I talked mostly about sheep-dogs."

Lucy became Warden of Pleshey at the end of this year, and
Evelyn was very much concerned with finding her staff, getting
new books for the Library, and strengthening the hands of the new
Warden on many points.

She found time to make a little collection among her friends
for a gift to Mrs. Harvey. Perhaps this is the right moment to
quote from Evelyn's own appreciation of Mrs. Harvey.

She was one of those rare personalities who possess and are
able to communicate to others something of the radiant
delight of Christianity. Supernatural joy is perhaps the rarest,
as it is certainly one of the most precious of all spiritual qualities. There must be many retreatants to Pleshey, including
the shy and doubtful visitors of the first years of the movement whom she welcomed with such love and skill—who
first learned what this joy could be by contact with Mrs.
Harvey; with her exultant yet reverent delight in all that per-
tained to the worship of God, her passionate love of beauty
and unquenchable spirit of rejoicing.

At the end of the year Mrs. Plunket Greene's letters from von
Hügel were published under the title *Letters to a Niece*. It was a
book which brought to Evelyn "an extraordinary sense of contact
with the Baron's spirit; a sense too of the power and intensity of

his nature, the greatness of that passion for God which consumed him, and the depth of the riches he had to bestow." In her review of the book in the *Spectator* she quoted some sayings of the Baron which seemed to her most typical of him.

> Let us rest content. We have not got to invent God, nor to hold Him. He holds us. We shall never be able to explain God though we can apprehend Him more and more through the spiritual life. I want you to hold very clearly the otherness of God, and the littleness of men. If you don't get that you can't have adoration, and you cannot have religion without adoration.
>
> Christianity is a heroism. People seem to think sometimes it is a dear darling, not to be grumpy, not to be impatient, not to be violent life; a sort of wishy washy sentimental affair. Stuff and nonsense! Christianity is not that. Christianity is an immense warning; a tremendous heroism.

Evelyn Underhill in the Conductor's room at Pleshey

Evelyn Underhill with Bishop Frere at the Anglo-Russian
Conference, 1938

16

RELIGIOUS EDITOR

In 1929 Evelyn began a bit of work which gave her great satisfaction and which she continued to do for three years. "You'll be amused to hear," she wrote to Lucy, "that I have been appointed Religious Editor of the *Spectator*, and all that side of the paper is now to be in my hands. I trust it won't mean an awful lot of work, it is rather an opportunity to get the things one wishes said before the public."

She had been writing and reviewing steadily for the *Spectator*—at the time edited by Sir Evelyn Wrench—all through 1928, but this new appointment followed a series of articles which she arranged and got up in the early spring of '29. She had secured a list of great names for these articles on religion: Archbishop Temple, the Abbé Bremond, Oliver Quick, Canon Barry (now Bishop of Southwell), the Dean of Westminster, and Professor A. E. Taylor as a summer-up. She wrote the editorial which opened the series herself, and also contributed an article on the Witness of the Saints. Of this last article she wrote to Lucy: "I'm so glad you liked the Saints. It was written in a state of dreary exhaustion and I felt sure it was utter rot. However, as time was up I sent it off, and by some miracle people do rather seem to cotton to it. One never can tell. I wanted to do something rather specially good and then couldn't."

She was exhausting herself with a ceaseless pressure of work. "Addresses for Salisbury, and for the Association for Promoting Retreats, all the Pleshey addresses and articles for several things are all waiting. In between I do scraps of *Mysticism* (for a new edition)."

During this summer of '29 she got to Downside Abbey, where

the Baron's grave was, and made a friend of the Abbot, Dom John Chapman, for whom she had a very great admiration.

"Downside was most lovely," she wrote to Lucy, "a bit of Heaven. And the Abbot a contemplative saint, with the simplicity of a child, and full of naughty wit. He was fearfully kind to me, and his talk had a depth and richness which made ordinary spirituality seem woefully thin."

Lucy Menzies was settling in to her new office as Warden of Pleshey. Evelyn, a little anxious as always lest this child of hers should wear herself to shreds, writes of the house prayers and Lucy's own prayers in the chapel: "I think regularity in the *Opus Dei* is important. In your own times in chapel when it is a strain, I should not attempt actual prayer, but just read a bit and just be there. As to advising people, if it is put into one's hand one just has to do it in simple trust that if one keeps on as quietly as possible God will do it through one, and that one's own insufficiency does not matter much."

In this year she brought out a little book made from some retreat addresses called *The House of the Soul*. It was the first book definitely made from retreat addresses, the forerunner of *The Golden Sequence, Abba,* and *The School of Charity*. It has a very lovely simplicity. In her House of the Soul there are two floors:

> a ground floor, a natural life, biologically conditioned, with animal instincts and affinities; and this life is very important, for it is the product of Divine creativity—its builder and maker is God. But we know that we have an upper floor, a supernatural life, with supernatural possibilities, a capacity for God, and that this, man's peculiar prerogative, is more important still.

She writes of "our human vocation, so utterly a part of the fugitive and creaturely life of this planet, and yet so deeply coloured by Eternity."

Of Hope, she writes:

> Migration is not an easy or a pleasant thing for a tiny bird to face. It must turn deliberately from solid land, from food,

shelter, a certain measure of security, and fly across an ocean unfriendly to its life, destitute of everything it needs. We make much of the heroism and endurance of our airmen and explorers. Perhaps one day man will rival the adventurous hope of the willow wren and chiff chaff; an ounce and a half of living courage, launching out with amazing confidence to a prospect of storms, hardship, exhaustion, perhaps starvation and death…the tiny bird, before conditions force it — not driven by fear, but drawn by Hope, commits itself with perfect confidence to that infinite ocean of air; where all familiar landmarks will vanish, and if its strength fails it must be lost.

This book was dedicated to Laura Rose, who had perhaps heard the addresses.

She enjoyed a visit to Truro to Lis Escop at the end of the yachting holiday. Since the Baron's death she had come to rely on the Bishop of Truro (Walter Frere) for spiritual counsel. They were both fine sharp instruments for God's purposes, and understood each other very well. A packet of Walter Frere's letters she kept till her death. He was writing to her about the ever-growing responsibility of the people who came to her for help, in these words:

> It is in working for others that you can lose yourself and learn in a sense to consider your own state as irrelevant, when you are commandeered for a task. Fancy the opposite policy! Assuring ourselves that our state was sufficiently satisfactory before we would learn to do a job. Impossible…. Your state is worse still directly you stop to think of it in any self-regarding way. That isn't penitence. Penitence is a swift prostration, and then on again. Don't let your mind then hang about your faults or hover over your sins or state of wickedness. St. Paul boldly forgets in order to reach forward. He was so sane and bold over it. The opposite is a nastiness— fit for flies more than people.

I think he must have advised her in her pioneer work of taking retreats, for I find her writing to Lucy: "My Bishop thinks I don't get enough time for myself when conducting—but it really is impossible."

She wrote to Lucy about her visit to Lis Escop:

> I enjoyed Truro immensely. There were nice people staying there, and we went forth like a caravan in four cars to see old churches and picnic on the cliffs at Trevose Head. The Bishop was wonderful as ever and I had a very satisfying talk to him on Sunday afternoon, and of course he said Mass every morning. He had just got a very lovely new wireless which was not doing all it should. Hubert made him a new aerial which brought in Berlin, Leipzig, Toulouse, and hosts of other stations to his almost childish joy. So the benefits of the visit were not hopelessly on one side. He would have made a splendid Van Eyck portrait as he sat last night in his Mirfield habit, with his ascetic ivory white face, absorbed in moving the dial and getting fresh places: but I fear he is not a bit well. He eats hardly anything.

In the next year she was writing, during an illness: "My own dear Bishop came and sat by my bed on Saturday and talked like the saint he is, and gave me his blessing, and says he will come again this week, and that's quite enough compensation for one little illness."

Through Bishop Frere at a later stage she came into touch with the Russian Orthodox Church. There is a picture of them sitting together at one of the gatherings of the Society of St. Alban and St. Sergius at High Leigh. How much she loved the emphasis on worship and the other-worldly sense of the Orthodox Church is shown in her book, *Worship.* Bishop Frere certainly helped her to write the section on the Orthodox Church, and brought her into the movement for closer unity between the two Churches.

She was involved in celebration of the jubilee of King's College in July, including a tea party on the terrace at Somerset House, and a grand procession and thanksgiving service in the Abbey. She was rather embarrassed by finding herself in the van of the procession, as theology was the senior faculty, and hearing mutterings of "Who is that lady?" It pleased her that the Archbishop, in dedicating the new hostel chapel, quoted the Baron's words about Adoration. "They needed it," she writes tersely, "for the service was highbrow to a degree that would have served excellently for Unitarians, Christ being not once mentioned or addressed."

The "Baby" Austin took them to Northern France for a holiday this year, pottering about and finding treasures unmentioned in guidebooks, with St. Joan and St. Martin as their pilgrimage saints;

> It's quite a nice district for saints [she wrote to Clara Smith]. We went to St. Martin's tomb at Tours, and at a tiny old dead place called Candes at the confluence of the Vienne and Loire, found a *miraculously* beautiful Angevin church built over the cell in which he died.
>
> Nice little hotel here with five cats and a lovely fluffy white rabbit, who has a day hutch in the *cour* and a night hutch in the kitchen, which glows with burnished copper and provides very good food of the normal French kind. Some of our food has been far from normal. I think our most startling meal was at the hotel of the Fairy Melusine at Lusignan—radishes, large dish of mussels (refused and exchanged for two fresh sardines), fried pigs' trotters (one each), pork chops, saucissons, cheese, grapes. The Fairy Melusine's view of knives and forks was, of course, very economical—and as to her idea of sanitation!!!!
>
> She was run hard by St. Savin, where *déjeuner* began with two little baked potatoes, and went on to ham and gherkins. But St. Savin had the most miraculous Romanesque Abbey. I don't suppose anything so exciting as that will happen now, as we are on beaten tracks.

17

CHIEFLY ABOUT RETREATS

As we get near to the last decade of Evelyn's working life, it would perhaps be as well to take a long look at her to try to see what those who were looking at her saw, and what those who were hearing her heard.

First, what did she look like in the 'thirties? Slight and thin she was, as I think she always had been, and not very tall, her body carrying her spirit with as little fuss about it as possible. She had discarded her little lace caps and, as her friends will remember, had had her hair cut short to counteract the reverential reviews of one of her books. For her retreats she still drew on her mother's stocks of lace, and she made herself delicate small headdresses falling to the shoulder. She had a transforming smile which made her pale interesting face gleam with life. If one looks at the early pictures of her at the time of her wedding, and then remembers that expression, so vivid and humorous, of the 'thirties, one realizes what the Holy Spirit can make of the human countenance. She was delightful to look at when she was speaking, her face expressed her meaning so enchantingly. She would finish a sentence with some fearfully disconcerting question, thrown out almost with a toss of the head and a half laugh. Her eyes and her way of looking at people were arresting; some people found them formidable. They searched and knew you, but to those very many people whom she loved, her look of affection was unforgettable, one of the loveliest things about her. She had a preference for blue and grey and silver clothes, whether they were tweed coats and skirts, which she liked for the country, or the rather severe rich stuffs of her retreat dresses. She liked her clothes, and Lucy Menzies used to spoil her by making just the sort of cosily knitted ones that she loved for yacht or car journeys. It was a pity that she was not more photogenic, but the camera is often outfaced by the vivid and swift creatures of the Spirit. There is a moment in *Pilgrim's Progress:* Mr. Greatheart takes up a sword belonging to one of the pilgrims and describes it as a "right Jerusalem blade," a word that brings Evelyn to the mind. What we were seeing in the 'thirties was that finely tempered sword outwearing its sheath.

Her clear voice was easy to listen to and very expressive, and she was always audible without any strain. When she went to prepare for her first broadcast, in some trepidation, the B.B.C. officials were struck by its quality and gave her the minimum of rehearsal. Her style was now economical though often very lovely. She never hesitated, and one got the impression of something most perfectly prepared, the proportions of her addresses were so just and satisfying. I think she could never have been boring, sometimes perhaps over-critical, cutting to things that she didn't like, rather wickedly amused by the tiresome and the over-godly, very much down on the complacent or the arrogant. She had learnt to be homely in a peculiarly telling way in her illustrations, but she had lovely profound words for great moments, not purple but perhaps snow-white patches for her mountain tops. She loved words, as a poet loves them, but words, as the saints discovered, must also be humbled before God. For primarily her greatest gift to us all was her sense of God, the God who is to be adored, loved, trusted. The "overagainstness" which the Baron had commended to her, came through to her hearers with overwhelming but peaceful insistence.

Lucy Menzies, writing of Evelyn's retreats at Pleshey while she was Warden says:

> In my time at Pleshey she generally gave three retreats there every year, at Passiontide, the Sunday after Ascension, and All Saints. She prepared for these retreats months beforehand. Everything must combine to focus the retreatants' whole attention to God, nothing must be left to chance. She generally arrived the day before, with everything arranged— hymns, readings, the sheet of suggested meditations given to each retreatant—even the room each was to occupy, for she knew the house intimately with its little rooms called after the virtues. (It was she who named the rooms which came

into being when we built the new chapel—*Adoration,* where
the altar had stood, *Compassion,* where confessions had been
heard, and so on.)

When the actual retreat was about to begin, after she had
welcomed each member of it, I remember the expectancy in
the chapel as her quiet voice broke its stillness. And it was all
so natural, nothing forced or "over pious." One remembers
gratefully the smile with which she encouraged those she
happened to pass in the garden; the gay humour with which
she drove home the deepest spiritual truths; the bracing selfless counsel she gave in the conductor's room.... She always
claimed at Pleshey the privilege of acting as sacristan and she
was generally the last to leave the chapel, long after her flock
were safely in bed.... She brought to Pleshey people from all
walks of life—students, "rich young things," clergy, artists,
anyone in fact who had a capacity for God.

"I never sat under her in retreat," wrote her cousin Francis
Underhill, Bishop of Bath and Wells, "but I have spoken with
many who have done so and have heard of the delicious shafts
of humour, almost asides which lightened the depth of her
teaching—those little quick witty phrases which illustrated not
only her spoken but her written word."

Often she brought to retreats some picture to be hung or
pinned to the notice board. I sent her a poem by A. E., which was
often pinned up. She had a special book of prayers that she had
collected which went to retreats with her, for she did not say
Matins and Evensong at retreats, but read prayers from this special
collection. If there was anyone to play the organ or humbler har-
monium she liked to have hymns at a retreat, and a hymn practice
before it began. (Two hymns which she loved very much, "Love
of the Father," and "How shall I sing that Majesty," were not easy
to learn, but she was particular that we should get them at any rate
passably sung.)

I don't think she was lonely at Pleshey when Lucy Menzies was
there, for they were very dear and close to each other, but I had a
feeling that conducting a retreat was a lonely bit of work for God;

she wanted someone to come in and say good night and to exchange a word that was not so horridly responsible as the succession of interviews; not that she was at all formal in the interviews. I remember one heart-stricken retreatant who came to her saying: "Oh dear, I must be quite different!" to whom her reply was: "Must you, what a pity, I do like you so much as you are." Those who came to talk to her felt a firm hand held out. She was a guide who knew her mountain, and taught us that if we could be humble, obedient and courageous it might be possible for us also to reach the snow. Only there must be no silliness, no running on ahead but a humorous sense of our capacities and a humble acceptance of the Way.

In the early 'thirties she must have been taking seven or eight retreats in the year, some in lovely and congenial surroundings but some at places like dear, ugly Water Millock, redeemed by its delightful warden, Miss Willoughby, but with a chapel that was obviously the ex-billiard room, and a garden black with the grime of Bolton, Lancs.

In 1930 she came into touch with two groups of people who were new ground for her.

Her March plans included a quiet day at Westcott House, Cambridge. I think this was the first time she spoke to theological students; she certainly went after this to the Theological College at Lincoln, and quite often to King's College.

At Lincoln, I believe the students found her rather formidable; perhaps she had ideals for them beyond their reach, though not beyond the hopes and prayers of the warden, Leslie Owen, who became one of her great friends, and is mentioned in her book *Worship* as having helped over the lovely chapter on personal religion.

The other group who came to love her dearly was the Wives' Fellowship, a company of educated young married women. Maisie Fletcher, who was their secretary at this time, writes of her first interview with Evelyn:

> In the spring of 1930 I went, at the request of the Wives'
> Fellowship, to ask Evelyn Underhill if she could possibly

conduct a retreat which we were planning to have at
Canterbury. Her books had been a growing revelation to me
since I had read her *Life of the Spirit* on my way to India two
years before. I went with some trepidation to meet this distinguished writer and mystic, whose work was making such
a profound impression on the religious thought of the day.
And then I found myself sitting in that rather austere and yet
delightfully friendly sitting room at 50 Campden Hill
Square, talking with incredible ease on matters about which
it is often most hard to speak, because here words are most
inadequate. She could steer the frail craft of human longing
out into the deep waters of the Spirit with such humour and
vigour, and yet with penetrating understanding. I left her
after an hour with the exhilarating sense of entering a new
companionship, not just with her but with the great communion of seekers and finders. The retreat she took for us
was an immense experience for us all, the addresses were
afterwards developed into her book *The Golden Sequence*. She
took other retreats for us later, and it was after one of these
that she told me with great delight of a gay young woman
who came to see her after one address; and Evelyn asked her:
"I wonder what made you come to this?" and was enchanted
by the frank answer, "Oh well, you see my husband thought
I could do with a spot of rebirth."

In the final chapter of her book *Worship,* Evelyn writes of the
rediscovery in the Anglican communion after the first world war
of the realities of the interior life, and of "the creation of a nucleus
of ardent and spiritually educated Christians and the production of
a vast literature upon which they could feed." This was the work to
which she set herself in the 'thirties. On the whole, the addresses
to big meetings grew less and the work for individual souls and for
small groups of Christians grew more.

She conducted retreats at Moreton, Leiston Abbey, Glastonbury,
and Little Compton, as well as Pleshey and Water Millock. Her
powers as a retreat conductor were at their height, but eight
retreats in the year were a tremendous tax on her mind and soul,

and her rather frail body. She used the same material for all the retreats in one year, but each retreat meant new people to pray for, and possibly to direct. She used to keep a book of her retreatants and the retreats which they had attended, so that she knew how they were faring.

It was the year of the Lambeth Conference. The Encyclical had not pleased her, and she wrote to Audrey Duff in August, when she had got the report:

> The Lambeth report strikes me as much better than the Encyclical…but I'm very disappointed with the Liverpool-cum-Birmingham religious philosophy to which they seem to have committed the Church. Quite unsupernatural, very slightly Sacramental, and decidedly non-Catholic in its emphasis. Also far too much about reading and thinking and far too little about Prayer and Penitence.

In her article in the *Spectator* on the Lambeth Report, she could not disguise her disappointment that what she called the "Vertical" movement in religion was at a discount, and the "Horizontal" had it all its own way. She felt that the Conference had declined from the inspiration of its first sermon, that in the Encyclical, the bishops roundly stated their belief that we must humanize religion if we would recommend it to our generation. But she felt that this anthropocentric temper was more marked in the Encyclical than in the concise and workmanlike resolutions that accompanied it.

Of the Reports she felt that the one on Youth was admirable, and she commended the fact that official approval was extended to direct spiritual work by women other than deaconesses. This she felt might be "the quiet introduction of a far reaching reform." The view of marriage taken by the Report she felt to be both Christian and modem.

She quotes with delight the decisions on War: "War as a means of settling international disputes is incompatible with the teaching and example of our Lord Jesus Christ. The Christian conscience is now called upon to condemn War." "Surely," she exclaims, "St.

Francis congratulated George Fox when the news of that decision reached the Rose of Paradise."

On the South Indian Church, she writes: "Here we see the Lambeth Conference of 1930 holding out hands of fellowship on one side to the representatives of historic tradition, and on the other to those who are working for new conditions still to be. By such recognition, both of history and novelty, it surely proves its possession of the character of true life." She ends her article: "The subalpine pastures of the Holy Mountain must inevitably be a chief centre of interest for the assembled shepherds of the Church. But how much more attractive those pastures might appear to those who still avoid them, did their exponents point out, beyond the haystacks and the cowsheds, the solemn beauty of holiness, the splendour of the everlasting snows."

That summer she had also been to the Anglican Fellowship meeting at Oxford. Her paper was published in *Theology,* and later much of it, too, was incorporated in *The Golden Sequence.* "As far as I could gather," she writes rather ruefully to Audrey Duff, "each of the papers on various aspects of the doctrine of the Spirit was going to be incompatible with the rest.... Dr. Buchman was present, and an object of general interest, but kept very quiet. Mr. Morgan of Selly Oak, and Fr. Winslow of Christa Seva Sangha, were the people I most enjoyed meeting."

She snatched a week-end at Truro with Bishop Frere during the yachting month, which proved wet and chilly, but she never failed to give her father her company while he was still sailing his yacht. She had learnt to make something of the yachting weeks, and, of course, Hubert and her father were delightfully happy. She once told me that Hubert's idea of bliss was "messing about in a boat"; even a little boat on a Westmorland tarn served, but he sometimes went off for a private orgy of sailing, or for a spell of work on the *Implacable* at Portsmouth.

18

THE GOLDEN SEQUENCE
AND A VISIT TO NORWAY

The book which Evelyn was writing in 1931 was *The Golden Sequence,* a book based on the lovely hymn, *Veni, Sancte Spiritus,* which was known through the Middle Ages by that name. She wrote in the Preface: "This is a personal little book; its aim is not the establishment of some new thesis. It merely represents the precipitation of my own thoughts as they have moved to and fro during the last few years across a line which has the spiritual doctrine of St. John of the Cross at one end, and Professor Whitehead at the other.... It consists in what ancient writers on these themes used to call 'Considerations.'"

She had in mind some of the great changes of thought that were bound to follow "the new proportion in which the Universe is seen by us, and which have deeply affected our attitude towards the things which do not change." "A good bit of it," she wrote to Elizabeth Rendel, "is just what I've had to find out and live through." Some of the themes in *The Golden Sequence* she had explored during the retreat which she gave to the Wives' Fellowship, and the address to the Anglican Fellowship in the summer of 1930, but all this was recast for the book. I always felt that this book was a special one for her, very much her own. She didn't expect it to have a very large number of readers (though it went quite quickly into a second edition). When I asked her for whom she was writing it she mentioned the names of a few dear friends who would understand and love it, as indeed they did. It was dedicated to the dearest of these friends, Lucy Menzies.

I first met Evelyn and Hubert at my sister Maisie Fletcher's house in the spring of 1931. They came to dine there, and we had a very friendly evening, and a few days after Evelyn came to see a little play of mine which Martin Browne was playing in at a school of Religious Drama somewhere in Kensington. I suppose it was a few weeks later that I had my first letter from her. I must have said in a letter how oddly my writing ran ahead of my experience, for she also confessed, "Yes, I too arrive several years later at the experience of things I said, I don't know why. All my poems were based on no experience at all—it is a funny business, isn't it? But I think self-abandonment is the real answer to everything, one just does and says what one has to do and be. My dear Franciscan saint (Maria) says: 'The point about Jesus is he can utilize everything, even our fatigue.' How I wish you could come to my Water Millock Retreat, July 10–13. Bolton can't be *very* far from you."

I went, of course. In that year she was giving a set of addresses that she never made into a book. The Ascent of the Mountain from the Purgatorio: "We all know the general scheme of that wonderful journey, how Dante clambered up from terrace to terrace, not forced by God's justice, but drawn by His love, and by his own passionate longing to correspond with that love."

My own feeling of despair at the thought of this mountaineering somehow went away during the first day under the magnetism and loveliness of her teaching and praying. The mountain was no less high, the climbing no less arduous, but somehow one wanted to try. She was very much horrified to find that I had never read Dante, and made several attempts to remedy this, none of which I am afraid succeeded.

It was in this year that she wrote the letter to Dom John Chapman, the Abbot of Downside, which tells us as much as we shall ever know of her reasons for staying in the Anglican Church. I remember her telling me that in the 'thirties various Roman Catholic friends tried again to persuade her to change her obedience, telling her that all her work for souls was wasted if not harmful, since it was heretical. The Rev. R. Somerset Ward recollects that, when she first came to consult him, she was still troubled by those who made this suggestion. The Abbot of Downside was not one of these; and she was so generously grateful to Rome for so much of her own training under von Hügel that she must have been glad to make her position clear to him.

> I have been for years now [she wrote] a practising Anglo-Catholic…and solidly believe in the Catholic status of the Anglican Church as to Orders and Sacraments, little as I appreciate many of the things done among us. It seems to be a respectable suburb of the City of God—but all the same part of Greater London. I appreciate the superior food, etc., to be had nearer the centre of things. But the whole point to me is in the fact that the Lord has put me here, keeps on giving me more and more jobs to do for souls here, and has never given me orders to move. In fact when I have been inclined to think of this, something has always stopped me: and if I did it, it would be purely out of self-interest and self-will. I know what the push of God is like, and should obey it if it came—at least I trust and believe so.

Meanwhile there were some things in the Anglican Church which gave her deep pleasure. She had always felt that the revival of the religious orders was one of the really vital things that had grown out of the Tractarian revival. Now on the way north she and Hubert put in at Kelham.

> We went round by Kelham and saw their new chapel. It's awfully impressive, intensely austere, all done by line and plain surfaces—not a statue—not even of Our Lady, no stations, the Blessed Sacrament reserved in a tiny oratory we were not allowed to see. The whole church is dominated by Jagger's wonderful rood (one gets no idea of this from the small photographs). Our Lord bound to the Cross with cords, a living figure, full of intense power, and looking straight into the eyes of whoever looks up at Him—and Mary an ecstasy of worship and John crushed by penitence and grief—the effect against the purple apse wall is simply marvellous.

Evelyn and Hubert made a complete break with their usual

holiday plans by going to Norway for their holiday in 1931. There was fishing in boats for Hubert, and flowers and mountains for them both, and, rather to Evelyn's surprise, churches going back to the eleventh century.

"There was a half-hour's pause," she writes to Lucy, "in one village and the driver casually recommended the church, which we found to be one of the oldest of the wooden churches with an eleventh-century Romanesque font brought by the Vikings, and a most touchingly beautiful rood."

There were some adventures too:

> Stalheim was a wonderful place—the hotel perched at the top of a 1,000-ft. cliff and looking down the Naerodal, one of those solemn rock valleys which seem like an approach to the Inferno. Our arrival was adventurous: as when we reached the foot of the cliff the car stopped, and the driver said calmly: "I go no further—from here you walk." He then pointed to heaven and said, "There is the hotel." It was 9 p.m. and pretty dark, but light enough to make it obvious that the climb was far beyond me! and not alluring to any but the young and strong. In the end we got a horse from a farm which scrambled slowly up the thirteen steep zigzags. The high valleys at the top were splendid, and I would like to stay there for days. We got one very good walk among the summer pastures, and saw the cows and goats being called down from the tops for milking.

From Lesjaskog she wrote to Audrey Duff:

> We are in a lovely high valley right on the Watershed, with a six mile lake on which I am now floating, the forests of pine and silver birch all round, and a beautiful rocky river.... Marvellous peace and solitude, not another boat or human being on this enormous lake, only a grebe and a dunlin.... The plants are mostly English moorland and subalpine sorts, wild monkshood everywhere in the forest, stagshorn moss, butter wort, cranberry and so on, and very good ferns.... Our wooden hotel is partly farm, and the cows and calves

wander pleasantly about in front of the door.... It's a purely
Norwegian place, no English and no tourist atmosphere.
There's a white wooden church with its own row of stalls
and during Sunday service nice pony faces were looking
out. I did not attend, tho' perhaps it would have been an
interesting experience.

Part of their journey, she says, was through the Kristin
Lavransdatter country, very little changed since the fourteenth
century. She wrote to me later in the year, "Norway has the qui-
etest forests in the world and the clearest green and wonderful
light. It was a *great* success."

She was quite practical enough on behalf of the Church to
write about other things besides theology and devotion; and she
put a plea into the *Spectator* in August of that year for the churches
in the new building areas. She had a standard about her churches,
simple though they might have to be.

All experienced persons know that every church can ultimately be placed in one of two classes—the Mouldy or the
Beloved. The Mouldy are generally locked during the week,
a needless precaution—when we try to enter we are met by
one of the most devitalizing and intimidating atmospheres
that human nature can produce. The Beloved are generally
open, and not very often empty. There may be many things
in them which do not please a fastidious taste, but here the
spiritual has been made homely.... And we are now being
offered an unparalleled opportunity to turn our backs with
decision on the Mouldy, and to create in fresh surroundings,
maintain, and fill with reverence and homeliness the wel-
coming church which alone will always conquer and alone
is always loved.

Week after week and month by month hundreds of families are being transplanted from the slums to the new areas.
It is a move to better conditions of bodily health, but often
to those of spiritual starvation. Help must come from outside
if this chance is to be promptly taken, and taken in the right
way. The alternative is a vast addition to heathen England. All

the outward signs of material civilization are hurrying into existence; only the embodiment of the spiritual lags behind.

The more difficult, haphazard, and unlovely the conditions of outward existence, the more imperative surely the need for these visible homes of the Spirit; and the more direct the obligation laid upon the Christians to see that their brothers and sisters have access to these, the ordained distributing centres of strength, sweetness, and light.

Towards the end of the year she was writing to Elizabeth Rendel:

I must write to you for the beloved All Saints; I really think after Easter the most darling feast of all the year, don't you? This has been an awfully busy month, and now I cease external activities till Lent—such a joy, and have a little time to think, and browse, and struggle to write my new book *[The Golden Sequence]*. The Church Congress was a queer affair [she was speaking at it]. I rather took against the atmosphere...there was a lot of high thinking done, and much talk of being modern, but our Lord and the Sacraments got left out. Since then I've been to Birmingham, and preached in the pulpit of a Wesleyan Chapel, and lived through awful moments while the minister described me to God in an extempore prayer; and I've given a Franciscan lecture at the Guildhouse and lots of other things.

I went to the Slavonic Mass at Westminster Cathedral this morning, a marvellous sight and experience which carried one back 1,000 years or more, and was full of beauty, but extraordinarily difficult to bring (I thought) into any relation with the Gospels, which shows the extent to which one unconsciously Westernizes one's faith.

She gave her first broadcast, and was pleased in writing to Lucy to find that it was to be on St. Lucy's Day. She never became a frequent broadcaster, but later she did a series on the Spiritual Life which were published as a book.

She was writing very lovingly to Lucy, who was rather ill and tired over Christmas. She was a very delightful person to give presents to, and received them in this spirit:

Beloved child—Your letter and most beautiful parcel arrived yesterday, and were promptly dealt with. Tony (the orange Persian) is delighted with his, and sends you many purrs, and I was so deeply touched to think of Giles [L. M.'s dog] negotiating Woolworth's and making such a very useful choice! Please kiss his nose for his Aunt. And I love the beautiful Assisi cloth, and am tempted (though it's much too good) to put it on the little table in the study. The hankies will go to—for best use and will not be lost. But I do feel horrified at an invalid struggling with the mental travail needed for such a lovely and elaborate parcel, and all its doing up.... I love the wren, and lavender bags are heavenly and in my clothes already.

I was changing house that autumn so I don't think I was in London or saw her. I went in November to a little house in Westmorland called Far Park, which Evelyn loved and where she paid me four most heart-warming visits, twice with Hubert, once with Lucy and once alone. We began very early to exchange works, I sending her religious plays, poems, and sometimes prayers, and she repaying me with much more important volumes, and pamphlets and bits of MSS. to read. I think just then she found it comfortable to be friends with someone who was writing, however slightly and irregularly, about the things that she cared about.

How wonderful that you are doing a Passion play, and let me think of it [she wrote to me in the spring of '32]. Seems to me making such things as this does count for people like you, as part of the Opus Dei, just as much as what you *think* is prayer. It is given to stimulate other people's sense of God, and so adds to the total prayer energy which is the ultimate job. Anyhow I always console myself like that when I find myself spending the whole time in having happy notions for addresses, instead of attending to Him in a more obvious way. P'raps it's part of the price we have to pay for our particular vocation? for it sometimes is a bit of a cross, isn't it? The retreats are going to be very simple...a pilgrimage round a cathedral where the Absolute Light shines through the windows of the different

mysteries of our Lord's life—and then hits *us*. [This was the set
of retreat addresses published after her death as *The Light of
Christ*.]

Evelyn came to stay at Far Park for two days in the middle of
April just before her retreat at Water Millock, to which we went
on together.

It was my first spring at Far Park and great fun to share with
her the quantities of white violets on the little terrace, and the daf-
fodils in the steep orchard. Up behind was the fell, and going
slowly she could walk up and see the lovely Kentmere hills to
which we paid a nearer visit one day.

One evening I read her what I had done of the Passion play, and
found what depth of sympathy and understanding she had for
anyone who was trying to write. She was quite critical, and I
altered a good many things because they grated on her. I think it
was her first acquaintance with religious drama.

We exchanged a good many lovely things that we had collected, including prayers that she had thought worthy of a place in
her copy of Bishop Andrewes, which was interlarded with things
that she loved.

She had said to me quite often that her natural bent was not
Christocentric, so that the addresses at Water Millock were a surprise to me in their beautiful adoration of our Lord, and their
understanding devotion to Him. As usual she had spent herself,
and wrote later:

> Water Millock did turn out to be rather tiring the next day,
> which happened to be packed with people, and so on, but
> I've now got back to normal, and am struggling with my
> chapter on Adoration which won't say just what I want it to.
> As you seemed to feel so strongly about the duty of reading
> MSS., might I send you a bit to look at if I get hopelessly
> stuck. Please give my grateful love to Far Park, and the white
> violets.

She sent the Adoration chapter, and I ventured to suggest that perhaps there might be more of a place in it for the adoring of God
through Christ. This is her very humble answer:

I'm so instinctively pulled to the Theocentric side, and my
soul goes off so naturally in that direction when left to itself,
that anything I do, try to do, is sure to be thin on the
Christocentric side. And yet, just because this book is so personal, I felt rather reluctant to alter it much. You see I come
to Christ through God, whereas quite obviously lots of people come to God through Christ. But I can't show them how
to do that. All I know is the reverse route.

She was at Blakeney, which she always loved, when she wrote:

The immense salt marshes looking like sheets of greenish
opal, and white clouds of terns, and the larks always shouting
Alleluia. But yesterday we went to Walsingham, and saw the
newly opened shrine "England's Nazareth," desperately
mediaeval and hot housey and intense—and I tried so hard
to feel religious about it, and completely failed.... It was nice
to get back to the larks.

It was a tiring summer, the retreats costing in different ways:

Little Compton was nice. Two quite lovely and deep ones,
and others good. And for the first time in any retreat of mine
we had the Blessed Sacrament on the altar all the time. I
thought, poor fool that I am, how lovely it would be! But as
it went on, and the awful power of that white eternity
seemed more and more overwhelming, it seemed to make
noisy nonsense of everything I was trying to say; and I ended
feeling like a cross between a monkey and a parrot. Everyone
else seemed quite calm and happy, so it was evidently all right
for them. But I felt like Angela when she kept saying to her
secretary: "Brother, I blaspheme, I blaspheme."
    Pleshey was terrifically heavy [she wrote later] but well
worth while. No one with much lift; general sensation of
hauling along sacks of spiritual potatoes. So I am too
depleted and jumpy to write coherently.
    My book is done [she writes at the end of May] except
for a last read through and will, I think, go to Methuen next
week. I think the weeks after one has finished a book are

rather nasty, don't you? I feel depleted, and spiritually down
at heel, and sure I shall never do anything more.

By the time she got her holiday, again in Norway, she was according to herself: "so nervous, hagridden, and wretched" that she felt
only an animal existence was possible. But Norway was an effi-
cient cure, and she wrote to me from Maristria later:

I've recovered my power of walking up hill, isn't it marvellous, and have been on the mountain tops at snow level, seeing my little darling plants in their own homes again, and
earn my lunch among the glacial buttercups. It was difficult
to believe it! Such divine loveliness, it gives one an agonized
yearning, don't you think, just like enclosed contemplative
convents. So near St. John of the Cross, "Nada, Nada, Dios,
Dios," only one never can reach that.

The Golden Sequence came out in the end of September. "I'm
very pleased that you liked the beginning of the Sequence," she
wrote to me. "I'm just at the stage of thinking how bad it is and
how horrid it looks, and that no one will be able to finish it. No
reviews yet so one can't tell whether people will catch the idea."
(She was delighted to hear later that one of our mutual friends,
Phyllis Ponsonby, had read it through four times in six months.) It
was well received on the whole but with some reservations,
mainly about its soundness. Nearly all the reviews thought it beautiful and stimulating to the spirit, but not all thought it sound.
Bishop Barry praised it wholeheartedly, so did the reviewer in the
Guardian, but the review Evelyn liked best herself was one by
Gerald Hibbert in the *Friend*.

She went in the November of this year to speak at a conference
called by the Central Council for Women's Church Work. I think
many people must have wondered if she would make some definite suggestions about women being used as retreat conductors,
though I think people knew that she never contemplated the
priesthood for women.

"As to the Ministry of Women Address," she wrote to Audrey Duff, "the Bishop of Carlisle had come to hear me, and pounced at once and demanded it for the Archbishop's Commission, so it must go there as soon as I can. Many seemed to like it, but others, including I fear D. S. (who had spoken just before) looked rather like stuffed monkeys. All I said was: 'It's God we want to get recognized, not us'; which after all is obvious, isn't it?"

She was terribly anxious that women should not emphasize their desire for status in the Church, and neglect the standard of devotion and spiritual life that such work demanded. "If a new era in women's life in the Church really is opening, do not let us come to it inwardly unprepared, because we are in such a hurry to begin.

"For improvement in our position, or mere multiplication of women serving in the Church will do nothing to extend the Kingdom unless those who enter on this career are really light-bringing souls."

This address was afterwards published in *Mixed Pasture*.

The *Spectator* had a new editor during this year, and this led to her giving up the religious editorship of the paper, though she still wrote some reviews for them.

Before the year's end she made another important contact, and spurred on by me, went down to see Fr. Somerset Ward, who later became her director. It was a happy meeting. She wrote to me: "I have had a wonderful day with Mr. Somerset Ward. I think he is the most remarkable sound specialist I've met since the Baron, and the thrilling thing is that though apparently so utterly unlike, their method of direction and point of view is very close.

"He certainly cleared my mind a lot, and concluded by delivering a rousing and fatherly lecture on the well-known subject of overstrain. I felt it to have been a most profitable day, and am very grateful to him and to you."

It was the second warning that she had had, as Fr. Talbot had told her when she went to make her retreat, that she was attempting far too much.

19

THE LAST RETREATS AND *WORSHIP*

There was no place in England more dear to Evelyn than Pleshey, and so it was a very special pleasure when the new chapel for which Lucy had been working ever since her appointment as Warden was consecrated in the spring of 1933. The old chapel had been much loved by her but it was too small to hold all the larger companies of retreatants who were using the house. The new chapel was very beautiful and simple. There was nothing in it that was not lovely. Evelyn went down just before it was consecrated to share in the prayer, and the vigil that Lucy had planned, and stayed for the consecration day. She wrote to Lucy on her return:

> I hope you are not quite worn out…but even so it would be worth it after offering such a lovely present to God. It was all quite perfect, and "I would have you observe," as Fr. Somerset Ward would say, that the outstanding spirit of this chapel witnesses directly to the creative quality of your prayer, however little you may feel that you get out of it. This is the oblation He has wanted from you, and has got; and it is going to get Him lots and lots of souls. So no more going into the garden to eat worms.
>
> The night watch was wonderful I thought. You ought to feel very proud and happy.

Quite early in the year she went to give the Walter Seton Memorial lecture at University College. She had always loved and studied St. Francis and always jibbed at the pseudo St. Francis built up by some of his admirers.

"Maisie came to my St. Francis lecture," she wrote to me, "and was a great support. It was a large audience, but, I felt, a bit stodgy, and rather startled by having St. Francis shown them as chiefly Christian."

This lecture was later published in *Mixed Pasture*. It ends with one of those stories of the saints of which Evelyn seemed to have such a boundless supply, a story not of St. Francis himself, but of his follower Angela of Foligno.

> When she knew that she was dying, Angela called all her spiritual children to her, and blessed them all and said to them: "Make yourselves small! Make yourselves small!" And after that she lay very still, and they heard her murmuring, "No creature is sufficient! No intelligence, even of angels or of archangels is sufficient!" Those who were round her asked, "What is it, Mother, for which the intelligence of angels and archangels is not sufficient?" And she said, "To understand."

She was trying to assess at this time in a paper read before the Newcastle Theological Society some of the things which the Oxford Movement had brought into English Church life in the hundred years since Keble's great sermon.

> We may allow that the Oxford Movement has meant for English Religion the restoration of two great essentials of spiritual life. It has given a renewed contact with history and tradition, bringing new access to the common treasury of the church, and a new appreciation of all we have to learn from those who have gone before. It has revived that rich liturgic and sacramental worship in which, as in some living work of art, the Church's corporate life of adoration and sacrifice is expressed. All this has meant—or rather is meaning, for there is much work to be done yet—a gradual penetration of the Anglican mind by the profound truth that God works through History, and that a great religious tradition gathering the insights and experiences of countless souls, is one of the chief instruments through which He feeds and moulds the spirit of man.
>
> But the final test of a religious movement is not to be sought in the realms of doctrine and practice but in the souls that it forms.
>
> The appearance among us of heroic souls, the many

decisive vocations to poverty, chastity, and obedience—and
also the widespread desire for a revival of the life of prayer,
and uneasy realization of its necessity, which has now covered England with a network of retreat houses, and brings
eager pupils to all who offer instruction on the inner life—
all this, I am sure, is very closely connected with the restoration of the forgotten ideal of Christian asceticism in its true
sense, which we owe ultimately to the Tractarians.

The following letter to F. H. seems to belong to this period and
is dated 1933 in the book of letters:

> The Church of Rome must always have a sort of attraction
> for those who love prayer because it *does* understand and
> emphasize worship. *But* the whole question of course is, not
> "What attracts and would help me?" but "Where can I serve
> God best?"—and usually the answer to that is, "Where He
> has put me."…It is obvious that people who can pray and
> help others to are desperately needed in the C. of E. And to
> leave that job because the devotional atmosphere of Rome is
> attractive, is simply to abandon the trenches and go back to
> Barracks. If all the Tractarians had imitated Newman's spiri-
> tual selfishness, English religion today (unless God had raised
> up other reformers) would be as dead as mutton! There is a
> great deal still to be done and a great deal to put up with,
> and the diet is often none too good—but we are here to feed
> His sheep where we find them, not to look for comfy quar-
> ters! At least that is my firm belief! And the life of prayer can
> be developed in the C. of E. as well as anywhere else if we
> really mean it.

It was the centenary year of the Oxford Movement and Evelyn
found herself drawn into some of the events, rather unwillingly to
start with.

> I went to the great Evensong at the Stadium yesterday. Don't
> know why one does these things—when I got there didn't
> like it. It all felt very undevout and queer, though rather

beautiful to look at, especially the Bishop of St. Albans (Michael Furse) most splendid in scarlet and gold, and sitting on his canopied throne like a Renaissance Cardinal.

But she did enjoy some of the meetings in the end, though she had looked forward to them with some misgiving.

"Quite a novelty for me," she wrote to me, "but I greatly enjoyed them. Fr. Ted [Talbot] on the fourteenth was really thrilling and inspiring."

But to return to the spring: Evelyn's first retreat in the new chapel at Pleshey was on 31 March, and the addresses were afterwards published in her book, *The School of Charity,* which was the Bishop of London's Lent Book for 1934. She found the new chapel a great delight, and already it had a feeling of a "beloved" church. This was only the second retreat to be held in it, indeed we had to dissuade Evelyn from kneeling on the bare stones, which she loved to do, as the floor was scarcely dry. I always thought this set of addresses was one of her most masterly in its shape and scope. To present the creed, the "iron ration of religion," she called it, in six addresses with no feeling of compression or crowding her material, was a spiritual feat of no mean kind. I had missed my train, and expected to arrive in disgrace, but one of my clearest memories of Pleshey is the welcome that I got from her and Lucy at the door of the Retreat House.

She went down later with me to see my Passion play acted in a church in Brighton. There were some unforgettably lovely things in this performance, which Martin Browne was directing. Evelyn had written a Foreword to the play; she considered this work of mine rather as her child, I think, and wrote about it in her own specially generous way at Easter:

> Oh, how perfectly lovely to have been able to do that, and how firmly you ought to remind yourself that it was given to you to do, and you did it, when you aren't feeling specially happy inside.
>
> Yes, I feel just like you about work, it isn't oneself that does it, just as in some queer way it isn't oneself that prays.

But I feel I've got to say: "Let me use it properly," as well as, "don't let me drop it," and "let me give it back to you," like the child's present that the mother has really paid for.

She had two nice breaks that spring, one with Hubert near Dorchester on Thames, about which she wrote to me: "This is being a lovely holiday, both sacred and profane. Such a heavenly country for drives and walks—such downs, and prehistoric castles and soft pinky tree tops in the forest, and larch and primroses and so on, cowslips just beginning…all very important! And a very nice church to go to every morning." It was here, Clara Smith remembers, that the old servants of the house got out the best silver in their honour, a compliment which Hubert appreciated completely.

They were down at Blakeney at Whitsuntide, writing a real bird letter to Audrey Duff, which shows her as a fairly competent bird watcher, a habit she had fostered on the cruises, and one which brought her and Hubert very close to each other.

> We have been twice on the private marsh, which this year has the largest colony of Sandwich terns in England, about 750 nests. They are hatching out rapidly, and one finds little striped fluffy chicks flattening themselves everywhere, and one has to walk about on the tips of one's toes. The infant blackheaded gulls are even nicer, balls of tabby down, and very enterprising, striding across the sand at great speed. The terns all nest together on one patch, a solid mass of dazzling white and little black heads. We found redshank and ringed plover nests, too, and there is a nice party of turnstones on the edge of the shore, also whimbrel and oyster catchers. The Christopher Dawsons are at Sheringham, and we took them out on the marsh today, and they were thrilled to the core.

Walter Fletcher died at Whitsuntide in this year and my sister, Maisie Fletcher, was very much in Evelyn's mind and heart. She wrote to her: "Oh, yes, I do feel so much that the truth seekers will get a lovely welcome, and enter into a power of self-forgetful appreciation far beyond most of the pious. Did anyone ever tell you how when darling Professor Lethaby was going he said suddenly: 'I think the word we shall use most in Heaven will be "Oh!"'"

Norway was the summer holiday place, and again a great success, though when they stayed a few days at Rothbury on the way home she wrote:

> It's dreadfully insular, I know, but I'm always so pleased to get back to English hills, even after Norway. They are homely and intimate, and more full of a kind of spirit I can easily taste and feed on. All the same we had a wonderful month (in Norway). It was nice having Lucy, and she did enjoy it, and was able to do quite a nice bit of hill walking, and get again the solemn mountain top feeling which is like nothing else in life; and she hadn't had it for years and years. We saw more of the country and farms and people and animals than we'd done in other years.

Evelyn and Hubert came to stay with me on their way south: "If you've any odd jobs," she had written, "of the handy-man type, keep them for H., who loves anything of that kind, small mendings and carpenterings and all that, and will be kept quiet and happy for hours."

It was a very satisfying visit. Hubert mended our furniture, and fished in my brother's tarn, and one day drove us over to see Ursula Luard-Selby (sister of Barbara Gnospelius) whose rare flower drawings had fascinated Evelyn. The Luard-Selbys were at Troutbeck Vicarage, and we drove up to the head of that lovely valley. We visited my family, lunching with my old Aunt Mary because, as Evelyn said, Hubert loved going out to luncheon with old ladies. My yellow kitten, of course, took to them at once and spent a lot of time on Hubert's knee. I remember reading them a dialect play that I had on the stocks. We picked a great many blackberries, and Evelyn and I got in a great deal of satisfying talk. It will be seen that they were easy guests.

Mixed Pasture was just about to come out. It contained various articles and addresses which Evelyn had given over the past few years. Perhaps the most valuable part of it was two articles on von

Hügel, but it also had the Thurgarton Walter Hilton, and the St. Francis lecture already quoted.

She was also occupied with seeing the proofs of *The School of Charity* through the press.

Making a picture of this year of her life, I should like to include her exquisite and touching care for Ursula Luard-Selby, whom we had visited in September, and who lost her little three-year-old boy a few weeks later. Though they had only seen each other for an hour, they seemed to be specially close to each other.

"Oh poor Ursula," she wrote to me. "Of course I wrote at once, but what can one say. He looked such a transparent migrant little child, I'm not surprised he wasn't to be kept.... Yes, I felt, too, in an odd way there's something links us; perhaps it's something we both know about flowers."

To Ursula she wrote:

> I have just heard of your great pain. There is nothing that one dare say to you, but to send you love, and nothing that can make it any better. Except perhaps the thought of that perfect little life carried up in its unspoilt innocence to something better still. Like the flowers, who always seem to be telling us that they are going on to greater beauty, as I'm sure they are. Children must bring a very special gift to the eternal world equal to the great suffering of those who let them go.

Later she wrote:

> Don't try to be too brave about it, will you? Because that isn't any use in the long run. I'm sure it is for our weakness and need of Him that God loves us best, and it's being quite simple about our sufferings that gives Him the chance He loves of beginning with us all over again.
>
> I've had such lovely letters from Ursula, [she wrote at Christmas]...how grateful I feel for being allowed to be the one to try to help her. It all fitted together, didn't it. Our going there...and that feeling of some queer strong link between us.

Towards the end of 1933 she was approached by Dr. Matthews, Dean of St Paul's, who wanted her to write a book on Christian Worship for the Library of Constructive Theology, of which he was part editor.

The Dean wrote to me:

> I persuaded her to write *Worship,* and had a good deal to do with the book while it was in process of being written. As one might have expected, her approach was so definitely Catholic that I feared she might not be sympathetic enough with the Protestant tradition of worship, and for the purpose of this series it was important that this should not be too apparent. I think on the whole she was wonderfully ready to make the attempt, and, so far as I know, Nonconformists have found the book useful and stimulating.

Evelyn wrote to me early in 1934: "It looks as if I should do that Christian Worship book—rather exciting. R. S. W. strongly approves if they give me two or three years for it." And a little later: "I've definitely accepted the Christian Worship Book, and now feel frightened and incompetent, but shan't attempt to start before Easter."

As usual she had her hands full. She writes of three Lent addresses in Holy Trinity, Sloane Square, which "refuse to get nicely born," and of retreat addresses for Pleshey, half done. (This was the set afterwards published as *Abba.*)

Later, sending *The School of Charity,* she wrote:

> I'm afraid lots of people won't get past the cover, which gives me renewed horror every time I see it. [Actually the photograph on the jacket is the best that we possess of her.] In fact the whole thing, seeing it exhibited en masse in book shops and so forth, makes me feel miserable and naked, and I'm not enjoying it at all. I've an awful feeling God doesn't mean me to sell large editions and address crowds. Perhaps it's only my particular way of being made vile, which the *Church Times* plainly thinks I am. "First time the Bishop has recommended a book not written by a priest."

In the review in *Theology*, J. R. Pridie wrote of this book: "Its thought moves on the highest plane. But while it deals with Reality in its true sense, God, it is never out of touch with the actual conditions through which Reality is manifested. The Divine Generosity is a warmer term even than the Divine Charity, and a sense of that generosity glows and sparkles all through this beautiful exposition of the verities of Faith."

She and Lucy were planning a visit to Palestine to take place after the Pleshey retreat, but all that plan was knocked out by a rather serious motor accident on a foggy day, which gave her a bad concussion.

> I was flung into the windscreen, and such is the hardness of my countenance I smashed it to bits. Result mild concussion and a face like a prizefighter in full employment...except for the mess made of work, etc., concussion is a lovely disease I think. You just lie in a "sleepy device," as the Cloud of Unknowing says, like a particularly contented baby in the arms of God, and don't care a straw about anything. However, this blissful state rapidly passing and I hope to get to Holy Trinity, Sloane Sq., for my address on Thursday.

She and Lucy didn't give up their pilgrimage at once, and she got down to do her Pleshey retreat and wrote about it: "Pleshey did go all right, quite wonderful, for I'd been pretty rotten before and again since; but those days a sound wave of strength took me through once I'd started and I never got rattled or lost my place or anything, so I'm very grateful to those who helped so much. Lucy, who'd felt anxious, said I looked more and more normal with each address."

But she paid for it afterwards, and found London noises rather unsupportable, so the Palestine Pilgrimage was given up and Lucy took her down to Burford. "I've retreated here for a week's trial, and perhaps a bit longer....Yesterday evening was marvellous, the tiny moon, and faint colours in the sky, and all the trees bursting their buds in a kind of very quiet Magnificat."

She and Lucy went on to Wantage to St. Michael's House, and she wrote to me on Maundy Thursday:

We got down here after lunch, and in spite of the terribly evident bright piety of our fellow guests, which nearly settled Lucy at tea, I like it very much. We are greatly spoilt, having each a nice warm bed-sitting room, and there is a very quiet bare chapel in which I spent a lovely silent evening while everyone else went to Tenebrae at the parish church. It feels very much prayed in and generally all right. We also went up to the Convent and saw my friends there who, in spite of Holy Week and the religious life, were in the highest spirits, in fact almost naughty. The little Reformatory girls kept strolling in and out of chapel, and kneeling down and adoring in the most homelike way, and the altar of repose was beautiful, a shrine full of flowers.

She wrote gratefully to Lucy after her Ascensiontide Retreat at Pleshey: "I feel as if I must have been an awful tax on you, not only those days, but all that time we were away, when you took such care of me and I fear often felt worried; anyhow you made a very good job of it and no one else could have as I know of."

She was back at work in June, taking her "rich ladies" retreat at Little Compton. Later, in London, after seeing Eliot's *Rock,* she wrote: "I was deeply impressed by the whole, especially the choruses. It is too long, I think—almost 3½ hours—and of course not all parts equally good, but a most moving performance all the same."

Ursula and I went to the retreat at Water Millock on the Lord's Prayer. It was the last that she held in that ugly and beloved place, where she had helped so many people.

The Pleshey Ascensiontide Retreat was lovely, so she said,

all so harmonious together somehow.... A variety of lovely things happened. One poor darling, torn for months with misery and self reproach over the sudden death of a husband she felt she had never done justice to, got back to full peace, and a sense of his presence and love. Of course—always make a good retreat, and we had a good lot of other first-class people too, my precious Diana for instance, and a most dear young chaplain so deeply reverent and real. He helped a lot.

[Diana Morshead, committed to her care by Bp. Frere, was a specially intimate and dear "child" and saw much of her in these years.]

But it was after this retreat, perhaps one of the best she ever had, that she wrote:

> With the strong approval of R. S. W. I've taken a very fierce decision. I'm going to have a complete year off from retreats in 1935, except one at Pleshey Ascensiontide for my regular "children" and retreatants, with meditation and directed prayers but no addresses. I think this ought to be nice—and a sort of feeling I've had lately that I just must make a break (this is my 11th year of them)—was brought to a head by Lucy and Marjorie Vernon writing to me quite independently to say that it had come to them so strongly that I ought to have a year off and devote myself to the Worship book, that they felt forced to tell me. So I referred the matter to R. S. W., who said he was quite clear I ought, from every point of view. I only hope everyone won't think I've become an R.C., or had a mental breakdown!!!

Evelyn began to scheme and to write her big book in the summer of 1934, as well as doing her retreat work. She had contributed earlier in the year to a study of the Oxford Group Movement edited by the Rev. H. A. M. Spencer, which also contained papers by Canon Raven, Professor Brown, and Monsignor Ronald Knox. Her article was a setting of the Group Movement in its historical place and comparing it with earlier revivals. The *Catholic Herald* review of the book notes that, "The best paper in this collection is Miss Evelyn Underhill's historical account of group movements in the past, Catholic and Heretical. She proves from the lessons of history that the group of ardent reformers is doomed to ultimate sterility if severed from the complete life of the Christian Church."

The Stuart Moores again chose Norway for their holiday journey. Evelyn seems to have been remarkably well there, and to have

thrown off the threat of asthma which was a perpetual anxiety
when she was working or speaking. They had Lucy Menzies with
them for part of the time and Evelyn's letters to her after she left
them are specially happy ones. She must have felt very fit to have
attempted the walk described in this letter from Molmen in mid-
August.

> On Wednesday we had a really glorious day—climbed to the
> top of the mountain above the lake...got to over 4,000 ft.
> There was no sun which made it easier, but marvellous cloud
> effects. First two hours slogging up through the wood...then
> out on the open hillside, and lunch among the cows, and then
> nearly two hours more climbing and plant hunting up the
> mountain face. At first everything seemed to be over, but
> when we got to the actual top, beyond the last cairn, it was
> marvellous. A wilderness of silver grey stones and peaty stuff,
> and all round us big rose-coloured cushions of *silene acaulis,*
> solid masses of bloom, thousands of little pink faces saying
> *Adoramus Te* quite distinctly; and under the stones lots of gla-
> cial ranunculus, also that beautiful red mountain azalea, one
> bit of andromeda hypriades, a lot of lennia borealis, and sev-
> eral others not identified. (That tiny gentian we found is
> called in Norwegian "Christ's Blue Eye.") We had a vast view
> of snow mountains...all very grand and sombre, violet, grey,
> and white, and wreathed with cloud; and every now and then
> a soft white one came over us, and shut everything out, and
> then melted mysteriously away. It was all very wonderful, and
> uncommonly like Tabor. I don't think anyone who doesn't
> care for mountains can quite understand the synoptics.
> Hubert is very happy, and has just fitted a weird new lee
> board to the boat, which is now christened H.M.S. Packing
> Case, and lives up to its name. I've done a little work, written
> the Sacrament bits of Chapters 2, and touched up the rest.

"I'm so grateful to you for reading *Worship* and approving of
it," she writes in another letter from Norway to Lucy. "I feel much
happier about it now; somehow I never can get over the feeling

that each new thing I write is probably nonsense, and your support and encouragement are a tremendous help."

She was worried about Lucy's fits of nervous exhaustion. She must have wondered whether the responsibility of Pleshey was too much for her rather chancy health. So many of her letters to Lucy at this date (as indeed always) were full of plans for her rest and restoration, expressed with the deep affection that she always felt for this "beloved Child."

She and Hubert came again to Far Park in September. She wrote to me on the way south: "I think Far Park the most peace giving house I ever stay in.... Hubert feels the same and is sending you affectionate and grateful respects. I've spent a lovely evening reading the Sarum Breviary, and *Murder at Lancaster Gate!*" Hubert had spent the visit in painting the disreputable Baby Austin.

Another kitten, James, had taken the place of my marmalade one who died in the spring, and Tony and Phil, Evelyn's cats of the moment, often sent him hints about deportment.

"I must stop," she ends her letter. "It's nice to think of you having James, who will, I'm sure grow up to be a real companion to you. He has it in him. Give him an affectionate stroke."

She sent bits of the big book to me to look at during the autumn, as she did to Lucy and Marjorie Vernon. We felt honoured, but with her it was always: "Thank you for reading this so quickly and kindly, and all you say." She found *Worship* a costly book to write; with her passion for truth and accuracy there was so much to verify and so many rather new points of view to consider. "I'm now beginning to struggle with the chapter on the Character of Christian Worship, and finding it distinctly tough," she wrote.

Writing to me on Christmas Day this year, she gives the feeling of 50 Campden Hill Square at Christmas time. She had prevailed gradually on all the householders in the Square to light up their windows "to welcome the Christ Child." I should think there was no other Square in London like it.

> Your white pussy is standing in the window together with a
> yellow tabby and a pekinese and two mice, all in the same
> work, given by various sympathetic souls to Tony, Phil, and
> me! Yesterday afternoon and evening when all the windows
> round the Square were lit up to welcome the Christchild,
> Phil lay on guard for four hours at the foot of the Tree,
> greatly edifying all passers-by, and saying: "I represent the
> Lion of the tribe of Judah." He has I think a good idea of
> religious drama. James will be interested.

(It was some Christmas about this time that two of her "children"
made her a cat's crèche with lots of worshipping small cats; she
loved this, and set it up with huge joy.)

> Christmas has been quiet and nice. I went with Agatha
> Norman to the Midnight Mass at St. Paul's, Vic. Gate. Such
> lots of people, and a quiet and moonlit night: and for once,
> by a miracle of kindness I felt in the right mood at the right
> time! Tomorrow afternoon we're going down to the tramps'
> colony, and on Saturday Hubert and I go away to Ashdown
> Forest for a lazy week, and then I go to Marjorie Vernon at
> Haslemere, and we shall read and work a bit, and get times
> in church together, and I shall go and see Fr. Ward and
> Deaconess Margaret—altogether a nice week.

She was writing to Lucy at the end of the year, looking ahead
into 1936 for her next series of retreats, and urging Lucy not to
wait for her but to do the Palestine Pilgrimage on her own.

"I don't feel it's any use your waiting for me, as I'm most doubtful about the whole thing. I hardly feel it suitable to leave Hubert
all to himself for so long a time. After all, he'd be nearly 67 in the
spring of '36." She still felt the mothering care for him of their
early days.

She had taken Elisabeth Leseur for her model in the tricky
business of fitting in home life with wider claims. The holidays
and weeks of rest with Hubert were, she felt, very much part of
the pattern which God had given to her.

Dorothy Swayne remembers how once when she was staying the night at Campden Hill Square, Evelyn switched off their intimate religious talk to welcome Hubert as he came in from work; and how natural it all seemed when Hubert enquired, "And now Miss Swayne, what would you like to drink?" Evelyn told Dorothy Swayne that she couldn't have some people to stay because they wouldn't realize that when Hubert came in, he must have the talk and attention that she loved to give him.

The year 1935 was to be the year of the big book. It must have felt strange to her not to be fitting in retreats and retreatants. In February she wrote to me:

> I cheered up and finished my Eucharist chapter (for the time being) and then discovered it was 10,000 words, so no wonder it seemed a long job. Now not quite sure what to tackle next, but a bit inclined to Biblical Worship. If you have any thoughts about good things to read for this do tell me. I had a lovely visit from the Bishop of Truro (Frere) on Monday, partly to deal with D. but also he made me tell him all about the book and gave me lots of good and expert advice. He seemed to have got over the wrench of giving up and looked much better in health than I dared to expect.

Lucy took Evelyn's advice and made her pilgrimage to Palestine by herself in the spring of 1935. The letters written to her there give a very good picture of Evelyn herself during that early spring.

She was wonderfully well, so perhaps the release from the strain of retreats had been a real relief to her. In early February she writes of "an Arctic Weekend, which I rather liked," and signs herself "in the pink." She had made an expedition to Richmond Park on her day off, she had planned a luncheon party, and paid a visit to Gwen Greene on the Baron's anniversary. All the time the writing of the book was pushing on, and she describes the difficult work on the Eucharist chapter to Lucy. She had found, rather to her surprise, that "the whole of modern devotions to the Blessed Sacrament was a purely mediaeval invention" and she is wondering how to deal with this rather uncomfortable discovery.

Lucy sent her tiny holy flowers from Jerusalem which she loved. She followed Lucy's steps most carefully. "I'm glad Bethany is still unspoilt, and wonder if you went to Emmaus; that is one of the bits I should most like to do."

Later there are visits from T. S. Eliot and Father Talbot, and an unfortunate tea party in high class Protestant circles. "Four women who could only be described as hard boiled Christians." In another letter she writes: "Took part of my day off at the National Gallery, which I hadn't entered for years. Saw the Wilton Diptych looking quite exquisite...the last time I saw it it was on the wall of a boudoir in Wilton House, a nest of Victorian monstrosities."

She was still hearing from the sisters at the Rifugio, and one of them sent her "a Saint and Beast story of Maria and a cricket which sits on her Dante and keeps her place...and was carried in procession on New Year's Eve sitting on a small cross."

She didn't shirk ordinary family troubles and writes of combined ops by herself and Hubert, who went to the rescue of an invalid cousin in acute difficulties with his household staff.

I was surprised to find Evelyn and Lucy on my doorstep one day in the Holy Week of this year. They had come up to spend the week at Dockwray, above Ullswater, and had come over to see me and to borrow some blankets, for they were very cold there. They stayed the night, and we talked a lot about Lucy's pilgrimage, and about the retreat that Evelyn was planning for her sole effort in 1935. We were to have the benefit of her studies and thinking and praying over the Eucharist chapter.

She wrote from Dockwray: "We are a thousand feet up in the fells, a lovely wild place with a darling old grey church, very small, growing out of the ground and so much prayed in by its dear and very humble priest and one or two others, that it gives you a marvellous welcome. The weather is perishing cold, and dreams of eiderdowns and woolly jackets haunt my prayers."

In May, Evelyn conducted her only retreat for the year. She had altered its form from that of her other retreats, but she did give four addresses at it, summing up for us much that she must have learnt in her study of the Eucharist for the Worship book. These addresses were on what she called the Rhythm of the Eucharist, the four great movements: the Offertory, the Intercession, the Consecration, and the Communion. Later they were put into her book, *The Mystery of Sacrifice.* She had been finding lovely prayers in the older liturgies, prayers which led her later to make the book of Eucharistic Prayers.

We had two days of silence, when the retreat addresses were given, and then a spare day for those who could stay, when we were allowed to talk in the garden. It was a great gathering of friends. Pleshey was at its loveliest, and I imagine none of us will ever forget the beauty and blessedness of those days. The deathless age-long shape of the Mystery of Sacrifice gave us a beauty of form for our Communions which I expect those of us who are still worshipping on earth use to this day.

Her book led her to make her own experiments in worship, and in June she wrote to one of her friends of her first Russian Orthodox Service.

> This morning was queer. A very grimy sordid Presbyterian Mission Hall in a mews over a garage, where the Russians are allowed once a fortnight to have the Liturgy. A very stage-property Ikonastasis, and a few modern Ikons. A dirty floor to kneel on, and a form along the wall...and in this two superb old priests and a deacon, clouds of incense, and at the Anaphora an overwhelming supernatural impression.

It was in this year that she joined the Anglo-Russian confraternity, probably encouraged by Bishop Frere. "Not much use really," she writes ruefully, "as I'm hopeless at societies and guilds, and always forget their rules and prayers. But they have a magazine with very good things in it, and also I am most interested in the Orthodox Church."

The Spiritual Letters of Dom John Chapman came out this year, and Evelyn reviewing them for *Theology* writes:

> All great direction of souls is at once traditional in doctrine and original in application. Abbot Chapman's mystical affinities are easily to be traced. He belongs to that group of

transcendental realists which includes among others the unknown author of the *Cloud of Unknowing,* St. John of the Cross (whose teachings these letters constantly reinterpret in modern terms), and De Caussade, whose works only became known to the Abbot in the last decade of his life, but to whose deep teaching on "abandon" his own views had long been drawing near. The letters now published…extend over a period of more than twenty years, and form, on the whole, one of the most important contributions to the study of religious experience which our generation has received…. The construction of freshness, lucidity, humour, and deep spirituality with which it is presented, and the robust, even disquieting common sense with which it is applied, give these letters a unique place among modern writings of this kind.

Evelyn and Hubert had their last holiday in Norway in August and September that year. They went back to the Molmen Hotel at Lesjaskog, where Hubert had had a boat built for him for sailing and fishing on the lake.

The boat is most successful [Evelyn writes]. Sail a bit on the small side for light winds, still we get along all right, and she goes well to windward, and is quite a pleasure to sail. She has created quite a sensation here, in fact we began to hear about her on the steamer after leaving Moldre. There seems to be plenty of fish this year, and so far H. has had a few each day, very convenient for supper which is apt to be rather a spartan meal.

Later they moved to Hjerkinn to join friends there at a much higher altitude, and Evelyn writes:

I'm so awfully pleased to be here 3,500 ft. up, and such exhilarating air, and one goes straight out on to the mountain, which is covered with darling little flowers. Tufts of grass of Parnassus everywhere, wee gentians, alpine aster, erigeron and your friend astragalus. It's so beautifully open with heavenly mountains all around and quite a lot of tracks and roads to start off. We hear there is a lake 8 kilos off, where I hope Hubert may get fishing to console him for exile from the boat. Myself I already feel twice as alive as I do at Lesjaskog.

Only the mosquitoes in the woods were rather fierce, but she loved the height and the wildness, and wrote when they returned to Lesjaskog: "I grieve to have left Hjerkinn, but Hubert has, of course, returned to his beloved lake; in fact he rushed down yesterday after our arrival and secured a small trout for supper."

Still there were joys at Lesjaskog. "We've found a lovely place called the Beacon Rock, a ledge of boulders and heather, and a small cliff with a view right over the whole lake. On Saturday we had a coffee picnic at the lake for Fru M. and Maret, and the smaller boy, and Hubert took them out sailing, a great joy. He really has had fun out of the boat and is looking very well."

And how was she? There's a paragraph in one letter that makes me think that the asthma was a threat even up in the mountains: "I simply don't know what I'd have done without Bronchovidrene, which is the only thing that really stops asthma, and goes out in my knapsack on long expeditions so as to be on the safe side.

"I feel quite pagan," she ends this last Norwegian letter (after this long unchurched period), "but very well and gay."

20

LAYING DOWN TOOLS

Evelyn's and Lucy's letters in the spring of 1936 were a duet of physical woes. Lucy had a succession of miserable attacks of illness as well as much spiritual dereliction, and Evelyn seemed to fall more into the grip of asthma and other chest troubles, especially when she was in London. All this year she was escaping from London when she could. One of the places where she found that she could work and really get on with the second half of *Worship* was the Central Deaconess House at Hindhead, where Margaret Wordsworth was at that time Head Deaconess. Evelyn found it a peace-giving place. "I've got a fearful lot to get through before the end of March," she wrote to Lucy. "Luckily, with their silence one can do it here." Miss Ursula Vardon, who was staying at the Deaconess House at the same time, wrote to me: "I sometimes shared the Quiet Room with her when I wanted to read or write letters. I remember on one occasion I felt obliged to apologize for having gone in and out several times. But she said that once she 'got going' nothing disturbed her, and she was obviously anxious that I should not feel she needed special consideration. I remember during that same visit she always insisted on doing her share of clearing meals, etc.; and also how she kept us amused by her stories at tea-time."

She had done a short broadcast on Mysticism in the early year; and though she clearly says in it: "The concern of the Mystics is with God. He is—that is what matters: not the ecstatic feelings which I may happen to have about Him," she writes ruefully to Lucy that "it produced the most insane collection of letters from every kind of crank, and the usual requests to read MSS., gifts of mystical pictures, bad Poems and so on," all of which she probably answered with her usual courtesy.

Her Septuagesima letter to Lucy begins with a wicked quotation:
"These three Sundays before Lent
Will prepare thee to repent." (And in brackets, "My favourite
hymn.")

But it also reports that the half of *Worship* is now revised, in
spite of worrying attacks of asthma. She cheers up the ailing and
harried Lucy by some sturdy advice.

> Don't think about being good. If you accept the very tire-
> some stuff the Lord is handing out to you that's all He wants
> at the moment. Let not your heart be troubled if you can
> help it, is the best N.T. bit for the moment, I think; but the
> more bovine and acquiescent you are the better. I know this
> will strike you as thin advice, but it's all I can give. Drop reli-
> gion for the time being and just be quiet, and wait a bit, and
> God will reveal Himself again, more richly and closely than
> ever before.

She managed to conduct three retreats during the year, though
she had to cancel the same number through illness, and she had
rather a cat-and-mouse summer with asthma. She writes from various country hideouts in England; for she and Hubert never got
back to the little boat on the Norwegian lake.

She came back with Marjorie Vernon to the Vernons' house in
Hampstead, partly to be under a Dr. Alexander, "who says," she
writes to Dorothy Swayne, "that he has never failed to relieve an
asthma case. At first it is all completely baffling, but I suppose one
will get hold of the idea in time."

While in London she was consulting with the B.B.C. about
three broadcasts, which were afterwards published in a book called
The Spiritual Life.

But quite often this year she was staying with Marjorie Vernon
at Worlington Rectory in North Devon.

> We are in the deepest depths of the country here—no
> beauty spots or attractions, no traffic, hardly a sound but
> birds, and the wind in the trees [she wrote to me]. It's mild,
> soft, rather moist, and seems exactly to suit me! and I'm very

happy indeed. The Rector has left behind a huge yellow cat, who would make two of Philip or James, and who has decided to treat me "as family." We have a little church practically in the garden; but alas! the custom is to keep it locked all the week, and the altar in dust sheets. However, we have removed these and find it a nice private oratory, which is rapidly acquiring atmosphere.

She wrote to Lucy about the Rectory:

We look out on a field with three cows, sloping down to the river and then a wooded hill. An old white house which could be simply charming were it not that the owners seem inspired by the Home Page in the *Daily Express,* and beyond that have filled all the available space with junk, mottoes, and bad little pictures. We have gathered armfuls and stowed them away. However, Marjorie having wickedly set aside the two best rooms for me, I'm extremely comfy, and now sitting in my own place with a little wood fire to keep the damp out.

But she was not entirely concerned with writing and personal troubles of her own and her friends this year.

Have you read Aldous Huxley's Peace pamphlet, *What are you going to do about it?* The end part I think fine, and just what all of us ought to do for a start. Do get it, it consoles one a bit for all the Ethiopian horrors, and Musso's "intuitively willed war," and the Church's tactful silence. It is all a horrible mystery; but more mysterious that immersed in such a seething pot, we can know and desire the Love of God. It seems to me on a vaster scale very like the contrasts of the 14th century: all the outbursts of violence and despotism and sin as a setting for the lives of some of those who have known most about God.

She had not been a Pacifist in the First World War, and I do not remember hearing her talk about it before this date, so Aldous Huxley may have set her thinking.

Later, writing to Lucy, who had to face a slight operation, and the prospect of having to resign from her work at Pleshey, she gives her the thoughts that must have been in her own mind often this summer, writing large to make her difficult handwriting more legible for Lucy's painful eyes.

> Though God at present gives you nothing of Himself that you can feel, He does and has given you power to do a wonderful work for Him at Pleshey, impossible if He had not been helping you in a very special way, and you can trust Him to care for it while you are away from it, without any anxiety. The sacrifice of laying it all down for a time is the gift He asks from you now, isn't it? So just give that with all the love and trust that you can; this will help Pleshey as well as being pleasing to God...every scrap you have to suffer can be added to the Cross.

Worship came out in the autumn. Bishop Barkway writing of this book says:

> When one compares *Worship* with *Mysticism,* the chief book of her earlier period, then the immense change of emphasis which has taken place in the intervening years is immediately obvious. The latter book is predominantly incarnational, institutional, and sacramental. The words used are different, for example the word *reality* which occurs so frequently in her first books is almost entirely absent. There is less stress on mysticism. It is strange to notice that the word is not to be found in the index, nor the word *contemplation.* To a youthful reader the style of the book may seem flat when compared with the earlier: there are no purple patches; but its deeper maturity makes this authoritative statement of her final point of view a much sounder exposition of the fundamental facts of life and religion.

> It was my happiness [wrote the Dean of St. Paul's about *Worship*] to have something to do with the production of this book. There were two difficulties—the first to persuade her that she had something to say on the subject, and the second

to persuade her to give adequate attention to non-sacramental worship.

She wrote herself in the Preface of the book:

Some of the friends and fellow students who have read these chapters have been inclined to blame me for giving too sympathetic and uncritical accounts of types of worship which were not their own. It has been pointed out to me that I have failed to denounce the shortcomings of Judaism with Christian thoroughness, that I have left almost unnoticed primitive and superstitious elements which survive in Catholic and Orthodox worship—that I have not emphasized as I should the liturgic and sacramental shortcomings of the Protestant sects. But my wish has been to show all these as chapels of various types of one Cathedral of the Spirit, and dwell on the particular structure of each, the love which has gone to their adornment, the shelter that they can give to many kinds of adoring souls, not on the shabby hassocks, the crude pictures and paper flowers. Each great form of Christian cultus is here regarded, to use an Ignatian simile, as a "contemplation to procure the love of God"; for its object is to lead human souls by different ways to that act of pure adoration which is the consummation of Worship…. In every form of worship—even the least adequate, the positive element, man's upward and outward movement of adoration, self-oblation, and dependence exceeds in importance the negative element which is inevitably present with it.

And she succeeded in making *Worship* pre-eminently a fair and just book, an unprejudiced survey. It has a mountain-top view of the longing adoration of man for God. "Get above" this and that, George Fox used to write to his Quakers, and Evelyn did manage to get above the quarrels and the scornfulness and superiorities that have disfigured Christian Worship, to give the wide view from the heights. She had never been a narrow Christian, she had seen as much as any great teacher of her time of the varying Christian bodies. Her friends were asked to pray for "My Baptist ministers,

My Wesleyan Church workers," as well as for Anglican ventures. Her first retreat was given to an interdenominational company; Presbyterian Lucy, and Sorella Maria, the Franciscan, both lived in her early affections.

She divided her book into two parts, which might be considered as the theory and practice of Worship.

In the first part she dealt with The Nature of Worship, Ritual and Symbol, Sacrament and Sacrifice, The Characters, Principles, and Liturgical Elements in Christian Worship. The rest of the first part is a study of the Eucharist, and of Personal Worship. Then in the second half she begins with the Jewish Worship, and the earliest Christian Worship, and continues with Catholic Worship, Worship in the Reformed Churches, Free Church Worship, Quakerism, and finally The Anglican Tradition.

It was a tremendous book to write, and no wonder it cost her much in strength and energy. It was a book that demanded all her scholarship, and all her willingness to learn new aspects of things. She was in a position to get authoritative help from all sorts of Christian thinkers. She mentions specially Bishop Frere, Dr. W. R. Maltby, Dr. Nicholas Zernov, Bishop Leslie Owen. But she also used to send bits of it to me and to others, to see how it struck the ordinary Christian.

The chapter on the Anglican Tradition, which she had found a tough subject to tackle, shows how well she had studied the relation of the Church of England to the English Character. She was, after all, an English woman: though she had drawn her religious life from sources all over the world, she was bred of people who came from the very heart of England, she knew English people well.

> The peculiar character of Anglicanism [she wrote] is a true
> expression of certain paradoxical attributes of the English
> mind—its tendency to conservatism in respect of the past,
> and passion for freedom in respect of the present—its law-
> abiding faithfulness to established custom, and recoil from
> expressed dominance; its reverence for the institutions which
> incorporate its life, and inveterate individualism in living that

life; its moral and practical bent. All these characteristics can be studied in any rural parish today. The English mind will neither have too much authority, nor too much novelty; it will love the past, and frequently turn back to it, but it will insist on interpreting the lessons of the past in its own way. It will accept the duty of ordered worship, but resist mere ceremonial for its own sake. It will listen with respect to its spiritual teachers, but will not tolerate interference with the liberty and deep reserve of the individual soul.

She talks about the "…true Anglican spirit with its peculiar brand of reverence, sobriety, moral earnestness, and sturdy realism."

Later in the same chapter she writes:

The new life which entered the Church of England with the Tractarian movement has now penetrated and transformed in various ways and degrees the whole temper of her worship, and brought it back into harmony with Catholic tradition. This achievement has won its greatest triumphs at the centre…in an ordered worship which is faithful to the spirit of the Book of Common Prayer. That worship, at once biblical and sacramental, carries through all that is best in the spirit of the past, yet preserves the flexible and synthetic character of Anglicanism.

It was here in the centre that she had found herself able to work and give, and to train souls. She never felt really at home among the extreme Anglo-Catholics, but preferred the great tradition which descended through Andrewes, Jeremy Taylor, and Ken.

Worship has a very striking concluding chapter.

If Christianity be indeed the disclosure of the Eternal God to men, it follows that the Eucharistic principle, the free offering and consecration of the natural life, that it may become the sensible vehicle of the Divine life must radiate beyond its ritual expression; gradually penetrating and transforming all the actions of humanity. This will mean that every sacrificial life, whatever its apparent incentive, is woven into the garment of the Church's worship.

Christian Worship then, both personal and corporate, as it achieves consciousness of its full vocation will expand to bring within its ever-widening radius, and lift towards God, more and more sacrificial material from every level of life; thus bit by bit achieving that Incarnation of the Eternal with the Temporal which is the Divine Creative goal.

In the autumn of this year she went to speak to the Worcester Diocesan Clergy Convention at Oxford and gave two addresses, which were afterwards printed in *Theology.*

Part of Evelyn's vocation had always been this speaking to the clergy, and to ordinands—it is part of the regular pattern of her life—and she was one of the only women of her time whom the clergy were ready to hear. These two addresses—"The Priest's Life of Prayer" and "Prayer in the Parish"—were, I think, her last addresses to a group of clergy or ministers. Evelyn had an exalted vision of the priestly vocation.

> A priest's life of prayer [she said to this gathering of clergy] is, in a peculiar sense, part of the great mystery of the Incarnation. He is meant to be one of the channels, by and through which the Eternal God, manifested in time, acts within the human world, reaches out, seeks, touches and transforms human souls. His real position in the parish is that of a dedicated agent of the Divine Love. The Spirit of Christ, indirectly in his Church, is to act through him.

She gave in the second of these addresses much of her own experience in the direction of souls, and a great deal of practical wisdom. These two addresses were printed as a separate pamphlet because they had been so much loved by those who heard them.

21

The Sword Outwears the Sheath

A batch of letters which Evelyn wrote to Lucy, who made another expedition to Palestine in the spring of 1937, show her making a gallant fight against the asthma which was, alas, getting a deeper hold upon her. But she was cheered by the reception given to *Worship*.

> My own excitement has been that *Worship* was chosen Religious Book of the Month in America, which ought to mean pretty wide circulation, and it's had quite a splendid R.C. review in *Blackfriars* and is, I hear, to have another in the *Criterion*.
>
> Nédoncelle's book on the Baron (the one Marjorie Vernon translated) is published today by Longmans. It reads very well and is nicely produced, and has a lovely photograph I hadn't ever seen as a frontispiece.

And on 15 February: "All well here. My broadcasts *(The Spiritual Life)* were published today, and are much in evidence in the book-shops. They look fairly quiet now as pictures are gone and angels are rationed."

The cats emerge in these letters. "Wonderful scene this a.m. to celebrate Tony's tenth birthday. Breakfast carried up to my room, with ten candles and two saucers of sardines, both cats brushed and sleek and wearing their collars followed. Phil allowed Tony to clear up his saucer, though usually the opposite course is followed, clearly recognizing that it was his day, and afterwards gazed with indulgent interest while T. tried to demonstrate his youth by playing with the cord of my dressing gown."

Again in a rather different strain in these letters to Lucy: "I see Harold [Buxton, Bishop of Gibraltar] has been examining conditions in Spain, and seems to think the Spanish Church got what was coming to it, ruling by fear, and squeezing money out of the peasants' hands for Masses to save their souls from Purgatory. It's all so very like our own Reformation in the violence and complete variance of the things said on each side."

But the fight for health all that year was rather a losing battle: "I've been in bed three and a half weeks," she confesses to Lucy, "low grade 'flu and asthma and bronchitis, and seemed to be going on fine when yesterday the germ broke out vigorously and destroyed all hope of being well enough to go away for Easter. Hubert is, of course, going to the Ship, so that will be all right. He has been very tired, and not too well."

Indeed on Good Friday she was writing: "Must get well quick, ready for Hubert's month in bed." But she got to what she calls "the crock's Mass" at Easter, and began to go for drives, and "Hubert is enjoying himself, and feels perfectly well and is eating huge meals...so disconcerting when it is agreed he had to lie in bed and live on porridge."

But it was a year of cancellations and she could not take the Ascensiontide Retreat at Pleshey: "Dr. B. says any use of my voice will be quite impossible. Really quite amusing isn't it, the way things pile up on us." Still, after a spell in the country at Whitsuntide, both she and Hubert got a clean bill of health from the doctor, and I think it must have been then that she completed the work on *The Mystery of Sacrifice,* which was ready for the publisher by the autumn. Writing was so much part of her that she would do it if she could, and Clara Smith's invaluable help with transcribing and typing made it possible for this, which was one of the loveliest of her sets of retreat addresses, to be made ready for publication this summer.

In September or late August she and Hubert went north to Blanchland, but though they loved the strange little monastery village they were neither of them well there, perhaps it lay too much in a hollow, and they went on to their beloved Cheviots to Wooler.

"This is a lovely place," she wrote to Lucy, "full of colour in this breezy September weather, with bright sun on the hills and harvest fields." But there again she had a night of bad asthma, and she said reluctantly, "I'm afraid the north is going to be no good to me any more."

Before leaving Northumberland she made one vital contact, and wrote to G. F. from Rothbury:

> Before leaving I made friends with an old Deaconess there who has just settled into one of the cottages to live the contemplative life. She spoke to me after Mass on Sunday. Her idea is three hours in church every morning, of which the first is entirely spent in getting rid of distractions.
>
> The Deaconess is an old pet...she is going to pray for you and me every day. I thought we might as well have the benefit of it. I felt very abashed on being told that everything she knew about prayer she had learnt from me, as obviously she knew infinitely more than I do.... I told her I was rather having to leave off active work, and she said: "Oh well, God has something else for you. After all, it doesn't matter in the least what one does so long as it's what He wants."

She wrote to me: "It was horrid not being able to come to you, but quite definitely wouldn't have been a good plan. I got down south, and had ten days in my Slindon cottage with Gwynedd Richards, which were delightful in themselves, with the lovely autumn woods and fields, and the downs which I adore—though hygienically not quite the success I hoped."

She had written to Lucy from Slindon:

> I must do some regular work there. I've still got that Mercier lecture to do and final touches to my Eucharist book. It's queer how the holidays haven't invigorated people this year, but perhaps it's only advancing age. Hubert went back to his dear "Implacable" and has now returned home in very good fettle indeed. We both got home yesterday and are settling in for the winter. Tony and Phil pleased to see dining-room meals again.... My little Eucharist book goes to the publishers tomorrow. I've called it *The Mystery of Sacrifice*. I *do* hope you'll like it. Now for the moment I've only got odd jobs. Greatly daring, I've undertaken to give the Mercier

Memorial lecture at Whitelands College on October 8th: *Education and the Spirit of Worship,* and only hope I'll have voice enough when the time comes. Do think of it. I wonder whether you feel as I do that the most difficult thing about rocky health is not the bits when one is really ill and has something to get one's teeth into, but the ceaseless uncertainty about whether one will be able to carry out one's undertakings, and the general shortening of the working day! This isn't worth calling a cross, and I fear has no intercessory value at all; but it is a bit of discipline! and perhaps has value in preparing for further and more useful suffering and stripping.

During this autumn when Lucy was having to face the prospect of resigning from Pleshey, Evelyn wrote to her when both were facing the apparent end of the work they loved.

"You and I have both been allowed a good run of active work, but the real test is giving it up, and passively accepting God's action, and work, and the suffering that usually goes with it.... After all, our Lord Himself had to leave His work to twelve quite inferior disciples. We have to learn to accept for ourselves all that that means, before we are really abandoned to God." Her next years were spent for the most part in learning to accept this, and all that it meant.

Rocky health or not, she did manage to deliver the Winifred Mercier Lecture. It is a notable piece of writing, and develops that theme with which she ended her Epilogue to *Worship:*

> In the days that are coming, I am sure that Christianity will have to move out from the churches and chapels, or rather spread out far beyond the devotional focus of its life, and justify itself as a complete philosophy of existence, beautifying and enriching all levels of being, physical, social and mental as well as spiritual, telling the truth about God and Man, and casting its transfiguring radiance on the whole of that world in which man has to live. It must in fact have the courage to apply its own inherent Sacramentation, without limitation, to the whole mixed experience of humanity, and in the light

of this interpretation show men the way out of their confusions, miseries, and sins. Only those who have learned to look at the Eternal with the disinterested loving gaze, the objective unpossessive delight of Worship, who do see the stuff of common life with the light shining through it, will be able to do that.

The Spirit of Worship is the very spirit of Exploration. It has never finished discovering and adoring the ever new perfections of that which it loves. "My beloved is like strange islands!" said St. John of the Cross, in one of his great poems. Islands in an uncharted ocean, found by the intrepid navigators after a long and difficult voyage, which has made great demands on faith, courage, and perseverance; islands that reveal beauties that we had never dreamed of and a life of independent loveliness, to which our dim everyday existence gives no clue; yet never reveal everything, always have some unanswered questions, keep their ultimate secret still.

This was perhaps the last considerable bit of writing that she did; it shows how undimmed her mind and imagination and spiritual insight were, in spite of the constant fight for breath. It is a noble bit of work, full of the quotations from the saints that she loved and full, too, of the wisdom that came to her as she wrote her big book—a vision of the great stream of Worship overflowing the banks of ritual and liturgy and flowing out like some river of Life to allay the dust and heat of the mechanized world.

One choice letter must be quoted: "Did I tell you the jewel we got from the new list of Tulips— 'The Bishop,' a bloom of great substance. Blue base with white halo, bourne on a stiff and upright stem."

She had some weeks in the summer of 1937 staying with Marjorie Vernon at Lawn House, Hampstead. This was the house to which she came with the Vernons in the spring of 1940, and in which she lived till her death in the summer of 1941. Marjorie Vernon began in this year to be her special guardian, as she continued to be till the end of her life. Evelyn found her companionship supporting, and was stimulated by her company. As her health grew more shaky she came to depend more and more on this friend, who was able to give her such constant care. Marjorie Vernon came to know Evelyn through Phyllis Potter, who arranged their first meeting together so that Mrs. Vernon should be able to talk to Evelyn about religious difficulties. The next day they both wrote to Phyllis Potter saying that they had had a delightful talk but that neither of them had felt able to say anything about religion, so what? However, the next time they met they got down to it at once. Evelyn could be diffident with certain people in spite of her long experience of helping souls.

Sometime in this year she read a book *Concerning Himself* by Maisie Spens. She wrote:

> Am reading Maisie Spens. She is difficult but full of stuff. A quite new attitude on our Lord's personality and action. Basic idea that His sayings arise from and point back to His inner experiences and life of prayer. We shall like discussing it.

Quite soon she was corresponding with her and sending her *Worship.*

> Of course, now that it [*Worship*] is walking about in its street clothes, so to speak, I am mainly conscious of the strands of thought I did not develop in it, though they are there in germ for anyone who will take the trouble to make them sprout. If there is one thing I seem to have learnt in the course of my spiritual wanderings, it is the oblique nature of all religious formulations without exception, and the deep underlying unity of all supernatural experience.

In Maisie Spens she found a friend who was thinking as deeply as she did herself about Reunion. She wrote to her at Whitsuntide:

> The basis of reunion must be interior, secret, out of the reach of all ecclesiastical controversies. I think you have had a wonderful inspiration in basing it on our Lord's own prayer, which, as you say, includes and overpasses the sacramental, and indeed all else.... I think you will have to wait and brood over it all a little longer, and see if light comes. Things are

moving in the supernatural world. Don't you feel this, in spite of all that seems so hostile to religion?

And later:

> For the development of unity in and through the Praying Christ, I do agree that a widespread group of praying souls, Orders, and Individuals is necessary; still more that these should belong to *all* Christian Communions.
>
> Note that an unusual number of Christians of all types…will be in England this summer at Oxford for the Church and State, and at Edinburgh for the World Conference. The Religious Orders should be most important for you. Of course use my name if you feel it is any use in making contacts.

At the end of the year they actually met. "Maisie Spens came to tea. I think there is something very special about her."

22

DOCTOR OF DIVINITY AND PACIFIST

The year 1938 brought her a quite unexpected honour. Aberdeen University made her a Doctor of Divinity. She wrote to Lucy Menzies from Lyme Regis where she was searching for sunshine on 23 February.

> Your beautiful telegram just come, and completely bewildered me, till I thought to resort to *The Times* where I found the news.... I think they must be dotty! Have not heard a word about it so far, but I suppose I shouldn't be written to till the Senate had agreed to the idea. Can't help wishing it had been St. Andrews, so nice to be in the same glory hole as the Baron. I think Maude Royden and I will be the only female D.D.s, a pretty pass I must say.... I suppose I shall have to go to Aberdeen—not an enticing notion in March, and further still, it's doubtful whether D.D. robes can be hired for small ladies.

She writes later to Lucy that her doctor wouldn't let her go to Aberdeen.

> It would have been fun to have been capped with Epstein, wouldn't it? No, thank you very much, I don't want to have the red robe—probably there will never be an occasion for wearing it, and if one does occur I'll just hire the smallest made and put a few tucks in. The hat is known, to my horror, as the John Knox cap! a piece of knowledge to be buried as quickly as possible. Hubert is wildly excited, and rushing round telling people.

She had written to Lucy about a retreat which she was planning to share with Fr. Sprott, taking certain interviews and leading the Meditations but not giving addresses.

"I do hope you will be at my retreat" (really Fr. Sprott's Retreat). "I should simply hate it if you were not, and expect you to be there, and do the music and the sacristy part. It may be my last one for all we know. I don't feel as if I were going to do much more of that work. What will take its place I have no idea. I am going on peacefully. Agatha was very nice and we got some drives, but I must say I love my bits of solitude. I get very little work done."

Still on her doctorate she wrote to Lucy: "Not so much of the Frau Doctor stuff, please. I do not wish to be addressed as Dr. E. U. I think it is swanky and revolting, and quite against Matt. 23:8. A discreet D.D. is as far as I care to go. Rather sad not to be at the graduation. The present Lord Rector used to pull my hair when I was small."

She never got to Aberdeen, though they postponed her ceremony for a year. She was back in London for Easter but not up to any work.

She got to the Anglo-Russian Conference at High Leigh, but Diana Morshead, who was looking after her there said that it was more than she could manage, and she had to leave before it was over.

"I was at the Anglo-Russian Conference," she wrote to D. E., "where one was kept very much on the run. It was thrilling and the Orthodox services quite unimaginably lovely." Bishop Frere was there too, and they were photographed together in the garden.

That summer she wrote one of her best sort of letters to a young priest, George Reindorp,[7] at the time of his ordination.

> It has been a crucial week for you, hasn't it? when you had to make the choice, which will colour all your life, whether you will be *(a)* a real priest, offered to God, standing before His altar as a sacrifice to Him to be used for His people's needs, or *(b)* a thoroughly nice young clergyman. How splendid that He pressed you to choose *(a)*. Having done so you can feel quite sure that although there will be very dark and dreary bits to get through, in all real necessities He will provide the support and light you need.

> Will you please remember you are always welcome here,
> and have only to say when you want to talk, or just sit for a
> bit and get your breath. It is sometimes useful to have an
> auxiliary home. [Dear 50 C.H.S. was such an auxiliary to so
> many people.]

She was consulting a Dr. Livingstone about her asthma and had
a rather miserable and quite fruitless interlude in the Brompton
Hospital, while her study was stripped of all its treasures which
might harbour dust. She only stipulated that her little embroidered
"Eternity" and her crucifix might remain, a choice which seems
strangely significant. I remember going to see her there and finding it severely empty.

She read that autumn C. S. Lewis' *Out of the Silent Planet* and
wrote to him: "It is so very seldom that one comes across a writer
of sufficient imaginative power to give one a new slant on Reality;
and this is just what you seem to have achieved. And what is more,
you have not done it in a solemn, oppressive way, but with a
delightful combination of beauty, humour and deep seriousness."

On 3 August of that year she went with the Vernons to a house
called Highden, near Washington in Sussex. It was to be her base
in the strange first months of the war; she nearly died there in the
spring of 1940. Altogether it is a place to be reckoned with in the
story of her last few years. Here are her first impressions of it in a
letter to Lucy Menzies:

> We arrived very happily yesterday. It is less than two hours'
> drive from London—a quite lovely place, completely
> enclosed by downs and beech woods, no roads in sight, and
> only one farm and a school. Modern house, full of light and
> air, immense windows, loggia in which I am now sitting with
> a heavenly view.... We are six miles from the sea. I am at
> present for a quiet life and haven't been beyond the house
> yet, but am getting on fine. Hubert is, as usual, very happy on
> *Implacable*.[8]

A little later she writes again from Highden:

> After a very heavy misty day yesterday, the lovely weather has

come back. We drove up on the downs this a.m., and sat in the shade of a beech tree for a bit. This is so far my limit, and most of the day I lie about on the loggia. We find Storrington Church, 3½ miles away, has three weekday Masses, and I'm hoping to attempt this on Friday, but the stern doctor has given Marjorie orders that after early Mass I'm to be put straight to bed for the day, which is rather discouraging.

Exploring the ancient Liturgies for the prayers included in the Mystery of Sacrifice had led to her wish to translate and publish more of these beautiful worshipping prayers, and Roland Vernon, who was a considerable scholar, began to help her to translate these. She wrote to Lucy: "He has done twelve from the Gelasian Sacramentary. He is very literal, but won't take quite enough notice of the fact that the results have got to be used as prayers, and therefore must not sound too odd."

Between them they did manage to catch the rhythm and beauty which belong to the old forms. I expect that Evelyn was responsible for the shaping of them, and Roland Vernon for giving her the closest meaning of the actual words. At all events, the little book belongs to this summer, and to the peace and space of Highden. "Roland really has slaved at translating my liturgic prayers, which are now making progress," she wrote to Lucy.

The Highden sojourn came to end in late September, and she went back after the anxious week of Munich to Campden Hill Square. "I shan't be frightfully busy," she writes to Lucy, "as I only have to revise my collects, and write their introduction, and do the usual autumn reviews."

The Christmas of 1938 was the last one that she spent at 50 Campden Hill Square, the last time the candles were lighted in the windows, and the cat's crèche set out. Charles Williams puts two enchanting letters about the cat's crèche into this year, though I should have been inclined to put them earlier. Still, here they are, too typical of her to be omitted.

The Cat's Crèche is too enchanting and will be lit up at teatime on Christmas Eve, and be the success of the day!

Thank you so much. My Irish Margaret [her Cook] gazed at it, and then said, "See the little cats making their offering to our Lord, and sure it's Himself is fond of animals!" After a pause—"I should think the lady who made this is a good living person."

And the letter of thanks from the cats enclosed with the above said:

Honoured Miss, We both thank you most purrily for our beautiful Crib, expressing as it does in drama our deepest feelings. We note that, like the story of Daniel in the Lions' Den, the lesson for us is one of self-control. It is, as you say, the abnegation of will involved in walking up with a *live* mouse that really counts (in fact the offering of a *dead* mouse often involving a certain temptation to pride). Gazing upon this scene and making it the material of our meditation, we hope in time to learn the real nature of the sacrifice of a troubled spirit, and perhaps the other bit will happen later. It may interest you to know, dear Miss, that as a matter of fact, owing to weight and well-fedness, victims are not often come by. The local mice and birds continue their careers unhindered. Fish we agree is different. But then they have that upstairs. Now dear Miss, with rubs and purrs, and hoping your Christmas mat will be provided with all your pet foods,

> We are, your affectionate cats,
> Tony Puss
> Philip Argent.

The year 1939 began with a spell at Campden Hill Square: "All notion of going away in January has been given up, particularly because I won't be ready for it yet awhile. So it has seemed better to scrap the whole plan and stay comfortably fixed in one's own home."

It was a time of poor health both for Hubert and herself, but there is not much self-pity in her letters, only a longing to get across to Lucy what she herself was making of her new experience of the Cross.

> I do know how difficult it is to lay down tools, accept limitation of illness, etc., feel one is no longer able to be useful, and face a blank future. But surely all this is of the very essence of the Cross, and you are never nearer to Christ than when you just accept it. It can be a life more redeeming and more pleasing to God, tho' not to us, than the best that was achieved by the Warden of Pleshey. I feel you would be happier if you thought more of the active side of your inactivity.

This letter goes on to show how valuable she was finding it to have someone younger like Marjorie Vernon to keep her company at this time.

> As to the particular thing that you can't do things for *me*, take me away and so on, after all one must face the crude facts which are that we are both rather physical crocks now, and one crock can't look after another. I absolutely need a robust person to rely on, whom I don't have to spare, and knock up in a few days if I don't have it. I daren't go away, for instance, with Hubert. All this is part of the limitation business, and we must just accept it, do what we can, and help where we can.
>
> No call to worry about me, [she ends briskly] I'm quite convalescent.

She went down to Salisbury with Marjorie Vernon in February, and had a specially delicious little snatch of country, which she enjoyed hugely as usual.

"We had extraordinary good luck with the weather, lunch picnics and two teas—not bad for February—really hot sun out of the wind, and lots of prims and pussy willows, and lambs. I got quite vigorous and scrambled up hills, and had no trace of asthma."

It was her last country spring, with her own special delights laid on, primroses and lambs, and it is a little gust of joy that had to give way to the labour of settling up her father's house after his death, and writing for the papers, and getting *Abba* into shape. Her father's death marked the end of a relationship in which she had been generous. She had inherited from him some of her distinctive characteristics, her keen brain, her workman-like habits, and the physical likeness between them was marked. She had always given him a good share of her holidays, and luncheon with him on Sundays was a fixture when she was well and in London. The little book of Eucharistic Prayers came out in the early spring. It was small and handy to take to church in the pocket, full of loveliness of the kind that she had learnt to give to people. The short Preface is filled with that inspiring scholarship which is so characteristic. The book had been put together through times of very poor health, but it shows no signs of this, and is as spiritually workmanlike as all her books.

Something must be said of Evelyn's pacifism, which was a very sincere belief with her, and linked up to her deepest creed, and her interpretation of the meaning of the Cross.

She began about this time to belong to the Anglican Pacifist Fellowship, and wrote a pamphlet for them called *The Church and War.* As later letters will show, she remained a pacifist to the end of her life, and did not, as so many people did, change her views in the turmoil of war. I think her paper for the Anglican Pacifist Fellowship belongs to the summer of 1939, but as early as 1937 she was writing of Dick Sheppard's death as a great loss to pacifism, so she probably held pacifist views for some time before expressing them in writing. These are extracts from her pamphlet:

> If she remains true to her supernatural call, the Church cannot acquiesce in War—for War, however camouflaged or excused, must always mean the effort of a group of men to achieve their purpose...by inflicting destruction and death on another group of men.
>
> Fear not him that can kill the body, says the Church—or so at least the Church ought to say. Yet armament factories working full-time announce to the world that we do

fear him very much indeed, and are determined, if it comes to the point, to kill his body before he can kill ours. This attitude is one with which the Christian Church can never come to terms; for questions of expediency, practicality, national prestige, and national safety, do not concern her.

She believed in legitimate police action:

> It is often difficult to define the boundary which divides legitimate police action from military action, nevertheless, Christians must try to find that boundary and to observe it. It is the Church's hour; and she will not face it, because like the hour of birth it means risk, travail, inevitable pain. We are forced to the bitter conclusion that the members of the visible Church, as a body, are not good enough, nor brave enough to risk everything for that which they know to be the Will of God, and the teaching of Christ.

She herself continued till her death to feel committed, and her paper ends with an appeal to Communicant Christians to join the Anglican Pacifist Fellowship.

She was in touch with another pacifist company, the Fellowship of Reconciliation, and wrote for them a *Meditation of Peace,* one of her really lovely bits of late writing. It ends:

> "O Lamb of God that taketh away the sins of the World, Grant us Thy Peace." That is a tremendous prayer to take upon our lips: the prayer of heroic love. It means peace bought at a great price; the peace of the Cross, of absolute acceptance, utter abandonment to God, a peace inseparable from sacrifice. The true pacifist is a redeemer, and must accept with joy the redeemer's lot. He, too, is self-offered, without conditions, for the peace of the world.

23

THE PRAYER GROUP

In the summer of 1939, before she left London for Highden, she was given work to do that meant more and more to her in the coming war years. Every creative servant of God longs to leave behind in the world a living group, because such a living company has always been the authentic Christian pattern. Evelyn had formed in the people who came to her retreats one such group, and now that her retreat work was over and she must have been wondering what sort of thing she could be given, with her poor health, to do for God, she was allowed to share in the making of another company, perhaps even more lasting because more closely knit, and a company reproducing itself to this day, and forming new groups of praying and thinking Christians.

It began with one of those cancellations that she so dreaded in 1937, that year when she wrote to Dorothy Swayne about some event, "It is the only thing I haven't had to cancel this year." There was a week-end planned by the Girls' Diocesan Association, at which Evelyn was going to be a leader, and to which she was prevented from going by the usual bad attack of asthma. She sent as her deputy Agatha Norman, who was one of her most understanding friends. Some of the girls at the week-end, under this leadership, formed themselves into a company prepared to undertake some serious theological study and prayer together. Under Agatha Norman's guidance they worked on until 1939, when in the summer of that year, and Evelyn was having a short spell of better health, they asked again if she could help them with their prayers and study. Of course, she wanted to do this, and nearly all the members of the first study group must have met her then, for she came to a meeting in a house on Campden Hill, and also to two other meetings at Mary Sumner House. At the first meeting a very simple rule was planned under her guidance and accepted by the members; at the meetings in the chapel at Mary Sumner House she led their prayers. Their idea was that prayer and theological study should go hand in hand. Those who have read this book will know how this would be after Evelyn's own heart, for she loved people to use their minds, she liked to advise about books, and she had always felt that it was a special part of her life to teach people what she knew about prayer. This group became a great resource and outlet for her still active mind in the days of horror and illness and isolation, after her bad attack in 1940. The members were scattered by the war all over England, but they were united by a letter which Evelyn wrote for them at all the great feasts of the Church. The letters were published in the book that was brought out after her death, *The Fruits of the Spirit*. It was her last work for God, for the last letter was sent out about a month before she died, and probably because it had the strength of her offered suffering behind it this company has formed others on the like lines, and the work is growing still, with its quiet gifts of study and prayer, influencing many people. All the groups owe a tremendous amount to the work of Agatha Norman, but all the early members felt the care that Evelyn was willing to give to them. She liked to have their letters asking questions, and quite a few of them came to see her at Lawn House.

At the Whitsuntide of 1940 she was sending them two great and lovely prayers to the Holy Spirit that she had found in her studies of the old liturgies, and in that heart-cracking summer she wrote to them: "If we put ourselves at God's disposal, His Holy Spirit prays in us, and now especially when the world is overwhelmed by the spirit of evil, and violence, this is one of the greatest things that we can do for our fellow men."

And again later in 1940, "The springs of war are in the invisible world, and it is there we must deal with it; remembering that those most responsible for its sins and horrors lie in the power of evil, and yet as our neighbours need our help. If all Christians concentrated their powers of prayer on the awful spiritual needs of the Dictators, the end of the war would be in sight."

At All Saints–tide in 1940, she is quoting for them von Hügel's: "All Saints' Day is the feast of every heroic soul, every heroic act inspired by God since God made man on earth....The day also of the saintly bit, the saintly moments, the beginnings of sanctity in souls not otherwise saints at all."

At Advent 1940 she wrote:

> We should think of the whole power and splendour of God as always pressing in on our small souls...but that power and splendour mostly reach us in homely inconspicuous ways; in the Sacraments, and in our prayers, joys, and sorrows and in all opportunities of loving service. This means that one of the most important things in our prayer is the eagerness and confidence with which we throw ourselves open to His perpetual coming. There should always be more waiting than striving in a Christian prayer.
>
> Because we are all the children of God [she wrote to them in her last letter at Easter 1941] we all have our part to play in His redemptive plan; the Church consists of those loving souls who have accepted this obligation, with all that it costs. Its members are all required to live each in their own way, through the sufferings and self-abandonment of the Cross; as the only real contribution which they can make to the redemption of the world. Christians, like their Master, must be ready to accept the worst that evil or cruelty can do to them, and vanquish it by the power of love.

She wrote an introduction to the Girls' Friendly Society's Manual of Prayer at my request, which was afterwards printed separately and called *A Note on Prayer.* One of the Chaplain's assistants during the war told me that she did not know what she would have done without this pamphlet. There was nothing else so real and simple to give to people who were beginning to pray.

24

The Last Years

Into the record of this last period at Campden Hill Square I should like to put some extracts from a little document made for Lucy Menzies by Maude Hance, Evelyn's parlourmaid, who stayed with her for twelve years and became a friend to all of us who went often to the house.

> I grew to love the work, and to live with her (E. S. M.) in the house was a great joy, also I loved to wait on her, and do all I could. It was a joy to live with her, and be a member of her household, or as Mrs. Stuart Moore used to say we were all to be like one family. Then I shall always remember when she had those bad times of asthma, she would look up at me with such a lovely smile on her face and would say "There, that is over again." Then being with her in so many of these bad times and often in her sickness which she bore so patiently made us grow to love one another, myself I often felt I did not want to be away from her…I always think she could see the good in others and help them in many ways. Living with her through all the troubles, sorrows, joys, happiness and difficulties that arose in our family life was to us a great blessing. We often would say, "We will never get another place like this" real home life in every way materially and spiritually. One joy is to think that I have lived with her, also that I was able to do all I could for her.

Maude used to go down to help at Pleshey in times of stress and would slip into chapel to hear the addresses, and one retreatant wrote to me that she remembers so clearly Evelyn and Maude going up the stairs at Pleshey, hand in hand, in perfect understanding.

When the house was shut up in 1939 she and her mother took the big tabby cat Philip to live with them. Alas for poor Philip, he came back to Lawn House for a day or two in 1940 and there finding no Maude and a strange household and cat, he strayed off into Hampstead, and was never seen again. Maude wrote to me later of that last year at 50 Campden Hill Square. "E. U. did have to give up a great deal of what she had loved, such as wild flowers and books in her room were only a few instead of all around her, as she loved so much to have them. But all the time love was growing on all sides towards E. U.," adds Maude.

Evelyn left 50 Campden Hill Square in July to go down to Highden again with the Vernons. She never thought then that she was leaving it for the last time. She meant to come back there, and left all her treasures and books behind. But she never lived there again, for she and Hubert came back to London with the Vernons to share their house in Hampstead after her very serious illness in 1940.

The house in Campden Hill Square had been in a very special sense the place of her ministry. Her books had been written and her prayers had been said in the upstairs study. (She once told me that she often knelt to write, half-praying, half-writing, when she was alone there.[9]) In the sitting-room below she had had those vivid discerning talks with all sorts of people who came to her for direction and counsel, and found her so encouraging a listener, and pierced through the truth with her, discovered that one could laugh over spiritual dilemmas, and in her company began to love God.

It was the friendliest of houses, and often full of distinguished company, though you didn't need to be distinguished to be welcome there. In the early war years Barbara Gnospelius remembers meeting Edith Sitwell, Ralph Hodgson, May Sinclair (who also loved cats), Mrs. Belloc Lowndes and Naomi Royde Smith. Later came Bishop Frere, Fr. Talbot, T. S. Eliot, Algar Thorold. It was a house full of books and some of them might be detective novels, and some new poems, and some the deepest studies in theology. The cats of the moment, portly and dignified as I remember them kept you company by the fire.

Perhaps one day there will be a plaque to tell that a poet and writer lived there, but only those who experienced her care for souls will know the real secret of the place.

Charles Williams in his book of her letters quotes from the account of one of her visitors, who came to see her after one of her illnesses.

"As I entered, she got up and turned round, looking so fragile, as though 'a puff of wind might blow her away' might be literally true in her case, *but* the light simply streamed from her face, illuminated with a radiant smile."

It was also the place of her suffering, for she never balked at the fact that the people who *meant business* (her expression) in religion were bound to suffer. Here she spent those hours "apparently in prayer but really raging in hell," torn by attacks of unbelief, too much in the front line to escape these furious assaults of evil. Here she bore other people's sufferings with a depth of sympathy and a continuous concern, costly to herself. Here she wrote those very special letters, so humbly and yet with the authority of experience behind her. And here she read and studied, satisfying her own very formidable standard of scholarship, a quick but remarkably thorough worker. But it was never a house oppressed by her vocation, and it was also here that she had those cosy evenings with Hubert, each nursing a cat. The Sunday and Christmas Eve tea parties made the house a delightful meeting place. Here she received with such delight parcels of country flowers, and Lucy's spoiling presents, and revelled in hearing and recounting all sorts of ridiculous stories. And here she wrote solemn letters from the cats and articles for the newspapers in their names.

The door shuts on 50 Campden Hill Square; it only opens on Hubert collecting some of their treasures, because it may be requisitioned, on Marjorie Vernon and Clara Smith sorting through letters and papers after Evelyn's death. But the family, Maude and Margaret in the kitchen, Clara Smith preparing books for the press, and always as it seemed waiting anxiously not to miss the post, and Hubert hammering in the basement were never to be collected there again.

Evelyn went down to Highden with Marjorie Vernon towards the end of July, and Hubert went for a spell to the "Implacable." I cannot find anything to show that they anticipated the onset of war. During August, Evelyn was remarkably well, and able to walk about and enjoy the country. It was the beginning of a spell of good health that lasted for nearly six months. But when war broke out in September, she felt it as perhaps only pacifists can. "I knew you would be feeling the horror of the whole thing intensely," she wrote to Lucy. "It is all so awful, one dares not dwell on it. One of the things I mind most is the thousands of little families being ruined straight off by the exodus of people from the towns, shops, and so on."

It seemed useless to go back to London, as Evelyn was more likely to keep well in the country, and Hubert and Roland Vernon had almost no work, so both families decided to stay on at Highden, which was available for the winter.

> We go on here [she wrote to me]. I feel a bit troubled about it, as we are just safe and comfy in heavenly country, but not being any use. I am just finishing my little book on the Lord's Prayer. It is queer finishing a book now that was mostly written in the summer. One's whole outlook seems so changed in proportion, and the terrible sense of universal suffering and ruin seems to get into everything. I feel at times *(a)* that one should fight against this oppression, and *(b)* that it is to be accepted as one's share in the pain and horror of war, there's almost a feeling of guilt attached to enjoying things...but [she adds] we've got a kitten! black and white and fluffy of farm origin but full of friendliness.

She wrote to D. E.:

> I'm not surprised that you get fits of revolt against this whole terrible and senseless business. But I'm sure the only safe and sane way just now is to keep the imagination sternly in check, turn to God in blind faith, and hold on to Him in the dark as well as you can or better let Him hold you. You won't however be able to get away from feeling the suffering and the darkness. So best accept them, join them to the Cross, and offer them to God.

After a few weeks to her great happiness, but also rather to her consternation, she was given work to do that she had never done before, she writes again to D. E.:

> I have tumbled into quite a lot of work here. A weekly inter-cession service in the parish church beginning next Wed. at 3, also a weekly religious lesson in school, 11 to 14 year olds, 33 of them, taking the place of the vicar, who is too ill at present. This *terrifies* me as I have never taught children.

The service she made for the weekly intercession was published later and became one of the few that one could use wholeheart-edly during the next few years.

I'm not sure if she ever got quite happy with the children, but she was delighted when she asked the class, "Why do we praise God?" to get a reply from one child, "To cheer Him up." She loved the Intercession service, and found the women really responsive who came to it, and the Bishop of Chichester authorized the lit-tle service book for use in the diocese.

The black and white kitten began to follow the example of his predecessors and write for the papers.

> My dear Editor [literary editor of *Time and Tide*], here is the review of the Cat Books. I have tried my best but it is my first effort and I am very young: do please be lenient to its defects.
>
> Hoping this finds you well and frisky as it leaves me at present,
>
> I am, your obedient kitten,
> Michelangelo van Katzen-ellen-bogen.

And as usual she was wonderfully awake to lovely things. "So per-fect here this morning," she wrote to Lucy, "a white frost and cloudless sky, the sunrise with tiny silver moon shining was really marvellous. Though it is a monotonous life in some ways, being in this beauty and peace is wonderful."

Among her letters at this time was one to E. I. Watkin, telling of her reactions as a pacifist in a world submerged by the flood of war.

Don't you find these times very difficult for pacifists? The
War seems to enter into everything, and there are few things
that one can conscientiously do. Most of my quasi pacifist
friends are becoming more warlike, apparently feeling that
provocation is more important than principles, and that the
only way to combat sin in others is to commit sin ourselves.
The attitude of the Anglican Bishops has been disappointing,
though a great many of the clergy are strongly pacifist.

To Maisie Spens she wrote at this time:

At present the whole attitude of the Church strikes me as
getting steadily more sub-Christian, more and more forget-
ful of absolute standards and inclined to regard the B.E.F. as
the instrument of the Divine Will.…The more supernatural,
absolute, and non-utilitarian you can make your work the
better it will be! I particularly like what you said about physical suffering: that it is God's Will, and yet also is never His
Will. That paradox has to be held on to all the time—so that
we can accept even evil and imperfection as penetrated in
spite of themselves, by God's ruling Will and Grace and
turned thus to His final purpose, though still remaining in
themselves, and until redeemed, contrary to His intrinsic will
for life.

Yes, I am still entirely pacifist [she wrote to Fr. Curtis,
C.R., in January 1940] and more and more convinced that the
idea that this or any other war is "righteous" or will achieve
any creative result of a durable kind, is an illusion…but certainly it is difficult to say what one thinks the Finns ought to
have done.

The whole autumn had been a wonderful interval of good
health for her, the last she was ever to have, and she writes in early
January to Lucy: "I have had six months without doctors or
nurses, the first time such a thing has occurred for years."

Her book on the Lord's Prayer, *Abba,* came out in January, and
sold 1,500 in the first fortnight, and had specially good reviews.

The ones she liked were Violet Holdsworth's in the *Friend* and
E. I. Watkin's in the *Tablet*.

The foundation of this book was the retreat addresses that she
gave in 1935, but she had worked over it a good deal in the summer of 1939. It is her last considered utterance on the life of
prayer, and though it is a small book it is full of heavenly wisdom.
She is still quoting from the Mystics, and added to this are the
riches she had been discovering in her researches into the ancient
liturgics.

It is difficult to show its quality in short quotations, but these
may help to tell why it was so welcome: it sold 5,000 copies before
Easter.

> The crowds who followed Christ hoping for healing and
> counsel did not ask Him to teach them how to pray; nor did
> He give this prayer to them. It is not for those who want reli-
> gion to be helpful, who seek after signs; those who expect it
> to cure their diseases but are not prepared to share its cost.
> He gave it to those whom He was going to incorporate into
> His rescuing system, use in His ministry; the sons of the
> Kingdom, self-given to the purposes of God.
>
> The coming of the Kingdom is perpetual. Again and
> again freshness, novelty, power from beyond the world, break
> in by unexpected paths, bringing unexpected change. Those
> who cling to tradition and fear all novelty in God's relation
> with His world deny the creative activity of His Holy Spirit,
> and forget that what is now tradition was once innovation:
> that the real Christian is always a revolutionary, belongs to a
> new race, and has been given a new name and a new song.
>
> The biblical writers…give us the strange and haunting
> figure of Melchizedek, the King and Priest of Salem, of
> whom we are told so little yet feel we know so much. It is a
> picture which holds us by something which far transcends
> historic accuracy; something conveyed yet unexpressed, like
> the undertones of a great poem. Whilst the other kings are
> fighting, slaying, disputing their spoils, living the full animal

life of self-assertion and self-development, Melchizedek comes forth from his hilltop city, in a quiet majesty which we instinctively identify with holiness; bearing not any signs of power, but bread and wine. He is the meek and royal minister of a generous God. This thought of the King and Priest, unarmed and undemanding, bearing Bread and Wine from the Holy City to the poor fighters in the plain, cannot have been far from our Lord's mind when, on the eve of the turmoil and agony of the Passion, He blessed and broke the loaves, took the chalice "into His holy and venerable Hands" and gave thanks; and, with and in this token sacrifice, gave Himself to be for evermore the food of men, "named of God a high priest after the order of Melchizedek."

Her six months of health came suddenly to an end, as the cold deepened after Christmas. Perhaps as a result of an adventurous visit to Brighton to see the Glyndbourne Company in *The Beggar's Opera,* the asthma and lung trouble fell on her with terrible effect in February; so that she wrote to Lucy (shakily and in pencil) in early March:

> I have never been so ill, and didn't know one could be and survive it, and am still only beginning to feel alive. In the end they gave me the maximum dose of morphia, and I slept for 27 hours without moving.
>
> Not yet decided [she wrote a little later] if they can move me to London before Easter. I can read a bit. Got a lovely book called *Caribbean Treasure* by Sanderson. Lovely sunshine here pours into my room, and all the snowdrops and crocus are out. The vicar has been to give me my Communion.

She and Mrs. Vernon did not in the end reach London till after Easter. It was now more than ever important for her to be with someone who could give her the support and care which Mrs. Vernon was able to offer to her. She was obviously unfit to reopen her own house. This and the fact that it was a financial benefit to both families, made Evelyn and Hubert decide to share the Vernons' house, and Lawn House, Hampstead, became her last home.

Now begins her final sojourn. It was appropriate perhaps that she who had always been a Londoner should share the stress of the war years, in a London house, exposed to bombs, and noisy with anti-aircraft guns. The London blitz had not begun when she first came back there. It was decidedly part of her suffering and stripping that she never went home to her books and her beloved things, to the little garden at No. 50, and all the usual background of her life. She wrote to Violet Holdsworth who had given her her book, *Seas of the Moon:*

> Though I am not yet half-way through the sixties, illness plus age has come to mean a very thorough limitation of freedom, and general slowing down, and dependence upon others; none of which is altogether easy to a person who prefers to do everything for herself at express speed. But it's a marvellous discipline, and introduces one to a completely fresh series of tests and opportunities, and involves the discovery of so much devoted kindness.

It was the end of all sustained writing for her too, though she produced the regular letters to the prayer group.

> I am supposed to be writing a book on Christianity and the Spiritual Life for the Christian Challenge series, [she wrote to E. I. Watkin] but feel quite unable to get on with it partly because a long stretch of ill health has reduced my vitality, partly the difficulty of living in somebody else's house, as we are doing now with only a few of my books.

In the summer of 1940 she was writing to L. K.:

> I am still in my room but am up at last allowed to do nix and hardly move as everything makes me breathless, it transpires that the long illness destroyed the elasticity of my lungs and that takes ages to come back (so far as it does come back),

meanwhile one just has to stay put, and submit to having everything done for one. I can't say I like it much but it seems to be the Lord's idea for the present moment.

She was very much thrilled, in spite of her pacifism, by Dunkirk.

Even war, it seems, isn't spiritually sterile [she wrote to me]....Were you not thrilled by the accounts of the patient endurance and unselfishness at Dunkirk? no one pushing and trying to get away first—and the splendid work of the young Chaplains, going about those awful beaches helping the men and giving the Sacraments. There was something supernatural in all that, an eternal quality triumphing over the horror.... I can't settle to writing can you? One is too conscious of living on the brink of a precipice for it to have any reality.

In July, she was writing a letter in *Time and Tide*:

The Christian model is not the ecstatic warrior, but One who lived and worked in an occupied country, conforming to the requirements of the conqueror with humble tranquillity, who endured without resentment the worst that evil could do, and by this perfection of self abandonment revealed to us the best. The God whom Christians serve, far from being the "ally" of any one group of His children, has as His chief attribute an universal charity and "sendeth rain on the just and unjust." Moreover the noble army of martyrs were self-offered as victims, and did not oppose evil to evil, violence to violence. Therefore though many Christians find themselves driven to the use of force in the present crisis, they may feel chary of invoking religious sanctions for their military acts. In view of our past record can any of us dare to say that a victory of our arms would necessarily be a victory for the Spirit of God? The true religious attitude is rooted not merely in ecstatic devotion to an ideal, but above all in humility and love; in a deep sense of man's entire and filial dependence on that God Whose inscrutable purposes are being worked out through the tumults and disasters of history, and who can win His truest victories even through the apparent defeat of the good.

And to Dorothy Swayne she wrote at the same time:

People are so anxious at present to have the support of religious faith while performing irreligious acts, and to claim God as an ally who must be on their side, instead of abandoning themselves to his Will. The immense awakening to the need of prayer is of course one of the good results of the War, but if it is to remain at the natural level and be concerned mainly with our military success or defeat it will not do a great deal for us. We all, as you say, manage to ignore the "hard sayings" of the New Testament—but now they are coming true under our eyes.

I'm glad you liked my letter in *Time and Tide*. I thought ————'s demand that the Church should ginger us up into a frenzy like that of the young Nazis really dreadful. We have already adopted far too many of the ideas of the enemy, (i.e. in our shocking treatment of aliens) and if we are not careful will suffer a moral and spiritual if not a physical defeat.

I've had rather a thin summer, mostly shut up in my room, but have been a bit better lately.

But as the summer came to an end, and the London blitz began, there was quite a lot to bear in Hampstead, though Evelyn never forgot her friends who were sharing in the hardest conditions in Dockland.

She wrote to Nesta de Robeck in October:

This household has remained very lucky, and so far nothing has touched us, and we are now quite settled into a basement and ground floor existence. The whole district is practically without water since the Highgate Power Station was blown up last week. We fill buckets from the main in the morning, and live on it as best we can during the day. However there is a certain odd satisfaction in being reduced to primitive conditions and having to practise abstinence about something one has always taken for granted. Sitting very loose to possessions and much simplification of life is certainly one of the lessons the Lord is going to teach us through the war, and we are beginning to get on with it now...a peculiar mixture of prudence and resignation is required in the conduct of life.

In December she wrote to Maisie Fletcher who was living with a M.R.A. team in Cheshire.

This business of living in close proximity to all sorts and kinds of people which the war has brought about, does find out all sorts of resistances, and shows how right the *Theologia Germanica* was in fixing on the I, the me, and the mine as the root of all evil. I so sympathize with you about the pooling of your possessions! it is much harder than one dreams it to be. We only have a few of our things here, but I'm not yet quite reconciled to seeing my Blake on someone else's drawing-room wall—even though it is that of my dearest friend. We stayed through the blitz, sleeping downstairs with our suitcases by our sides; and at the end of it Hubert fell very ill, and I had rather an anxious time. However he has made a splendid recovery, and will soon be at work again. I have to lead a very enclosed life this winter; but am gradually settling down to the idea; and it is wonderful to have this joint home, and all the kindness and companionship one gets here.

Though it was an enclosed life her mind was not enclosed. She was reading and sometimes reviewing, she realized what was happening at things like the Malvern Conference, and helped a good deal to spread the prayer for reunion which Maisie Spens was fostering. She had her work to do in the offering of the pain and suffering to God.

I do understand [she wrote to Maisie Spens] your distinction between trying to visualize and grasp all the sufferings and horrors, and accepting the pain of them. At the beginning of the war I tried to do the first, with deplorable results. The second is done *to* one rather than *by* one which makes it all right and is simply one's share of the life of the Church at this time.

Quite a lot of people came to see her at Lawn House. Diana Morshead came up to London committees and visited her, and Gwynedd Richards was working in London and was with her quite often. Lucy came down from the North, and some of the Prayer Group made their way to her, and asked questions and got her advice. Maude came up from the country to see her. Fr. Somerset Ward came to direct her when he was in London. He told me how alarming some of her attacks of asthma were to her, and what courage it needed to stand up to them perhaps even more than was needed to stand up to the blitz. She didn't try to evade any suffering that was going on among those she loved in that awful winter of 1940–41.

> G. was here for the morning [she wrote to Lucy] utterly exhausted, and heartbroken by the horror and suffering she's having to deal with and the pure devilry of it all.
>
> She says the state of Dockland is quite past belief—the people are at the end of their tether and live in acute fear. She's in charge of a church hall full of them and says the dirt and squalor and hopeless misery is awful.
>
> A large window fell on V. cutting and bruising her a good bit but she keeps going. D. is there, and standing it well, also E. M. If you had time to write one of them a line, I think they'd like it. They feel so cut off and are really being heroic.

Her spirit remained undimmed. She was writing a little.

> I'm quite busy [she says in the same letter] writing the post-script for a book of essays on Peace which is being published this spring…and also producing an article on keeping Lent for our parish magazine! the vicar is so kind in coming to me every week I really couldn't refuse. After which the Lent Letter for the Prayer Group will have to be done.

An unexpected visit from T. S. Eliot gave her great pleasure:

He spends two nights a week with the Fabers in Frognal so says he will look in from time to time. Like everyone else he feels the scattering of his friends.

She still found energy for letters of direction.

I think you are privileged [she wrote to one of her family doing difficult war work] and standing up to the cost marvellously well. But it is costly. The compensating craving for some shelter and love seems just natural and rather humbling but not in the least sinful. No point in increasing strain by trying to behave more heroically than we really are, and rejecting the helps that nature provides. If Lawn House can give a bit of shelter and cherishing we shall feel very pleased, warmed through and honoured.

This is the first thing I should say [she wrote to another]. Just plain self forgetfulness is the greatest of graces. The true relation between the soul and God is the perfectly simple one of childlike dependence. Well then, *be* simple and dependent, acknowledge once and for all the plain fact that you have nothing of your own, offer your life to God and trust Him with the ins and outs of your soul as well as everything else! Cultivate a loving relation to Him in your daily life; don't be ferocious with yourself, because that is treating badly a precious if imperfect thing which God has made.

The spring went on, and she got out for little drives sometimes and saw snowdrops and crocuses. Her life seemed to be gentled by her acceptance which left her very humble.

At present, I think one can do little [she wrote to a pacifist friend] but try to live in charity, and do what one can for the suffering and bewildered. We are caught up in events far too great for us to grasp, and which have their origin in the demonic powers of the spiritual world. Let us hope that the end of all the horror and destruction may be a purification of life.

I remain pacifist [she wrote to another] but I quite see that at present the Christian world is not there. Like you I feel the final synthesis must reconcile the lion and the lamb—but meanwhile the crescendo of horror and evil and whole-sale destruction of beauty is hard to accept.

Anyhow I do feel [she wrote in one of her last letters] that trusting God *must* mean trusting Him through thick and thin.

Death came to her after a week of increasing weakness on 15 June in the Octave of Corpus Christi, one of her favourite Feasts.

Her last years had taught her to relinquish one thing after another, it was the Abandonment to the Will of God which one of her favourite writers, de Caussade, had taught her, the "stripping" which she knew how to accept. The priest, who used to bring her the Sacrament from Christ Church, Hampstead, wrote to me:

I shall always remember the joy and peace of those services, the sense of Worship and of the Presence of God, her humil-ity and serenity.... She taught me much.

Maude Hance (her maid) came to see her in the last weeks and wrote of her visit.

I did see her before she passed away in June, and still that calmness was there and a great understanding of one's life here on earth, and in the world to come.

At what cost of humble abandonment had she learnt this final serenity—she, whose early letters show her to be so quickly moved by impatience and passionate feeling.

I remember from my first retreat how much she had loved the short epitaph which the poet Henry Vaughan made for his grave. Gloria—Miserere.

It was thus that she felt the Christian death could be expressed—"Glory is the final word in religion," she had written in *Abba,* "as joy is its final state. No life, no intelligence reaches perfection, yet in each there is a promise of the Perfect. Each comes up to its limit and in so doing testifies to that which is beyond it—the Unlimited Splendour of the Abiding, the Glory of the Living God."

Epilogue

It is seventeen years now since Evelyn Underhill's death, and many of the people who knew and loved her most have crossed over into Eternity; but I have made some extracts from letters and writings of people still alive who cherish her memory and who know what they owe to her teaching and loving care.

A priest who knew her very well writes:

> It was in the last stage of her spiritual development that she reached the heights for which she had longed, and this was due very largely to the great work of spiritual direction to which God called her. She found in the care of those sent to her all the tenderness and pastoral anxiety which enabled her to rise above the intellect into a fuller communion with the love of God. This work which so enriched her has left its abiding mark on many lives, and made her worthy of that great reward which God gives to a good and faithful servant.

Another priest who came to know her as a young man, just after his ordination in 1937, says:

> Of course I was only on the fringe of her great and wonderful life; yet I felt I must write to you because I have realized that her prayers for me then, her care for my spiritual upbringing, her introduction to Fr. —— have influenced my whole life. I was privileged to take the Blessed Sacrament to E. U. several times. I remember so clearly, and it has remained a clear memory ever since, that nobody to whom I have ever ministered seemed to radiate so serene a calm as I went into her room. And invalid though she was…I always retain a feeling of her *zest* for the Christian religion and her fundamental common sense and humour…but it is the serene calm which I remember most.

The next impression comes from the principal of a school:

> No words can express the gratitude and love which were
> created by her touch, her presence, her teaching. Her gift of
> reaching minds struggling towards enlightenment was
> absolutely unique. She was a gateway to God. She had
> looked so long with such adoration and humility upon the
> things of Eternity that she reflected the vision to us who
> came year after year to her retreats. There is indeed a time-
> less touch on all she taught and wrote, and was. The years
> that have passed since she died have not dimmed her at all.
> She can still be found.

This from a Scottish friend who knew her in the 1920s.

> What made a deep impression upon me at the first meeting
> especially was her extreme naturalness. Indeed if she had a
> pose at all it was trying to hide this unique personality under
> a bush (which flamed out in spite of her efforts). I had the
> privilege of being under her for two years as my spiritual
> director (1921–23). Her methods are best described in her
> own parable of the successful gardener of roses.
>> "He tends each lovingly and carefully, providing the suit-
>> able soil for the roots, and pruning at the correct time."
> As a Scottish Presbyterian I am afraid I required a lot of
> pruning.

And another from a parson's wife: "Her touch was so delicately
right."

From her hostess when she went to take a Student Christian
Movement retreat at Cambridge:

> What a charming guest she was! There was a delicious
> homeliness about her. On her arrival she had quite an over-
> whelming welcome from our discerning old spaniel. As her
> hostess I was invited to be present in the Chapel when she
> give her retreat addresses. I appreciated this enormously, but
> even more having the ones I missed read to me at home, and

being able to discuss them with her. I remember the Chapel packed with keen young people listening intently.

Another old friend writes:

> I remember an episode which shows her quick wit. We were standing side by side handing over our coats, when we heard behind us two students discussing her. "Is Evelyn Underhill married, I wonder, and has she any children?" A quiet voice broke into their discussion: "Alas, no, my dears, only cats."

And here is a fellow writer speaking:

> My first memory of her was on that first visit in 1937, she already so established, and I a nobody, so much younger. After tea downstairs with her and her husband she took me up to her own study. I was very conscious that she had recently been ill, and of her then frailty, and my overriding feeling was that I must not stay and overtire her, so within a very few minutes I said that I must go. "Have you got something else to which you really must go this instant?" I had to confess that I hadn't. "Well of course you must stay. I *want* you to." After a further time which was so absorbing to me that I suddenly felt conscience stricken, and that though it had flown it must probably have been long by clock time, I said "this time, I must go at once, I must have tired you, the one thing I didn't want to do." "Tired me? oh no. It's so jolly, so real, you've refreshed me." And when I did go "Promise me that you will never come to London without ringing me up, and seeing if you can find time to come and see me." Not only was there all her generosity but the *humility* of that "seeing if *you* can spare time to come and see *me*."… It was such utterly unselfconscious humility, and part of her treating others as though they were more than equals. At one point on another visit, she said with childlike joy "Oh isn't this fun!" conveying her sense of enjoying others, a very great and special trait in her.

And a last word from one who worked with her constantly:

> Her friends will remember her as body, as well as reasonable,
> extraordinarily reasonable mind and soul: a thin creature
> with a pale face and dark eyes, a face that when she was truly
> interested (but she could be very easily and truly bored),
> would look like alabaster with a light behind it. She might
> be more aware than most of us of the unseen, but she was
> also passionately appreciative of the seen, and unexpectedly
> clever in some departments of practical life. Her friends did
> her sewing but she could bind books so beautifully as to win
> prizes at international exhibitions. She could not even begin
> to drive a car but she loved the excitement of sailing a small
> dinghy in a difficult sea. She was good at birds and when it
> was too calm to make sailing amusing her alternative was to
> drift silently up a Cornish creek and watch those black and
> white, orange legged waders who, she said, looked as if they
> had been dressed in Paris.

The owner of a green finger, she made a country garden out
of the unpromising strip of earth attached to her Campden Hill
house. Snow mountains, Bach, the Paradiso, and M. R. James
ghost stories were among her earthly adorations. Though she
demanded a great deal of solitude she could be a delightfully
sociable person, gay and witty, and liking conversation, a collec-
tor of friends. She was a most faithful correspondent, who really
wrote and answered letters, and her Christmas present list was
formidable. The last "real party" she ever went to was a *Time and
Tide* cocktail party at Lady Rhondda's Hampstead flat in the summer of 1939. She had been ill on and off that year, and it represented a return to the world. She said to me afterwards, "I loved
that party. I felt as though I'd really come alive again." Some people will think of her as their only reliable interpreter and guide
in the way of the Spirit. She hated religious jargon and woolly
phrase, and tried to avoid the technical language of theology,
while making the fundamentals of religion as clear as possible.

One of her favourite passages, one which she read as a prayer at all her retreats, was the sentence from à Kempis:

> Defend and keep the soul of Thy little servant among so many perils of this corruptible life, and Thy Grace going with him, direct him by the way of peace to the country of everlasting clearness.

Everlasting clearness would be for her an indispensable attribute of Heaven.

Acknowledgements

We are indebted to the following for permission to quote copyright material:

Messrs. J. M. Dent & Sons Ltd. and Messrs. E. P. Dutton & Co., Inc., for extracts from *Immanence* and *Theophanies* by Evelyn Underhill; Messrs. William Heinemaun Ltd. for extracts from *The Grey World* by Evelyn Underhill; and the executors of Evelyn Underhill and Messrs. Methuen & Co., Ltd., for extracts from *Mixed Pasture* by Evelyn Underhill.

We have been unable to trace the owners of the copyright in Baron von Hügel's letters to Evelyn Underhill, and we would welcome any information which would enable us to do so.

Notes

(These notes originally appeared as footnotes on the pages.)

1. Later Dean of Norwich (1909–11) and Bishop of Birmingham (1911–24).

2. The Archbishop of Canterbury's son who had become a Roman Catholic.

3. Father Geoffrey Curtis, C.R.

4. Mrs. Plunket Greene.

5. Dr. Maude Royden held a regular Evening Service on Sundays at the Guildhouse, Eccleston Square.

6. B. K. Conningham, Principal of the Theological College at Farnham, later Principal of Westcott Home, Cambridge.

7. Now Provost of Southwark.

8. *Implacable* was the naval Training Ship which H. S. M. visited often and which was one of the great interests in his life.

9. Here were some specially loved treasures, Maude Hance remembers. There was always kept on her writing desk, a picture in a frame with these words on it—"Think Golden thoughts and serve God with a quiet mind," and a picture with the word *Eternity* (this was the little delicately embroidered panel which a friend had had made for her). She left it to Lucy Menzies who left it to me.

Index

About SKYLIGHT PATHS Publishing

SkyLight Paths Publishing is creating a place where people of different spiritual traditions come together for challenge and inspiration, a place where we can help each other understand the mystery that lies at the heart of our existence.

Through spirituality, our religious beliefs are increasingly becoming a part of our lives—rather than *apart* from our lives. While many of us may be more interested than ever in spiritual growth, we may be less firmly planted in traditional religion. Yet, we do want to deepen our relationship to the sacred, to learn from our own as well as from other faith traditions, and to practice in new ways.

SkyLight Paths sees both believers and seekers as a community that increasingly transcends traditional boundaries of religion and denomination—people wanting to learn from each other, *walking together, finding the way.*

We at SkyLight Paths take great care to produce beautiful books that present meaningful spiritual content in a form that reflects the art of making high quality books. Therefore, we want to acknowledge those who contributed to the production of this book.

PRODUCTION
Tim Holtz, Martha McKinney & Bridgett Taylor

EDITORIAL
Amanda Dupuis, Polly Short Mahoney,
Lauren Seidman, Maura D. Shaw & Emily Wichland

COVER DESIGN
Drena Fagen, New York, New York

TEXT DESIGN
Bridgett Taylor

PRINTING & BINDING
Lake Book, Melrose Park, Illinois

Other Interesting Books—
Meditation/Prayer

Finding Grace at the Center: *The Beginning of Centering Prayer*
by *M. Basil Pennington,* OCSO, *Thomas Keating,* OCSO, and *Thomas E. Clarke,* SJ

The book that helped launch the Centering Prayer "movement." Explains the prayer of *The Cloud of Unknowing*, posture and relaxation, the three simple rules of centering prayer, and how to cultivate centering prayer throughout all aspects of your life. 5 x 7¼,112 pp, HC, ISBN 1-893361-69-1 **$14.95**

Three Gates to Meditation Practice
A Personal Journey into Sufism, Buddhism, and Judaism
by *David A. Cooper*

Here are over fifteen years from the journey of "post-denominational rabbi" David A. Cooper, author of *God Is a Verb*, and his wife, Shoshana—years in which the Coopers explored a rich variety of practices, from chanting Sufi *dhikr* to Buddhist Vipassanā meditation, to the study of Kabbalah and esoteric Judaism. Their experience demonstrates that the spiritual path is really completely within our reach, whoever we are, whatever we do—as long as we are willing to practice it. 5½ x 8½, 240 pp, Quality PB, ISBN 1-893361-22-5 **$16.95**

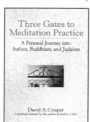

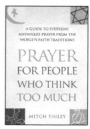

Silence, Simplicity & Solitude
A Complete Guide to Spiritual Retreat at Home
by *David A. Cooper*

Award-winning author David Cooper traces personal mystical retreat in all of the world's major traditions, describing the varieties of spiritual practices for modern spiritual seekers. Cooper shares the techniques and practices that encompass the personal spiritual retreat experience, allowing readers to enhance their meditation practices and create an effective, self-guided spiritual retreat in their own homes—without the instruction of a meditation teacher. 5½ x 8½, 336 pp, Quality PB, ISBN 1-893361-04-7 **$16.95**

Prayer for People Who Think Too Much
A Guide to Everyday, Anywhere Prayer from the World's Faith Traditions
by *Mitch Finley*

Takes a thoughtful look at how each major faith tradition incorporates prayer into *daily* life. Explores Christian sacraments, Jewish holy days, Muslim daily prayer, "mindfulness" in Buddhism, and more, to help you better understand and enhance your own prayer practices. "I love this book." —Caroline Myss, author of *Anatomy of the Spirit*
5½ x 8½, 224 pp, Quality PB, ISBN 1-893361-21-7 **$16.95**; HC, ISBN 1-893361-00-4 **$21.95**

Or phone, fax, mail or e-mail to: SKYLIGHT PATHS Publishing
Sunset Farm Offices, Route 4 • P.O. Box 237 • Woodstock, Vermont 05091
Tel: (802) 457-4000 • Fax: (802) 457-4004 • www.skylightpaths.com
Credit card orders: (800) 962-4544 (8:30AM–5:30PM ET Monday–Friday)
Generous discounts on quantity orders. SATISFACTION GUARANTEED. Prices subject to change.

Spiritual Biography

The Life of Evelyn Underhill
An Intimate Portrait of the Ground-Breaking Author of Mysticism
by *Margaret Cropper*; Foreword by *Dana Greene*

Evelyn Underhill was a passionate writer and teacher who wrote elegantly on mysticism, worship, and devotional life. This is the story of how she made her way toward spiritual maturity, from her early days of agnosticism to the years when her influence was felt throughout the world. 6 x 9, 288 pp, 5+ b/w photos, Quality PB, ISBN 1-893361-70-5 **$18.95**

Zen Effects: *The Life of Alan Watts*
by *Monica Furlong*

The first and only full-length biography of one of the most charismatic spiritual leaders of the twentieth century—now back in print!

Through his widely popular books and lectures, Alan Watts (1915–1973) did more to introduce Eastern philosophy and religion to Western minds than any figure before or since. Here is the only biography of this charismatic figure, who served as Zen teacher, Anglican priest, lecturer, academic, entertainer, a leader of the San Francisco renaissance, and author of more than 30 books, including *The Way of Zen, Psychotherapy East and West* and *The Spirit of Zen*. 6 x 9, 264 pp, Quality PB, ISBN 1-893361-32-2 **$16.95**

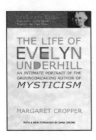   

Simone Weil: *A Modern Pilgrimage*
by *Robert Coles*

The extraordinary life of the spiritual philosopher who's been called both saint and madwoman.

The French writer and philosopher Simone Weil (1906–1943) devoted her life to a search for God—while avoiding membership in organized religion. Robert Coles' intriguing study of Weil details her short, eventful life, and is an insightful portrait of the beloved and controversial thinker whose life and writings influenced many (from T. S. Eliot to Adrienne Rich to Albert Camus), and continue to inspire seekers everywhere. 6 x 9, 208 pp, Quality PB, ISBN 1-893361-34-9 **$16.95**

Inspired Lives: *Exploring the Role of Faith and Spirituality in the Lives of Extraordinary People*
by *Joanna Laufer* and *Kenneth S. Lewis*

Contributors include *Ang Lee, Wynton Marsalis, Kathleen Norris, Hakeem Olajuwon, Christopher Parkening, Madeleine L'Engle, Doc Watson,* and many more

In this moving book, soul-searching conversations unearth the importance of spirituality and personal faith for more than forty artists and innovators who have made a real difference in our world through their work. 6 x 9, 256 pp, Quality PB, ISBN 1-893361-33-0 **$16.95**

Spiritual Practice

Women Pray
Voices through the Ages, from Many Faiths, Cultures, and Traditions
Edited and with introductions by *Monica Furlong*

Many ways—new and old—to communicate with the Divine.

This beautiful gift book celebrates the rich variety of ways women around the world have called out to the Divine—with words of joy, praise, gratitude, wonder, petition, longing, and even anger—from the ancient world up to our own time. Prayers from women of nearly every religious or spiritual background give us an eloquent expression of what it means to communicate with God. 5 x7¼,256 pp, Deluxe HC with ribbon marker, ISBN 1-893361-25-X **$19.95**

Praying with Our Hands: *Twenty-One Practices of Embodied Prayer from the World's Spiritual Traditions*
by *Jon M. Sweeney*; Photographs by *Jennifer J. Wilson*;
Foreword by *Mother Tessa Bielecki*; Afterword by *Taitetsu Unno, Ph.D.*

A spiritual guidebook for bringing prayer into our bodies.

This inspiring book of reflections and accompanying photographs shows us twenty-one simple ways of using our hands to speak to God, to enrich our devotion and ritual. All express the various approaches of the world's religious traditions to bringing the body into worship. Spiritual traditions represented include Anglican, Sufi, Zen, Roman Catholic, Yoga, Shaker, Hindu, Jewish, Pentecostal, Eastern Orthodox, and many others.
8 x 8, 96 pp, 22 duotone photographs, Quality PB, ISBN 1-893361-16-0 **$16.95**

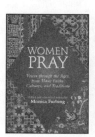   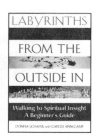

The Sacred Art of Listening
Forty Reflections for Cultivating a Spiritual Practice
by *Kay Lindahl*; Illustrations by *Amy Schnapper*

More than ever before, we need to embrace the skills and practice of listening. You will learn to: Speak clearly from your heart • Communicate with courage and compassion • Heighten your awareness for deep listening • Enhance your ability to listen to people with different belief systems. 8 x 8, 160 pp, Illus., Quality PB, ISBN 1-893361-44-6 **$16.95**

Labyrinths from the Outside In
Walking to Spiritual Insight—a Beginner's Guide
by *Donna Schaper* and *Carole Ann Camp*

The user-friendly, interfaith guide to making and using labyrinths— for meditation, prayer, and celebration.

Labyrinth walking is a spiritual exercise *anyone* can do. This accessible guide unlocks the mysteries of the labyrinth for all of us, providing ideas for using the labyrinth walk for prayer, meditation, and celebrations to mark the most important moments in life. Includes instructions for making a labyrinth of your own and finding one in your area.
6 x 9, 208 pp, b/w illus. and photographs, Quality PB, ISBN 1-893361-18-7 **$16.95**

Other Interesting Books—Spirituality

God Within: *Our Spiritual Future—As Told by Today's New Adults*
Edited by *Jon M. Sweeney* and *the Editors at SkyLight Paths*

Our faith, in our words.

The future of spirituality in America lies in the vision of the women and men who are the children of the "baby boomer" generation—born into the post–New-Age world of the 1970s and 1980s. This book gives voice to their spiritual energy, and allows readers of all ages to share in their passionate quests for faith and belief. This thought-provoking collection of writings, poetry, and art showcases the voices that are defining the future of religion, faith, and belief as we know it. 6 x 9, 176 pp, Quality PB, ISBN 1-893361-15-2 **$14.95**

Releasing the Creative Spirit: *Unleash the Creativity in Your Life*
by *Dan Wakefield*

From the author of *How Do We Know When It's God?*— a practical guide to accessing creative power in every area of your life.

Explodes the myths associated with the creative process and shows how everyone can uncover and develop their natural ability to create. Drawing on religion, psychology, and the arts, Dan Wakefield teaches us that the key to creation of any kind is clarity—of body, mind, and spirit—and he provides practical exercises that each of us can do to access that centered quality that allows creativity to shine. 7 x 10, 256 pp, Quality PB, ISBN 1-893361-36-5 **$16.95**

Spiritual Innovators: *Seventy-Five Extraordinary People Who Changed the World in the Past Century*
Edited by *Ira Rifkin* and *the Editors at SkyLight Paths*; Foreword by *Robert Coles*

Black Elk, H. H. the Dalai Lama, Dorothy Day, Gandhi, Thich Nhat Hanh, A. J. Heschel, Krishnamurti, C. S. Lewis, Thomas Merton, Desmond Tutu, Simone Weil, and many more.

Profiles of the most important spiritual leaders of the past one hundred years. An invaluable reference of twentieth-century religion and an inspiring resource for spiritual challenge today. Authoritative list of seventy-five includes mystics and martyrs, intellectuals and charismatics from the East and West. For each, includes a brief biography, inspiring quotes and resources for more in-depth study.
6 x 9, 304 pp, b/w photographs, Quality PB, ISBN 1-893361-50-0 **$16.95**; HC, ISBN 1-893361-43-8 **$24.95**

Or phone, fax, mail or e-mail to: SKYLIGHT PATHS Publishing
Sunset Farm Offices, Route 4 • P.O. Box 237 • Woodstock, Vermont 05091
Tel: (802) 457-4000 • Fax: (802) 457-4004 • www.skylightpaths.com
Credit card orders: (800) 962-4544 (8:30AM–5:30PM ET Monday–Friday)
Generous discounts on quantity orders. SATISFACTION GUARANTEED. Prices subject to change.